MANAGING CHANGE

Practical Strategies
for Competitive Advantage

Also available from ASQ Quality Press

Root Cause Analysis: Simplified Tools and Techniques
Bjørn Andersen

The Change Agents' Handbook: A Survival Guide for Quality Improvement Champions
David W. Hutton

Critical SHIFT: The Future of Quality in Organizational Performance
Lori L. Silverman with Annabeth L. Propst

Creativity, Innovation, and Quality
Paul E. Plsek

Let's Work Smarter, Not Harder: How to Engage Your Organization in the Execution of Change
Michael Caravatta

The Toolbox for the Mind: Finding and Implementing Creative Solutions in the Workplace
D. Keith Denton

Quality Problem Solving
Gerald F. Smith

Mapping Work Processes
Dianne Galloway

101 Good Ideas: How to Improve Just About Any Process
Karen Bemowski and Brad Stratton, editors

The Certified Quality Manager Handbook
ASQ-Quality Management Division

To request a complimentary catalog of ASQ Quality Press publications, call 800-248-1946, or visit our online bookstore at qualitypress.asq.org .

MANAGING CHANGE

Practical Strategies
for Competitive Advantage

KARI TUOMINEN

ASQ Quality Press
Milwaukee, Wisconsin

Managing Change: Practical Strategies for Competitive Advantage
Kari Tuominen

Library of Congress Cataloging-in-Publication Data

Tuominen, Kari, 1944–
  Managing change : practical strategies for competitive advantage / Kari Tuominen.
    p. cm.
  Includes index.
  ISBN 0-87389-470-7 (alk.)
    1. Organizational change. 2. Strategic planning. 3. Competition. 4. Industrial
  management. I. Title.

HD58.8 .T86 2000
658.4'06—dc21   99-056446

© 2000 by ASQ

All rights reserved. No part of this book may be reproduced in any form or by any means,
electronic, mechanical, photocopying, recording, or otherwise, without the prior written
permission of the publisher.

10 9 8 7 6 5 4 3 2 1

ISBN 0-87389-470-7

Acquisitions Editor: Ken Zielske
Project Editor: Annemieke Koudstaal
Production Administrator: Shawn Dohogne
Special Marketing Representative: David Luth

ASQ Mission: The American Society for Quality advances individual and organizational
performance excellence worldwide by providing opportunities for learning, quality
improvement, and knowledge exchange.

Attention: Bookstores, Wholesalers, Schools and Corporations:
ASQ Quality Press books, videotapes, audiotapes, and software are available at quantity
discounts with bulk purchases for business, educational, or instructional use. For information,
please contact ASQ Quality Press at 800-248-1946, or write to ASQ Quality Press,
P.O. Box 3005, Milwaukee, WI 53201-3005.

To place orders or to request a free copy of the ASQ Quality Press Publications Catalog,
including ASQ membership information, call 800-248-1946. Visit our web site at
www.asq.org or qualitypress.asq.org .

Printed in the United States of America

 Printed on acid-free paper

American Society for Quality

Quality Press
611 East Wisconsin Avenue
Milwaukee, Wisconsin 53202
Call toll free 800-248-1946
www.asq.org
qualitypress.asq.org
standardsgroup.asq.org

MANAGING CHANGE

PRACTICAL STRATEGIES FOR COMPETITIVE ADVANTAGE

Strategic management

Product management

Process management

Development management

The *successful* learn from others.
The *mediocre* learn from their own experiences.
Failures learn from no one.

BUILDING COMPETITIVE ADVANTAGE IN THE IMPLEMENTATION OF STRATEGY

It is often not the strategic plans themselves that compete against each other but, rather, the speed and quality with which they are implemented.

The world is full of plans, some better than others. Of these, very few are ever implemented. Still fewer are those that have been implemented at the right time and quickly enough to produce a genuine competitive advantage. Most simply enable firms to catch up with their competitors.

We don't have time; we have a battle going on.

FOREWORD

This book is aptly titled: *Managing Change: Practical Strategies for Competitive Advantage*. It has been written to help organizations focus on and make lasting change; however, making change is difficult. Any material that helps organizations overcome obstacles to change is useful and needed. Perhaps an analogy from medicine will make the point.

A doctor tells a patient that the high blood pressure diagnosed is a significant risk factor for stroke and heart disease. It is recommended that the patient lose weight, exercise, and drastically reduce the use of salt. Very often, the patient hears the physician's words but fails to heed the advice to make critical lifestyle changes.

Business enterprises, like the patient, are constantly being made aware of leading practices that clearly will improve measured performance. Books on change, benchmarking studies, consulting engagements, and conferences all provide prescriptions for improved performance; however, recommendations go unheeded and proven benefits are not realized. This book seeks not only to document the models and practices that will help organizations achieve successful change (but also to help organizations to actually implement them and reap the benefits).

This book stresses models and case studies to get its message to the reader. But the models are not to be used blindly. They are there to help understanding of complex, real-life conditions, which are messy. That is an added benefit of the book. It has been shown time and again that those who neglect models risk doing things over at added time and expense. Worse, they never change. The objective of the book is to show how significant change can be made in acceptable time, which is imperative in today's world.

But this is not just a book. This is a rich source of delivery mechanisms for the content of the material, including text summaries and notes, courses (including workshops and seminars), an application tool, and an assessment vehicle. The reader will find that these can be used selectively with various levels of management to implement a program for change.

The liberal use of artwork (figures, drawings, and graphs) for analysis, display, and decision is a welcome addition to show how the models and content can be applied creatively.

Readers should take their cues from the book's title; if they are interested in making change, here is a text worth studying. I commend it for their use.

Robert C. Camp, Ph.D., PE
Principal
Best Practice Institute
Rochester, NY, USA
Author of three books on benchmarking

ACKNOWLEDGMENTS

If I had not had the experience of working for various managers throughout my career, it would not have been possible for me to write this book. This book also gives me the opportunity to thank three of them in particular.

Sigurd Jörgensen was the first person I reported to. He was responsible for the development program at Rosenlew Metal Industry and was one of the leading proponents of industrial engineering in Finland. He had the ability to motivate his subordinates. Within the first few days of my career, he gave me some advice: "Approach your work from the point of view of becoming the best in the development field in Finland in three years' time." He did not demand this as such but just expected me to set my sights high and work accordingly. That was the start of my continuing interest in continuous learning in its various forms.

A good example of my first experience of learning from people better than I, and in this case from a real master, was during the second week of my career. I heard him give a presentation on a course; I taped it, transcribed the presentation from the tape, and reworked it to make it into a presentation I could use.

Here is another good example of his management style: during my interview, I had promised him I would learn Swedish. In my second week, he gave me two books in Swedish. They were about industrial engineering and how to organize it. He handed me the books, saying, "We should think about how to organize your development department and what its name should be. The department is relatively new, and it still has not got an official name. You should get some good tips from these books. Read them, come up with a proposal, and we will discuss it further." I cannot imagine a better way to motivate someone to learn Swedish. I took my dictionary in hand, and during the evenings I attacked the books and started to think about a name for my department.

The second person I would like to thank is the senior vice-president of Rosenlew and the division manager of Rosenlew Metal Industry, **Jaakko Koskinen.** He constantly gave me new opportunities by transferring me from one problem business unit to the next. In all of them, I had the opportunity to learn something new and to make significant and visible changes.

The third person I would like to thank is **Jaakko Heikinheimo,** for whom I worked for a long time and who, whatever the situation, gave his support and provided the opportunities to succeed and the freedom to fail, to correct my mistakes and to learn from them.

I would also like to thank my publisher, the illustrators, Lasse Malmberg, my son, Riku, and all who have helped produce this book for their valuable advice. I would like to pay particular thanks to my former colleagues, who produced the results that I have presented as mine in so many training sessions.

I would also like to thank the translators of this book, Keith Silverang and Paul M. McDonagh.

Finally, I would like to acknowledge Petri Lehtipuu for making my dreams come true.

Kari Tuominen

Welcome to the Book

Getting a Good Overview of the Subject

Because reading a book thoroughly takes time, it is important that you read this book *in two stages.* In the first stage, you will get a good overall impression of the contents of the book. After that, you can choose the most interesting parts to read in the order you prefer.

Read the front matter, pages x–xxvii. They present the objective of the book and problems to which the book provides solutions. You can find instructions for "*Quick Notes*" to other parts and chapters of the book on the first pages of the part or chapter.

> You can find instructions for "Quick Notes" on the following pages:
>
> | | |
> |---|---|
> | Page 1 | Holistic management |
> | Page 16 | Development models |
> | Page 22 | Strategic management |
> | Page 65 | Product management |
> | Page 134 | Process management |
> | Page 191 | Development management |
> | Page 228 | Management of change |
> | Page 247 | Systematic framework and specific targets |
> | Page 259 | Leadership brings change |
> | Page 273 | Results, not plans, provide solutions |
> | Page 289 | Managing my own change |

On the Internet at www.benchmarking.fi/book1/managingchange.htm, you can also find a synopsis of the book and a 10-step model for how organizations have used the book, as well as questionnaires (see page 15) presented in the book. The model shows how organizations can use the questionnaires for the development need survey to discover the organization's own opinion of both current and target performance, and the need for improvement. The model provides instructions for preparing and conducting the survey, summarizing the data, and how to run feedback sessions to analyze results and start up development actions. A PC program is available for documentation, calculation, and presentation of the data and comments in various forms.

Following are the contents, which list the main points of the book.

CONTENTS

THE OBJECTIVE OF THIS BOOK

REALIZING BUSINESS STRATEGY THROUGH CAPABILITY STRATEGIES

Companies have to develop their *business strategy* continually. The business strategy explains where the company operates and "what are the right things" the organization should be doing. Implementation of the selected business strategy for its part requires that the organization has the appropriate skills at the operational level and knows "how to do things correctly"—in other words, has mastered the necessary *capability strategy.*

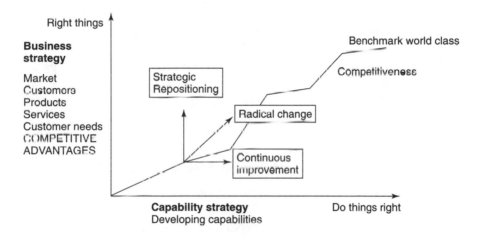

The implementation of a demanding business strategy in a tough competitive environment often requires exponential change in the organization's abilities. Exponential improvements are not achieved by doing things better but by doing them in a different way.

This book concentrates on the capability strategies associated with the *management of products and processes, as well as the continuous development of skills.* The book describes development models that can be used to double competency by doing things in a different way, not just by doing them better. The book places emphasis on a company's ability to implement the plans and objectives of its business strategy faster than its competitors can. The book can also be regarded as a vehicle for moving between business strategy and capability strategy.

A SOLID THEORETICAL FOUNDATION

"Learning by doing" is still a valid methodology, but if it is the only way to learn in your organization it is too slow, and it is expensive. This book has been born out of the author's enthusiasm to learn from others as well as from personal experience. Collecting other people's experiences, successes, and failures multiplies the opportunities for learning.

Many important development models and successful improvement programs have come about by learning from others' experiences. The following are a few examples.

JIT Was Created through Adapting the Successful Practices of Others

JIT was born when Toyota's production director, Taiichi Ohno, realized how American supermarkets operated: "We imagined each stage of the process as being like a warehouse for the next, and each stage could be filled up like a supermarket shelf as required." JIT was born as a result of a process of benchmarking.

In the 1980s, the West marveled at how the Japanese developed products in half the time, and their throughput times were just a fraction of those in the West. When Western consultants and researchers visited Japan, they came to understand Japanese production principles, which began to be known as the JIT production philosophy.

Benchmarking Was Developed through Modeling Internal Success

"Western" benchmarking was also born from the practical considerations of the time. At the end of the 1970s, Canon brought a copier onto the American market that sold for Rank Xerox's production cost. Xerox completely lost its competitive edge and was close to bankruptcy. This stimulated Xerox to compare itself with its competitors and learn from them. As well as competitors, Rank Xerox examined and learned from companies outside its own field. The result of this process of comparison and learning was that Xerox was able to make radical improvements in its competitiveness. As well as improving profitability, Xerox also modeled the process it had used to learn from those better than it, called benchmarking.

Motorola Learned from Its Japanese Rival

At the end of the 1980s, the Japanese brought out a car phone in America that sold for the same as it cost Motorola to produce its. Motorola accused the Japanese of dumping and managed to stop imports of Japanese car phones for 18 months. During that time, Motorola learned how the Japanese constructed and manufactured their car phones. Motorola's competitive capabilities, which we are now familiar with, were born.

ABB Learned from Motorola for Its Customer Focus Program

At the end of 1989, Gerhard Schulmayer left Motorola to become director of ABB's industrial segment in Zurich. He sold the idea of a comparable development program to the one Motorola had implemented to Percy Barnevik, president and CEO, ABB. This resulted in ABB's Customer Focus, T50, and Time for the Customer development programs. Today there are many companies, Volvo being one of the first, that have learned from ABB and launched their own time-based competition development programs.

Models for learning from one's own and others' experience have been developed and can be applied at both the organizational and the individual levels. The following are three models that are applied in this book.

Learning from One's Own Experience

Managing Change applies Kolb's models of learning from experiences and follows his model, adding the principles of benchmarking. According to D. Kolb, "You can learn by your own experiences. The learning may however be insignificant if you [cannot] formulate a theory for it, or understand the cause-and-effect relationship. It only remains a memory which cannot be used in other contexts."

The claim is based on the experiential learning cycle presented by Kolb in 1984. This has been used extensively to illustrate experience-based learning.

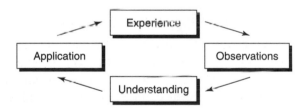

There are four stages to the learning cycle: One's own experience, observations based on it, thinking about it, and developing a theory or model on the basis of it. This understanding enables experience to be applied in very different conditions.

Learning from the Success of Others—Benchmarking

Learning from the experience of others follows the same principles: experience, observation, understanding, and application under other circumstances. Rank Xerox developed the benchmarking methodology to compare itself with and to learn from the best organizations. Benchmarking follows the same model as Kolb's experiential learning, which Rank Xerox extended to include learning from others' experience. The following shows the four-stage benchmarking model.

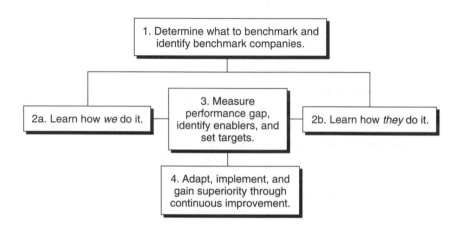

Modeling Individual Excellence—NLP

NLP (neurolinguistic programming) is a research movement that concentrates on the interactions of the operations of the brain and mind and the possibilities stemming from them. NLP is a model that can be used to study and improve human communication, as well as to study and alter mental operations. We often know *what* ought to happen to make something work better; NLP includes the information about *how* to make it all possible.

NLP concentrates on skills. NLP was born when mathematician Richard Bandler and linguist John Grinder asked what distinguishes someone who is skilled in an area from someone who possesses absolute mastery in the same field? They did not look for answers in people with innate ability but from the structures of human activity and experience. While examining "mastery," Bandler and Grinder succeeded in paring down the elements of this mastery to the level of the intuitive and subconscious parts and began to call themselves *modelers.*

With its foundations in modeling, NLP assumes that, if one person can do something, then in principle anyone else can do it, too. The question is one of how to model or open up a successful operating style. When modeling is successful, skills can be taught to people who did not previously possess them. Part 4, "Managing My Own Change," is based mainly on the underlying assumptions of NLP and the author's practical experience.

THE BOOK TAKES A LEARNING FROM EXPERIENCE APPROACH

The presentation in this book follows the Kolb experiential learning model presented earlier, supplemented with the principles of benchmarking.
The case studies in this book are taken from the author's and other people's experiences. The development models that follow them have been born out of observation of the author's and other's experiences and by learning from experts in this field.

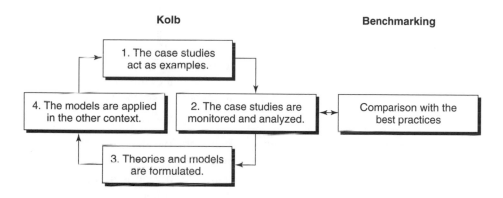

THE NEED FOR CHANGE AND CONTINUOUS IMPROVEMENT OF MANAGEMENT SKILLS

The ability to change has always been key to a company's ability to survive and prosper. However, change and renewal in themselves are not sufficient. The need for change must be recognized in time, change must be focused on issues that are important to the company's success, and change must be implemented with competitive speed and quality. In order to satisfy these demands, the management of change requires a sufficient level of *management skills*. These skills are developed by *managing change*. They can be developed both through one's own experience and by learning from the experiences of others. In order to exploit his or her own and other people's experiences, the manager of change must create development models, which can be used to direct, guide, and implement the development of the company.

This book presents examples, theory, and models of the management of change and development. It tries to present them in a form the reader can use to base his or her own models on and to adapt them to his or her own programs of change. The aim is to encourage the reader to learn from his or her own and other people's experiences and so move toward a continuously learning and developing organization. The book links theory and practice. In particular, it builds a bridge between planning and implementation. It uses experience to illustrate the latest development and change management models.

FOR WHOM IS THE BOOK INTENDED?

This book is for managers, supervisors, and development professionals who

1. Have a burning desire for their company to succeed
2. Know that continuing success comes only from constant and rapid renewal
3. Want to create understandable and stimulating models of corporate development for themselves and their organizations
4. Know that the management of significant change separates the real managers from the herd
5. Want to develop themselves continuously by managing the renewal of their organizations
6. Want to exploit all the resources available to them without prejudice and to participate in the continuous renewal of everyone in the company
7. Want to learn unreservedly from their own and other people's experiences

The book will benefit experienced managers of change who want to improve and extend their own development models exploiting their own and other people's experience. The book is also suitable for younger and less experienced managers who want to accelerate the development of their own models by learning from other people's experience.

For each subject, the book briefly presents the theory that is relevant to the matter at hand. It is assumed, however, that the reader will study these questions in depth using other sources; therefore, the theories are summarized.

This book is not intended for managers, supervisors, and development professionals who

1. Want to keep promises given to the board or their immediate manager so as to save their jobs
2. Believe strongly that the company's success depends only on whether it is going through "good or bad times"
3. Believe that the various development models are useless and that it is sufficient to get the deal at a good price and manufacture at low cost
4. Manage significant change by delegating to department heads
5. Want others to change in accordance with the strategy
6. Expect others to implement management's plans
7. Believe that you can learn only by doing it yourself

If you fall into this group, read the book, anyway. Maybe it will give you some new and practical thoughts for improvement, which you can apply within your organization.

WHY DO SO MANY DEVELOPMENT PROJECTS FAIL?

Many people have developed and improved themselves and their organizations, but too few have been able to generate significant and measurable results using systematic development programs. There are good reasons for this. The plan never got off the ground. The plan was started but it failed the first hurdle. The plan was implemented but after a while it became obvious that nothing had actually changed. The list goes on.

Why does such a small proportion (only one-fifth, as many studies show) of implemented programs yield noticeable results? Research, literature, and the author's line management experience reveal that the answer lies in the following three areas:

1. Holistic management
2. Development capabilities
3. Skills of change management

More detailed explanations are presented in the following pages.

Holistic Project Management

The reasons that development programs fail are often found in the managers' backgrounds. One has good skills in strategic planning and new market entry. Another understands product development, and a third knows production and how to improve it. A fourth is familiar with financial management and personnel development.

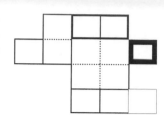

The organization can generate a good business idea for the company. However, it is not able to identify the skills or development program needed to bring the new idea to fruition. It knows business strategy but not competence strategy.

One important reason that development programs fail is that there is a lack of holistic understanding. One area is understood well, but not the others:

- There are ideas, but it takes too long for them to become innovations.
- The R&D works, but the products are not commercialized.
- The R&D is successful, but manufacturing and delivery are slow or of poor quality.
- The company is good at cutting costs but not at continuously developing its processes.
- The company can develop but fails to select the right targets for development.
- The company may be able to start a development program but lacks the skills to implement change.

As well as having their own areas of expertise, the best managers also understand the big picture. They know how the different areas link with each other. They know how to manage the whole, so that annual targets are achieved. They also know how the whole must be improved in order to meet future targets.

Successful Managers Are Masters of Holistic Management

The following page is the whole picture. The various parts and their interdependencies are covered in the first part of the book and are illustrated with case studies.

MASTER OF HOLISTIC MANAGEMENT

Strategic management

Markets, customers, customer needs, products, services, and competitive advantages

Product management

Competitiveness, ease of manufacture, and flexibility

Process management

Quality, efficiency, flexibility, and enthusiasm

Development management

Business idea, products, processes, and competencies

Development Capabilities

The business idea is excellent, the development plans are good, and there is enthusiasm for improvement, but development skills are lacking. This is another important reason that development programs fail.

"I haven't got time for it." That is what we say, when, in fact, we do not know what we should be doing. We usually do what we know we can do. We explain away our lack of skills by saying there is not enough time. We do not admit that we do not know how to do something and do not have time to learn.

If you have implemented a project that lasted, for example, a year, ask yourself this: "How much time would I have needed if I had had the skills one year ago that I have now?" You would have needed a fraction of the time you actually used; wouldn't you agree?

A development program should be rolled out once, and it must proceed rapidly. If it fails once, it is hard to restart it. Enthusiasm and belief in it evaporate with failure. In order to ensure implementation, development programs must follow tested development models.

Successful organizations understand this and know these models. They have benchmarked themselves against even better companies, have applied the results to their own needs, and are continuously developing.

Successful Managers Are Masters of Development

The following list is a summary of the stages of a development model. They are covered in more detail in the second part of the book and are illustrated with examples.

MASTER OF DEVLEOPMENT

Strategic management

1. Determine development topic and targets.
2. Create commitment.
3. Turn targets into measurable projects.
4. Evaluate the program.
5. Launch the development program.
6. Execute the program and follow up.
7. Exchange development experiences.
8. Finalize the program.
9. Continue management commitment.

Product management

1. Recognizing the need for change
2. Determining the customer requirements
3. Planning of the program and setting targets
4. Specifying and modeling the customer requirements
5. Product design
6. Sales design
7. Defining the organization and the production strategy
8. Developing the process
9. Continuous capability improvement
10. Establishment and continuous development

Process management

1. Organizing for the improvement program
2. Defining the project
3. Defining and measuring the process
4. Developing the process
5. Continuous measuring and learning
6. Continuous improvement of the process
7. Managing individual processes
8. Managing the process

Development management

Benchmarking

1. Determine what to benchmark.
2. Identify benchmark companies.
3. Measure performance gap.
4. Identify enablers resulting in excellence.
5. Learn how *we* do it.
6. Learn how *they* do it.
7. Establish performance goals.
8. Adapt and implement.
9. Continue development to gain superiority.
10. Start again with higher targets.

Skills of Change Management

Many managers have succeeded in circumstances in which major changes were not needed. Others have succeeded in circumstances in which continuous improvement was not of critical importance. They have taken good advantage of the skills that were already available. They have found suitable markets and customers whom the skills they had could be used to serve. These managers would not necessarily succeed again if their companies' skills were no longer sufficient. Customers' needs change, and competition becomes significantly tougher. They may buy a couple of firms, but integrating them to become a functioning entity does not work, and so it goes on.

Change is managed in a different way: sooner or later, these managers will have to manage change as well. In these circumstances, they may not notice that change is not managed using the same methods as for day-to-day business. They are used to managing through a hierarchical organization. The management tools used have been tar-gets, responsibility, authority, and delegation. When major change occurs, it is these tools that are subject to continuous change. Many things to be changed cannot be delegated. They do not change rapidly, nor do they do it on their own. Change can affect structures, power, boundaries of responsibility, performance measurement, compensation systems, and so on, right through to corporate cultures and values. They are the result of long change processes, which someone has to manage.

Different change situations need their own management methods: improvement in great leaps has to be managed differently than is continuous development. Cuts are managed differently than are quality programs. Local changes are managed differently than are global changes. The manager has to recognize what kind of change is being dealt with and manage it accordingly. He or she must be able to achieve both the budgeted targets and the long-term development targets.

Skills in Change Management Separate Successful Leaders from Average Ones

The change management model includes the main skills that are needed when applying the various development models. This subject is covered in more detail in the third part of the book.

MASTER OF CHANGE MANAGEMENT

1. **A systematic framework and specific targets.**
   - Identify the true need for change.
   - Create a challenging and inspiring vision.
   - Show your commitment through your involvement and interest in learning.
   - Be ready to compromise.
   - Raise your targets.
   - Prepare challenging plans.
   - Timing is everything.
   - Identify and exploit development resources.
   - Invest in development professionals.
   - Provide development training.
   - Organize for change.
2. **Leadership brings change.**
   - The driven leader has vision and can pass it on.
   - The driven leader has desire.
   - The driven leader listens to others.
   - The driven leader seeks change in him- or herself.
   - The driven leader rises to a challenge.
   - The driven leader finds challenge lovers.
   - Challenge lovers get things done.
   - Everyone must get involved.
   - Champions have what it takes.
   - Prepare for conflicts.
   - Inform and communicate.
   - Maintain the need for change.
   - The right values lead to the best solutions.
3. **Results, not plans, provide solutions.**
   - The perfect plan does not exist.
   - Be sure everyone is committed.
   - Start from several directions simultaneously.
   - Initiate open measurement immediately.
   - Start at once.
   - Initiate a pilot program.
   - Go for quick implementation.
   - Have a long-term horizon.
   - Reward even for a brave attempt.
   - Move toward ongoing improvement.

Part 1

HOLISTIC MANAGEMENT

QUICK NOTES

Pages 2–15. Read headings, illustrations, tables, and the text in *italics*.

1

Chapter 1

ORGANIZATION—A COMBINATION OF MANAGEMENT MODELS

SUMMARY

A business is an entity that can be divided in many ways. Traditionally, we have understood the business as a whole in terms of its organizational chart. The organizational chart lays out the activities of the business: product development, marketing, production, and so on, as well as identifying the power relationships among the people in the organization. The organizational chart, though, describes very little that is of interest to the customer. Instead of the organization, I have tried to describe the whole using four *management models: strategic* management, *product* management, *process* management, *and development* management.

Strategic Management

Strategic management is the ability to define a company's *business idea,* formulate plans to implement the idea, and bring the plans to fruition. The business idea and associated objectives and development plans should be formulated and promulgated so that everyone can implement them enthusiastically in their own work.

Product Management

Through our company's products and services, we create added value for our customers. Our products and service have to fulfill our customers' needs and expectations better than our competitors' products and services can. The product range and the way in which the products are made have a critical impact on the company's business processes, as well as on cost efficiency and quality.

Process Management

Products and services are born out of product development and production processes, which the other processes support. The structure of the processes and the expertise embodied in them determine cycle times, flexibility, cost efficiency, and the quality as perceived by the customer.

Development Management

A company must continually develop its business idea, products, and processes, as well as the skills of its employees. For example, a company develops its *business idea* by selecting new markets and customer segments. It improves its *products* by designing them to meet specific customer requirements. It improves its *delivery process* by reducing through-put times. It develops the *skills* of its employees by having its salespeople learn about their customers' processes.

The following is a simplified diagram of the content of these *management models*.

Strategic management

Markets, customers, customer needs, products, services, and competitive advantages

We have a vision of what we want to be;
we share the targets and know how to reach them.

Product management

Competitiveness, produceability, and flexibility

Our products meet expectations better
than those of our competitors,
and they are designed
for efficient production and delivery.

Process management

Quality, efficiency, flexibility, and enthusiasm

Our processes produce customer satisfaction
better than those of our competitors,
and they work with a high level of efficiency
and flexibility. People enjoy their work.

Development management

Business idea, products, processes, and competencies

We manage the development leaps
and continuous improvement in order to remain constantly
ahead of our customers and our competitors.

The Model for Holistic Management

IDENTIFYING INTERACTIONS

These four models are the pillars that support the operations of every company. They are strongly interdependent, and the interdependencies must be taken into account when developing them. These interdependencies are not shown by an organizational chart. Following are some examples:

- A company's competitive advantage is recognizing new market opportunities well before its competitors *(strategic management)*. To exploit these opportunities, the company must be able to develop customer-specific products for global markets *(product management)* and get them through the product development process and onto the market quickly *(process management)*.
- The situation can also be the other way around. A company has mastered product innovation *(product management)* and can get products through product development and onto the market quickly *(process management)*. It then has to be able to identify appropriate markets and customer segments as well, and to do it in good time, often years before the product launch *(strategic management)*.
- A company has mastery of product or manufacturing technology that could give a decisive competitive advantage *(process management)*. It is then necessary to be able to design the products so that the technological advantage can be exploited *(product management)*.
- A company is able to reduce its delivery times by delivering from stock *(process management)*. It needs to be able to improve its production process so that the products its customers need can be delivered directly without stockpiling *(development management)*.
- A company has halved the throughput times in its production process and can make deliveries very rapidly *(process management)*. However, the competitive situation demands that delivery times be halved again over the next few years *(development management)*.

As well as identifying the development targets described, the company has to have the skills to implement them. It must find change management skills from within. This subject is covered in Part 3 of this book.

Case Study: The Bakers

The Bakers is a chain of Finnish bakers with 30 bakeries all over Finland. There are 10 in-store bakeries, and their number is increasing quickly. The Bakers is also expanding into Scandinavian markets. The example is taken from a real firm, but the details have been changed significantly.

The major *business objectives* set for the operating management of The Bakers by the firm's owners are as follows:

- Twenty percent growth in five years by expanding throughout Scandinavia and becoming the third largest bakery chain
- Ten percent growth in three years by developing organic products for the Finnish market
- Status as the clear market leader in Finland within three years
- Improvements in cost efficiency in order to maintain current high levels of profitability in spite of the need to fund growth

---

In order to achieve these objectives, the *business idea* was defined, as were the product, process, and development management success factors needed to support it. On the following pages, each success factor is explained with the aid of a picture, a short account of the theory, and an example from The Bakers. The description of the general principles underlying the success factors are shown in *italics*. The descriptions of The Bakers are in roman script.

The *success factors* describe the situation that can create competitive advantage, cost efficiency, and flexibility. The actual *development models* are presented in Part 2 of the book.

The model and its example give the best results if you try to substitute your own organization's success factors for those of The Bakers. You will observe that the model does not give perfect answers in every situation, but you need to extend it by formulating your own model for each case. The model provides a good jumping off point for a concerted effort to think about your own company's success factors, their interdependencies, and their development targets.

Strategic Management

1. Markets and customers

Markets define the area where we want to operate. Our products, services, and way of operating have to be adapted to the needs of our selected market.

2. Products and services

Products and services form the core of our competitive advantage. They must satisfy our customers' needs and expectations better than do those of our competitors.

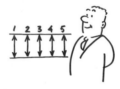

3. Customer needs and expectations

The customer will select a range of suppliers whose products and services meet his or her needs. From this range, the customer will select the supplier who can also best fulfill his or her expectations.

4. Competitive advantage

Competitive advantages are the features of our products, services, and operation that clearly differentiate us from our competitors. Our products, services, and way of working clearly give the customer better value added than do those of our competitors.

The definition of the *business idea* is the basis for the definition of the current and required success factors. In order to achieve the strategic objectives, the operating management has to define two *business ideas.* The first depicts the present business idea; the second is the business idea toward which the company is striving using its own development activities in order to fulfill its strategic objectives. The business idea describes the company's selected markets and customers as well as the products and services that will fulfill its customers' needs and expectations. It also spells out the main *competitive advantages* on which the company competes.

Strategic Choice	Current Business Idea	Target Business Idea
Markets	Finland	Expand into Sweden and Norway
Customers	Chain stores Retailers Consumers	The same customer groups
Products	Bread Cakes Confectionery	Add organic products
Services	Delivery of frozen goods to in-store bakeries	Health education for shops as well
Needs and expectations	Hunger Enjoyment Gifts	Health as well
Competitive advantage	Flavor and broad range of breads Fresh cakes Confectionery designed for local tastes Close customer relations	Healthy and nourishing bakery products as well

The company will expand within Finland and into the Swedish and Norwegian markets. As well as its existing product range, the company plans to develop an organic range of products aimed at satisfying customers' health concerns. A new service is health education in shops to promote sales of the organic products. A new competitive advantage will be the health and nutrition aspects of the bakery products. This is also expected to improve further the traditional image of The Bakers.

In order to implement the selected business idea, the company has to develop its product range, products, and production strategy as described in the following section.

Product Management

1. Product range

Our product range meets the demands of our selected markets and customers better than does that of our competitors. Our product range comprises a limited number of basic products, each of which provides sufficient choice for our customers.

Our position as the main local supplier is supported by our broad product range. About half of our product range consist of nationally recognized brands and the remainder are local products. Products for different customers are differentiated from each other either by differences in the product or in the packaging.

Product Group	Product Line	Products	Brands
Bread	White Wheat	10 pcs. 15 pcs.	20 pcs. 30 pcs.
Cakes	With fillings Without fillings	20 15	40 30
Confectionery products	Gateaux Soft confectionery Biscuits	5 5 5	10 10 10

2. Production strategy

The structure of our products allows for flexible planning and production at various locations as necessary. The location of our production guarantees local flexibility and overall efficiency.

Bread is baked in five specialist bakeries. The recipes for the products and their manufacturing techniques mean that all products, including those to be sold under customers' brand names, can be produced in the same bakery without lengthy changeover times or major changes in ingredients. Cakes are produced centrally as frozen products and delivered to be baked by local bakeries and in-store bakeries. With a few exceptions, confectionery products are produced by local subcontractors.

3. Competitiveness

Our products meet customers' expectations with regard to technology and quality and are clearly better than those of our competitors. We are able to design and produce products in response to particular customer requirements economically and quickly.

The competitive advantages our products enjoy are taste and a broad product range for bread, freshness for cakes, and confectionery designed to appeal to local tastes. Our recipe bank enables us to design and produce rapidly and economically in response to specific demands from our customers for certain cakes and confectionery products.

4. Produceability

The structure of our products enables us to produce a broad product range and gives us the ability to respond to customers' demands quickly and economically. Our products are designed for economic production in which speed, reliability, and high quality are easy to achieve.

The recipes and packaging for our bread and cakes enable us to use automatic production and give us products of consistent quality. The recipes for our confectionery products are easy to swap between subcontractors and give us flexible local products for local customers.

Products must be taken quickly from product development to the market, they must be produced efficiently, and they must generate continued customer satisfaction as described in the following section.

Process Management

1. Processes for creating customer satisfaction

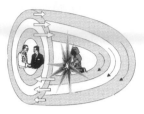

Our core process starts from customer needs and ends in customer satisfaction. Our processes are a part of our customers' processes.

Our processes are part of the chain store's marketing process, the retailer's sales and purchasing processes, and the consumer's nourishment, health, and enjoyment processes. Customer needs and expectations are defined for every core process:

Core Processes	Chain Store	Retailer	Consumer
Sales support			
Product development			
Production			
Distribution			

2. Processes extend across departments, business units, and enterprises

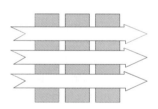

We do not compete alone but are part of a business chain that has competing chains. Our objective is the overall financial viability of the process chain.

We are part of a business chain: farmer, grain merchant, mill, *bakery,* chain store, retailer, and consumer. Our chain has many competing chains. The amount of money at the disposal of the whole chain has fallen 70 percent in 10 years. The chain must develop as a whole, irrespective of who owns each part of it.

3. Measuring for a feedback loop for learning

The main measures of the quality of the process are customer satisfaction and comparison against competitors. The main measures of the efficiency of our processes are throughput times, costs, and flexibility. We implement repair and preventive measures rapidly.

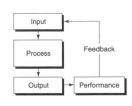

Measurement of customer satisfaction and comparison with our local and national competitors are carried out every month by means of feedback, which we get from each customer twice a year. Other feedback is also collected and analyzed as a continuous process.

The main measures of the efficiency of our process are throughput times, costs, and flexibility. Time standards are set for repair and preventive measures.

4. Processes must be organized

Our processes have an owner who is responsible for the objectives of the process and its continuous development. Each process has a development group that participates in the continual development of its processes.

Our 4 core processes and 10 support processes are organized as follows:

Process	Process Owner	Development Team	Quality Measures	Efficiency Measures
Core Processes				
1. Sales support				
2. R&D				
3. Production				
4. Distribution				
Support Processes				
1. Training, etc.				

In order to keep our operations competitive, we have to continually develop our business idea, products, processes, as well as everybody's skills in accordance with the principles presented in the following section.

Development Management

1. Developing the business idea

We continually develop our business idea in order to achieve our strategic objectives. We apply the best methodologies to the development of the business idea, learning them through benchmarking against first-rank companies.

Our business objectives for growth and international expansion require a renewal of our business idea. We must specify our new markets and target customer groups, identify their needs and expectations, and then develop the products, services, processes, and skills that will satisfy them. We used the Finnish sweet industry's expansion into the Scandinavian markets as our benchmark.

2. Developing products

We continually develop products that assist with the implementation of our business idea. We apply the best methodologies to our product development, learning them through benchmarking against first-rank companies.

We developed a range of breads specifically for the Swedish market. We carried out research to define customer needs and expectations. We carried out competitive benchmarking in the Norwegian market. That assisted us in setting objectives for product range and quality.

We developed a range of organic products for the Finnish market.

We learned the Quality Function Deployment (QFD) technique for transforming customer requirements into product and process features. We benchmarked ourselves against appropriate exponents of the QFD technique.

3. Developing processes

We continually develop processes that assist with the implementation of our business idea. We apply the best methodologies to our process development, learning them through benchmarking against first-rank companies.

We developed the core processes in our Finnish operations to world-class level before the major expansions into Norway and Sweden. We benchmark against the corresponding processes in our own company, against our competitors, and against companies from outside the sector. We use internal benchmarking to transfer our process skills to the new markets in Norway and Sweden.

We develop the processes needed for our organic products in Finland by working closely with farmers, mills, and our customers. We look for the best practice in corresponding processes within the Finnish bakery sector.

4. Developing competencies and skills

We continually develop our personal skills, which assist with the implementation of our business idea. We continually develop participative learning and development methodologies and encourage everyone to develop and learn from those more knowledgeable than them.

We improve our employees' Swedish and Norwegian language skills and their knowledge of the national cultures. We establish a special development and training program to improve the skills of our staff in strategic management, product development and process development. We improve our employees' knowledge of nutrition and organic products. These training programs are implemented simultaneously throughout Scandinavia.

MODELS AS PART OF A HOLISTIC VIEW

The development models presented in this book do not have a life of their own. The desired outcome of a development program is to be able to meet *customer* expectations better than *competitors*. This in turn requires multi-skilling. The *skill* base must also be sufficient to achieve a profitable operation and thus meet the expectations of the company's *owners* and *financiers*. The business operations must also be developed so that they meet the demands and expectations of the *community* as a whole.

In each model, the development objectives, limits, and opportunities take into consideration the requirements as well as the opportunities from competition, customers, owners, and the community. In addition, they require your own models, such as the management of customers, competitors, finance, employees, and the environment. However, these management areas are not treated specifically in this book.

SELF-EVALUATION QUESTIONS

This book presents a number of questions in each chapter. With the help of these questions, you can rank your organization in each area of management. You can evaluate both present and target performance, discuss the reasons for different opinions, and plan development projects. This provides a practical mechanism for ongoing self-analysis and improvement.

1. Evaluate the priority of each area on a scale of 1 to 5.
2. Evaluate the present performance capability of each area by marking it with a cross, and indicate your opinion as to the position of the target capability with a circle. The scale has been selected so that priority and target performance capabilities should correspond to each other.
3. Give what in your own estimation is the overall mark for the whole sector.

Example

Evaluation Criteria	Priority	Current and Target Performance				
		1	2	3	4	5
1. Do you know the customer satisfaction?	4		X		O	
2. Do you know the expectations of the customers?	5				X	O
3. Do you know the capabilities of fulfilling the expectations?	5				X	O
4. Etc.						

Evaluation Criteria	Priority	Current and Target Performance				
		1	2	3	4	5
1. Do you know the customer satisfaction?						
2. Do you know the expectations of the customers?						
3. Do you know the capabilities of fulfilling the expectations?						
4. Etc.						

		Current and Target Performance
x Your evaluation of the current performance level o Your target	Priority 1 Not significant 2 Significant 3 Important 4 Very important 5 Competitive advantage	1 Poor 2 Adequate 3 Good 4 Very good 5 Exceptional

Part 2

DEVELOPMENT MODELS

QUICK NOTES
Pages 17–19. Read the complete text.

Development models—Background, Purpose, and Contents

How Were the Book's Development Models Created?

The development models presented in this book (column 1) have been created on the principles of Kolb's experiential learning model. They have been created by combining corporate case studies (column 2) with other tested development models (column 3). These new models have then been applied in other companies in different circumstances (column 4).

1 Development Model of the Book	Experience Applied		4 Application of the Development Model of the Book
	2 Case Study	3 Development Model	
Part 1 Holistic Management	Rosenlew Rauma Ahlstrom	General Electric development model	The Bakers
Part 2 Chapter 2 Strategic Management	ABB	Model created by the author	ABB Ahlstrom Machinery Rosenlew Other organizations
Chapter 3 Product Management	Aquamaster-Rauma	Plus-modularization model by Innomat Ltd (acquired by i2 Technology, USA, 1998)	Trailer manufacturer
Chapter 4 Process Management	Ahlstrom Pumps	H. James Harrington The Rummler-Brache Group	Prostec
Chapter 5 Development Management	Rosenlew Household Appliances	Rank Xerox benchmarking model	Decathelete Rosenlew Tools
Part 3 Management of Organizational Change	Rosenlew Rauma Ahlstrom	Model created by the author	Examples
Part 4 Managing My Own Change		Model from NLP literature and training	Composing *Managing Change*

The development models are simply presented; the problems associated with them are not addressed, neither is any position taken with regard to the management of the development process. These questions are addressed for all the development models in Part 3, Management of Change.

Models Are Development Methods and Management Philosophies

The models presented in this book are not simply development methodologies. They also embody management principles that differ significantly from those we are used to. The models and the associated theory and case studies attempt to bring out the critical differences between the modes of thought. The following are some examples:

- *Strategic management* emphasizes the successful and rapid implementation of strategy as well as the part played by managers in directing it. The board normally tends to concentrate on strategic planning and delegates the implementation as an operational matter.
- Companies are used to selling whatever their products or services are. The main focus of attention is on the product. *Product management* focuses on selling what the customer needs. The focus shifts to understanding the customer's needs and fulfilling them with products designed to meet them.
- We are used to considering business activity as companies, business units, and departments. We then measure and evaluate performance within these limits. The primary focus is on the efficiency of one's own unit. In *Process management,* we reduce the significance of these boundaries, concentrate on the customer in our development, and measure and evaluate performance with respect to the process.
- In *development management,* the objective has been to improve on our own performance and simply pull development ideas out of thin air. In benchmarking, the objectives and opportunities are sought from outside the company, and the company learns from those better than itself. Management of development is management of learning.

Taking these principles on board is more about learning to throw out the past than acquiring new skills. We do not, however, want to give up what we already know and are familiar with, if we have no comprehension of a new and better way of working. If change seems to be too great, the risk of losing what we have seems greater to us than the gains we could acquire. We know what it is we are losing, but we do not know for certain what we are putting in its place.

The models give a holistic view. They explain the causal connections between various issues, and they ease the process of unlearning the old and acquiring new skills. The models create an understanding of, and feeling of comfort with, the shift to the new and untried. The fact that someone else has already trodden the proposed path bolsters courage. The models also allow transfer to the new operating philosophy in stages, which reduces the risk of failure.

Models Do Not Describe Reality

Remember, though, that the given models for development do not represent reality. They are far too simple for that. Reality is much more complicated. The models with their phases help us understand the whole, its parts, and their interrelationships.

The models should be applied but not followed blindly. You may cause more harm than good if you do not understand what you are doing. To make comprehension easier, each model has been presented with a short theory and case studies. The cases describe the development projects the model has been taken from, or where it has been applied.

Some managers get enthusiastic about a particular development model, assuming that the model will manage change. Since the manager's own change management skills are not sufficient or may have never been put to the test, failure is explained in terms of the deficiency of the model or its unsuitability.

Many managers resist these sorts of development models, saying, "We do not have time for all of that; our model must be simpler." They forget that reality is a dozen times more complicated. Reality does not become less complicated by simplifying the model. Those who get by on their own and consider the models worthless use far more time and resources to obtain the same results. Worse, they never reach the target. When a mere 10 percent of the workload that change really demands is set in front of them, they shy away from it.

The Models Are Designed to Accelerate Change

The aim of the models is to support the achievement of significant change at sufficient speed. Applying the model causes the development cycles to repeat, which speeds up the learning process. Experience shows that management is trained for strategic planning, not for strategy implementation. The idea behind the models is to develop the implementation skills of executives and decision makers.

The following four chapters of Part 2 (2–5) present four development models. There are short accounts of the theories and case studies from which the models have been developed. A description of the model's application within another organization is also included.

Chapter 2

STRATEGIC MANAGEMENT

Strategic management

Markets, customers, customer needs, products, services, and competitive advantages

Product management	**Process management**

Development management

The best way to foresee the future is to create it yourself.

Joel Birnbaum
Hewlett-Packard

Content Summary

The chapter illustrates the key concepts of implementing strategic management. The concept *business idea,* as it applies to strategic planning, is described. The book emphasizes how alignment between market opportunities and capabilities is needed to exploit identified opportunities, and it demonstrates the interaction of different capabilities. The book defines the essential skills of strategic management and emphasizes the importance of change management.

Asea Brown Boveri has achieved success in all its business areas. That success has followed from both strategic decisions and the implementation of systematically planned development programs targeted at executing the selected capability strategy. The case study describes one program called Customer Focus. The project was known as T50 in Sweden and as Time for the Customer in Finland. The case study doesn't aim to give a precise description of the program. It attempts to describe the key features, which we benchmarked when the equivalent global program (P500) in Rauma Ltd was started. We were especially interested in how a global program was planned, implemented, and managed at a consolidated corporation level. The company example is based on interviews.

The chapter describes the implementation of capability strategies in nine successive phases. The chapter is based on the above-mentioned case study and on the corresponding project (P500) carried out at Rauma Ltd.

The list of questions in the book will help you evaluate your organization's current and intended position, will form a basis for discussion on the reasons for differences in personal evaluations, and will help you plan your improvements.

INTRODUCTION TO STRATEGIC MANAGEMENT

Capability Strategies to Implement the Business Strategy

Strategic management can be divided into two categories:

1. *Business strategy* defines the business in which the organization operates and "the right things to do."
2. *Capability strategies* define the general capabilities and operational competencies of the organization—that is, "to do things right."

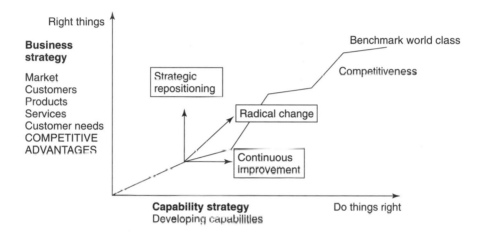

Business strategy includes the company's business idea.

The business idea represents the markets and customers chosen by the company and the products and services by which the customer demands and expectations are met. It also represents the competitive advantages with which they primarily compete.

The company aims to function according to its business idea, by which it meets the strategic goals. To achieve the new strategic goals, the company has to recreate its business idea. Every company has a business idea. In a successful company, the business idea is carefully planned; it is agreed on and committed to, and its elements are measurable.

The business idea decisions included in the business strategy need a capable organization in order to be fulfilled. For example, we can ask the following questions: Can we provide customer variable products to the global market needs? Are our products innovative enough and are we able to get them quickly to the market? Can we create permanent customer relations at the chosen market? Can we create effective production and distribution and their continuous improvement?

On the other hand, improving our competencies provides an opportunity to make changes in our business strategy. For example, improved product modularity can make it possible to approach new markets and customers, and improved cost efficiency makes it possible to enter a new market with intense competition. To be successful, the organization has to manage both the business and the capability strategy. Development according to only one standpoint does not significantly increase competitiveness.

The company carries out its capability strategy with the assistance of development projects.

Too often, development projects are started without ensuring how they support the business goals and the chosen business idea. Do the projects have any strategic meaning or not? Actually, the business idea does not even formally exist or there are various opinions of it.

The business idea concept is also a useful tool for getting personnel to understand how development, strategic goals, the business idea, and the securing of the future are connected to each other.

If you are responsible for a significant development project that is not a clear extension of the business idea, organize a participative process to define the present and future business ideas.

Understanding the Interactions

To ensure that the capability strategy chosen really supports the goals set in the business strategy, capability strategy and goals must be connected to each other by performance targets. When setting goals and making plans, the following interactions must be taken into account:

1. The *financial performance* meters indicate the results expected from the company by various interest groups. With their help, the strategic goals are set.
2. Permanent financial improvements are not born without improvements in the *process performance.*
3. The process performance is based on the process structure and the *capabilities* in it.
4. The performance improvements are just wishes without concrete *development projects.*

1. Financial Performance		Current	Target	Best
Sales	mFIM	600	700	800
Return on asset	%	5	20	24
Market share	%	10	40	60
Solidity	%	25	50	50
2. Process Performance		**Current**	**Target**	**Best**
Product development cycle time		12 months	6	8
Quotation cycle time		1 day	1 hour	1 day
Manufacturing cycle time		10 weeks	5	5
Delivery reliability		75%	100%	100%
3. Capabilities		**Current**	**Target**	**Best**
Customer process know-how		2	5	4
Leading-edge product technology		4	5	5
Leading-edge production technology		3	5	3
4. Development Programs		**Start-Up Date**		**Best**
1. Fast-to-market program		January 200x		Year A
2. JIT production program		April 200x		C
3. Product rationalization		April 200x		C

The strategic plan should not be approved if it does not include the evaluation and impact of interactions and a comparison with the best organizations. When presented in this way, strategic planning requires skills to answer multiple questions simultaneously, as illustrated in the next section.

Providing Answers in the Same Time Frame

> 1. In what should we perform better?
> 2. How much better?
> 3. How well could we perform it?
> 4. How do we manage and lead the change?

The capability to answer these questions in the same time frame is absent in most organizations, leading to the following failures:

> 1. The development project is a success, but its impact on reaching strategic targets is very minor.
> 2. The item to be developed is OK and achieved a 30 percent improvement, but the competitor is still 30 percent better.
> 3. The item is OK and achieved a 50 percent improvement, but someone in another type of industry is still 50 percent better in that area.
> 4. The topic and the goal have been set, and the plan is the best possible. All the other points may be in order, but the development effort is too ambitious, compared with the available development resources and capabilities.

The answer to the first question requires a good market, customer requirements, and competition situation awareness. The second question requires measured data from your own and your competitors' performance and information related to the customer's expectations. The third question requires benchmark knowledge from businesses within and outside industries. The fourth question requires change management skills applied in theory as in practice.

Next, a model is presented that shows how a development area can be found by identifying the interactions among the business targets, performances, the processes, and competencies.

Identifying Critical Issues for Improvement

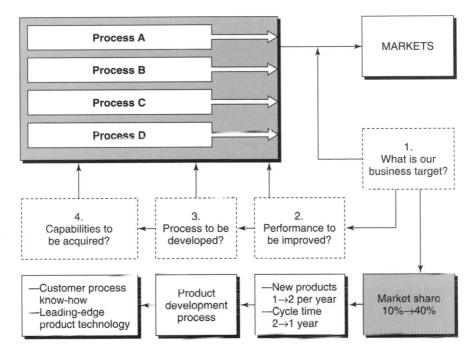

According to the diagram, a company's business target is to increase the market share from 10 percent to 40 percent. It would require doubling the number of new products developed per year, from one to two. To achieve this, the product development process cycle time has to be halved from two years to one. This could be achieved through developing the product development process—particularly, improving the knowledge of customer needs and mastering leading-edge product technology. An additional example appears on page 46.

The skill to answer presented questions and identify illustrated interactions requires an extensive participation of the people and a process of strategic planning deviating from the traditional one.

Basic Skills in Strategic Management

Companies compete with the content of their business idea and strategic plans. In most cases, the plans themselves do not compete with each other, but the speed and quality of their implementation do. The following are strategic management skills, by which the quality and speed of implementation are ensured:

1. Identifying the needs and opportunities to change the business idea
2. Defining business targets and supporting plans and getting everyone committed to them
3. Turning business targets into challenging and measurable development projects
4. Evaluating the value and attainability of the plans
5. Implementing development plans with competitive quality and speed
6. Learning from experiences

Strategic management is not an individual job of the manager. It is a team effort in which everyone must be involved. All employees must be committed to strategic management and willing to learn from their own and others' experiences. Even the best plan is no good if people are not committed to it and the plan is not realized.

The way in which a plan is made has a great impact on how committed the people are to realizing it: "I haven't been involved in program planning, and I don't understand its content. How could I carry out something that I don't even understand? I'm not convinced of the benefits of the plan and the attainability of that program. I'm not convinced, either, if I have a possibility to change anything, even if it is necessary."

The strategic planning and implementation leading to success, is no longer possible within organizational levels or on a departmental basis, because the customer of such planning is only the next organizational level up.

Change management starts at the preparation of the change plans.

Most company managers consider strategic management to be their most important task. In practice, it has primarily included only elements in the business idea related to the business strategy.

Strategic planning processes usually include 90 percent marketing opportunity planning. At most, 10 percent is used to define the capability development planning needed to use the opportunities. The implementation as a nonstragetic issue is delegated to middle management, the product development manager, the production manager, and equivalents.

Planning and implementation have generally lived their own lives. Typically, management has set the company's financial goals, middle management has set the improvement targets, and the development management has planned the necessary development projects. Often, a year passes but practically nothing has happened. The dusty plans are again dug from the shelves, and the replanning starts according to the scheduled year planning cycle.

The world is full of plans, some better than others. Of these, very few are ever implemented. Still fewer are those that have been created in a certain time frame, which also creates a competitive advantage, not just to reach the same level as competitors.

Growing numbers of managers have noticed the definition of capability requirements and development as a strategic question. They have realized that strategic management is not just planning. It is also converting plans into target-oriented and measurable development projects, as well as managing the implementation.

The information technology's lifetime is short. If a product's average lifetime is five years, 1/5 of the device and software base has to be replaced every year. Even if we wouldn't aim at growth at all, we would have to produce new, improved products at least by that amount per year.

Joel Birnbaum,
Research and Product Development Manager,
Hewlett-Packard

CASE STUDY: ABB, CUSTOMER FOCUS PROGRAM

The case study presented here is not aimed at providing an accurate description of the whole development program. Its goal is to give an example of how one international corporation launched its global development program, how it was managed, and what the prerequisites for success were.

The case study is based on interviews of the local program coordinators in Finland and Sweden and the coordinator of the whole global program in Zurich. The thoughts and phrases appearing in the text are based on statements given during the interviews—that is, on personal experiences of the interviewees.

Case Study Summary

How I see Customer Focus—Percy Barnevik

We are everything we say we are: we are big, global, local. That's a very good prerequisite for success, but it is not enough.

We are recognized as technology leaders in our core businesses. But as competition gets tougher, being only a technology leader will not guarantee our success in the future.

We all know who ultimately pays our salaries—the customer. It is our customers who determine whether we meet their needs and expectations.

From all this, we know the key to our long-term success and profitability: the

unconditional and total satisfaction of our customers with every contact they experience and every product or service they receive from us. Whatever we do must be aimed at satisfying their needs and expectations at an ever higher level. We have to be aware that this is a moving target, because their needs and expectations change. We must welcome such changes as opportunities for adding more and new values for our customers.

To instill this uncompromising customer-driven attitude throughout our group, we have started a process called "Customer Focus." To me, it is one of the most important processes that we have embarked on in our company. Quality and cycle time are vital elements of this process since improvement of both offers a huge potential for increasing customer satisfaction.

This booklet is intended to tell you what Customer Focus is all about. Please think of it also [as] an invitation for you to become part of the Customer Focus team.

Percy Barnevik
Percy Barnevik
President and CEO

The President and CEO of ABB, Mr. Percy Barnevik, opened the Customer Focus program with these words in a leaflet representing the program. Mr. Barnevik pointed out the link between the development program and the strategic goals of the corporation.

Start-up of the Development Program

ABB in its current form was founded in 1988. At the end of 1989, Mr. Gerhard Schulmayer of Motorola, U.S.A., moved to Zurich to lead the Business Segment Industry of ABB. He brought along the experience he had gained in Motorola from a corporatewide successful development program aiming at improvement of cycle times and quality. Within six months he was able to convince the CEO and president of the enterprise, Mr. Barnevik, with an idea of centrally led and supervised total quality management and time-based management programs—Motorola's success story as an example.

The kick-off meeting of the program took place in Zurich in May 1990. The meeting was attended by CEOs of all the country organizations. Percy Barnevik presented the goals of the development program, and Mr. Schulmayer presented experiences gained at Motorola. An outside consultant presented the principles of implementing the project. The principles of implementation were based on previously used and experienced development models and success stories (George Stalk, Thomas M. Hout: Competing Against Time).

In the beginning of July 1990, Mr. Barnevik was ready to give an order to implement the program with a planned schedule in all countries. Each country manager took responsibility for introducing the idea and for transferring Mr. Barnevik's instructions to the individual business units and companies.

Principles and Goals of the Development Program

The goal of ABB is to be superior in its business operations, as well as to be the best in continuous development. Being the leader means tough requirements, resources, and the use of experts. It also requires challenging targets, investments in development professionals, and uncompromised plan implementation and follow-up.

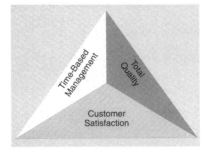

The instructions given from Zurich focused on achieving dramatic improvements in the most important performance criteria—for example, results related to customer satisfaction, process cycle times, and quality.

Results Achieved during the Development Program

The results achieved were significant, as can be seen from the table representing the results of the T50 projects in Sweden. The reduced cycle times have also been used in the competitive situation. For example, Cewe, a producer of meter instruments, has been able to increase its amount of export sales significantly, having achieved shorter delivery times. ABB Components has been able to introduce a new product to the market one year ahead of the original time schedule, resulting in an increased market share against the toughest competitor.

Substantial Time Reductions in Order Cycles		
	From	To
Standard LV switchgear	33 days	3 days
Tap changers	86	38
Standard AAC motors	47	20
Standard DC motors	30	15
Robots	20	15
Standard ABB masters	60	45
Instrument transformers	75	30
Surge arrestors	43	24
HVDC contracted for delivery	3 years	2 years

Case Study Description

Principles and Goals of the Development Program

The principles of the development program were presented in a 14-page leaflet "ABB Customer Focus, What It Means to Us," the contents of which were as follows:

---

1. How I See Customer Focus—Percy Barnevik
2. What Is Customer Focus?
3. What Is Total Customer Management?
4. What Is Time-Based Management?
5. How Do Customer Focus, TBM, and TQM Fit Together?
6. What Does This Mean to Our Group?
7. What Steps Are We Taking?
8. What Does It Mean to You?

ABB Sweden named its own program T50. ABB Sweden set a goal of reducing all cycle times by half by the end of 1993. The goals were met and even exceeded (see the table on page 33). The impact of the improvements on profitability was estimated to be 3 billion Swedish crowns.

The internal business unit ABB Control was used as a model when setting goals. ABB Control had been able to halve its cycle times before the T50 program. The best practices were also searched for some Swedish, European, American, and Japanese companies. Many were used for benchmarking in subsequent stages of the development program. Goals have been reached, and, in some cases even multiplied, as can be seen from the table in the previous section.

In Finland, the program was called "Aika asiakkaan käyttöön" ("Time for the Customer"). However, differing from the Swedish practice, development goals were set for the projects after conducting a pre-study. The goals set, however, were about on the same scale as the ones set in Sweden. The aim was to reach the goals by the end of 1992. Below is an example of the goals set.

ABB Strömberg Power/Relays Project was started in February, 1991

Performance	1990	June 1991	Target—1992
Delivery time (days)	30	15	5
Delivery reliability (%)	78	65	100
Proportion of stock of yearly turnover (%)	12	11	10
Proportion of defect costs of yearly turnover (%)	2	2	0
Proportion of R&D costs of yearly turnover (%)	16	?	10
Throughput time, product development	6 months–3 years	?	3–8 months

Development Models Based on Objectives

The launching of development programs was done country by country. Taking into account the targets given, the country organizations could select a development model of their own. A common development model within a country gave better possibilities for managing and directing the program, as well as for changing experiences.

The European countries selected cycle time as the main development target (time-based management). The United States, the U.K., and Canada focused on the development of quality (total quality management) by applying the Malcolm Baldrige Award Criteria. Europe later complemented its program with the quality issues; the countries that had started with quality continued with cycle time development.

Organizing the Development Program

The quality organization of the task force in Zurich was responsible for the coordination of the global program. A steering group was founded in each country, the country manager acting as chairperson.

In addition, a country coordinator was appointed in each country (10 in Europe), which reported to the steering group of his or her country and to the quality organization in Zurich. The task of the coordinators was to assist the management of each unit with the start-up and implementation of the project. Their task was also to ensure that the goals of each project were challenging enough and to monitor that the project was proceeding according to the plans and targets set.

The instructions and expectations from Zurich were very convincing and unambiguous; thus, it was not necessary to promote the idea of development projects to the managers of the Finnish companies—Mr. Percy Barnevik had already accomplished this. The task of the internal consultants was mainly to assist with the planning and implementation of each project. The country coordinators met in Zurich every other month, in which they could exchange experiences and report results.

In addition to a country coordinator, a management-level person was appointed to coordinate the implementation of the local T50 program in every ABB business unit in Sweden. In Sweden, the persons in charge of the T50 program met four times a year to exchange development experiences in a one-day seminar.

The management insisted that the started development program's costs and savings be taken into account in future business plans and budgets. The program control and follow-up was supposed to be a constant topic in the management group's agenda in every company.

Launching the Program with Extensive Training

One of the cornerstones for the successful program was the massive training and information given at both the corporate and unit levels. Zurich wanted to make sure that the message was understood correctly. The basic training for time-based management was arranged in Mannheim, Germany, in August–October 1990. Seven groups of 20 persons each participated in the training. In addition to the country coordinators, line managers, appointed full-time project managers, and internal consultants participated in the training.

The training was implemented by using 10 top-quality consultants, who through examples, theory, tested development models, and exercises demonstrated business process cycle time development.

Participants of the seminar were also given directions on how to start projects and what the implementation of the change required from the management.

In his opening speech in June 1990, the managing director of ABB Sweden, Bert-Olof Svanholmin, noticed that the development project to be started (T50) would most likely be the company's most significant task in the beginning of the decade. From the first day, it had to receive the attention and resources it required:

- Thirty people from Sweden participated in the training in Mannheim, Germany, in the autumn of 1990.
- One hundred people participated in equivalent training in Sweden in the spring of 1991.
- More than 1000 people participated in the one- to three-day training course on the same topics at the end of summer 1991.
- Thousands of participants attended the shorter sessions handling the same program.
- The program contents were displayed in brochures, bulletins, and staff leaflets.
- As a totally new information channel, public media were used. The company management believed that the management's message would reach the staff much better in this way than by internal bulletins. Second, the public media reached the customers, the suppliers, the stockholders, the potential new employees, and the public better in general. Third, the publicity increased the management's responsibility and the need to succeed. The price of losing the company's reputation would have been too great.

The development program got a great amount of press in the leading newspapers, magazines, trade unions' and business management's magazines, and radio and TV.

In Sweden, the prerequisites for success were considered to be the following:

- Commitment and involvement by top management
- An engaging vision
- Clear objectives
- A widespread sense of urgency—that is, awareness of the need to improve communication of vision and objectives
- A training program and qualified support
- Ownership of the change program by those who are affected by the change
- The order of the process as "top down, bottom up"

In the United States, the corresponding persons went to Motorola University in Chicago. (Motorola's entire management is trained at this university. Motorola also accepts outsiders for this management training system.)

Development Resources

The started development program would have a great strategic importance. It was decided that it should be given the required resources. The program could not be allowed to fail and had to be carried out on a tight schedule. In order to meet the demands Zurich required, the program would use the best possible consultants and development models, which were already proven to be effective elsewhere. Each country had to find the best consultants in the world, the ones that suited best the purpose.

Country management and country coordinators got their first contact with potential consultants at the training week at Mannheim. The country coordinator's task was to discuss and choose the best consultants in every country. In Finland, the selection was made during the autumn of 1990. (Among the international consultants, three could speak Finnish.)

Sweden, Finland, Germany, and Switzerland used mainly the same consultant. Another consultant worked in common with Italy and Austria. The companies in the United States mainly used a third consultant. The goal was to choose the consultants who best suited that country, but in limited numbers, to make it easier to exchange experiences.

By using external consultants at the project's inception, a big benefit was achieved in starting the development projects. As the program proceeded, difficulties arose among the international consultants with the cultural differences and knowledge of language. For this reason and for more favorable expenses, a special group was formed for the development program.

Supporting the country coordinators and at the disposal of the development program were the ABB's own consultants in six countries. In 1991, there was a total of 120 internal consultants, and the aim was to increase the number to 170 in 1993.

There was only one internal consultant in Finland's operation in 1991. In 1992, there were four, and the aim was to increase the number to 10 in 1993. Full-time project managers were assigned as internal consultants when the projects were completed. To transfer the experience from the especially successful development projects in Finland to other business units in ABB, Zurich wanted to raise the number of internal consultants.

Project Authorization

The development project had to meet the following criteria to be approved as a project in the program:

- Clear, far-reaching goals with respect to customer values and total cycle time
- A whole unit or division involved (or a pilot project that is expanded later)
- Development of competence
- Well-defined performance measurements
- A focus on achieving early results
- Application of proven development models
- Full-time project managers

Each of the country management groups approved the projects according to these criteria.

Starting the Development Projects

According to the goal, set in June 1990, at least one project had to be started in no less than half of the ABB units at the end of the year and in all of them at the end of summer 1991. All projects had to be reported to Zurich on being started.

The country coordinators' responsibility was to introduce the approval criteria to each unit's management group and to agree on which projects to start.

Using the given project criteria, the planned schedule, and the appointed country coordinators, the projects got started. An agreed-upon control method, oversaw that the plans were carried out and that the radical performance improvements were achieved.

During the spring of 1991, the prestudies of five projects were carried out in Finnish ABB units under the guidance of external consultants. According to the agreement, their task was to guide the preliminary studies so that corresponding studies could be made afterwards independently in various business units.

After the summer of 1991, six new projects were started in Finland independently. In a total of 11 development projects, 400 people were involved in the development work. In some projects, external consultants continued in a guiding role, with the aim being to finish the projects independently.

The consulting expenses were considerable, but they paid for themselves very quickly. As one of the unit managers said, "Consultants proved to be an excellent and fast way to analyze the situation or existing problems and to indicate development possibilities. The advantage was that they were systematic and used tested development methods. With their help we accomplished results in a month that could have taken a year to achieve by ourselves." The aim, however, was to use as few consultants as possible and run the projects on their own in the future.

In Sweden, the program was started with four pilot projects. The goal was to achieve good examples quickly. However, the fast progress in all Swedish ABB units diminished the significance of the example pilots. After a year from the start of the program in Sweden, there were 38 ongoing projects in which all the required criteria were met.

Exchanging Development Experiences

The transfer of development experiences occurred in many different ways:

1. Within ABB, projects were started on a purely country basis without connections to the business area organizations. In this way, they were able to start faster and to choose suitable consultants, development models, and procedures in each country. The aim was to have the support close by. The country-based synergy effects were greater than the business synergies (product and other business development took place by division). One of the reasons was that many business areas had not yet adopted their final organization. There were still many overlapping activities that had not yet been removed.

2. ABB's internal consultants were used crosswise in different countries. They were also used in the countries where there were no consultants. The aim was, with the assistance of internal consultants, to transfer knowledge, skills, and experience from one unit to another.

3. During the first year, ABB Sweden organized five half-day experience exchange seminars. A total of 2000 managers and supervisors attended the seminar.
4. In Sweden, one year after the project start, a one-day seminar was held. At this seminar, each unit manager and project leader presented his or her own project and the results achieved. Five hundred people participated in this seminar.
5. Well-documented project descriptions and achievements were used as internal success stories and were distributed to participants.
6. To exchange experiences, the program was a constant topic at the ABB's three-day management seminar and at the ABB units' managing directors' country meeting, held four times a year.

Measurement and Follow Up of the Results

What gets measured gets done.

Percy Barnevik, CEO, ABB

Measuring had great significance on setting goals, monitoring, and following up results. In the early stages, the number of started projects and participating divisions was the central performance indicator.

The units were allowed to define the best suitable project progress indicators by themselves. However, the following performance indicators were used in all units:

1. Cycle time
2. Delivery reliability
3. Inventory
4. Productivity
5. Quality costs

These key measurements were monitored in each country and reported to Zurich. Percy Barnevik might request them personally direct from each country. In many countries, the same key results were shown openly to all on the notice boards, and the achievements were linked to remuneration.

Conclusions

The first year's results already showed that the program's development goals were going to be achieved. According to the ABB Drives unit, the success was significantly influenced by the following factors:

- ABB's decentralized organization structure
- The HR policy and related development of competence, which paved the way for the program
- A time reduction target that was easy to comprehend on all levels
- Employees' perceptions of personal advantages in the program
- Company awareness of the Swedish economy and competitiveness within the ABB Group
- Management commitment and involvement
- Significant investment in training
- Proven development models
- Learning from others

> The winners will be the fast ones—
> not necessarily the big ones.
> However, when the
> big ones (ABB) become fast—
> watch out.
>
> *Percy Barnevik*

The differences between the successful and the mediocre enterprises are not born by applying new development models but by understanding, adapting, and uncompromisingly implementing the already existing ones.

MODEL OF IMPLEMENTATION OF THE CAPABILITY STRATEGIES

A nine-step model to realize the capability strategy through a development program, is presented in this section. The model assumes that a company's strategic goals and business idea have been defined according to the principles presented earlier. The model illustrates how to identify a development target and how to ensure that the development program (capability strategy) fulfills the strategic goals and enables you to realize the planned business idea (business strategy). The model also shows how to get the people committed, how to launch the program, and how to ensure effective implementation.

To illustrate the model, a set of examples is shown. The model and the examples give the best result if you replace them with the development program of your own organization.

Model of Implementation of the Capability Strategies

1. Determine development topic and targets.	**2. Create commitment.**
3. Turn targets into measurable projects.	**4. Evaluate the program.** 1. Meeting market requirements 2. Meeting capability requirements 3. Meeting financial requirements 4. Meeting attainability
5. Launch the development projects.	**6. Execute the program and follow up.**
7. Exchange development experiences.	**8. Finalize the program.**
9. Continue management commitment.	

Summary

1. **Determine development topic and targets.**

   The development topics and targets that support the strategic goals and the chosen business idea are defined. The strategic goals are broken down into performance targets. The processes and competence to be developed are defined.

2. **Create commitment.**

   The broad commitment to development plans and targets is ensured in all steps of the development model.

3. **Turn targets into measurable projects.**

   The development plans and targets are turned into measurable and challenging projects. The projects are planned and organized.

4. **Evaluate the program.**

   The development program is evaluated to ensure that it meets the market requirements, improves required competencies, achieves the financial objectives, and is attainable in a competitive time frame.

5. **Launch the development projects.**

   The management ensures that the projects are started according to the planned schedule.

6. **Execute the program and follow up.**

   The development projects are carried out, and their progress is monitored through measurements. The measurements indicate whether the projects are on the right track. These measurements also serve as a feedback system for learning.

7. **Exchange development experiences.**

   The experience obtained is documented and transmitted and internalized inside the company.

8. **Finalize the program.**

   It is ensured that the projects are completed and are guided on a continuous improvement trail.

9. **Continue management commitment.**

   Enthusiasm is maintained through the inspiring methods created by management.

1. Determine Development Topic and Targets

In this step, define the development topics and targets that support the strategic goals and business idea chosen. Break the strategic goals into required performances; identify the processes and competency to be developed.

To achieve the strategic goals and implement the chosen business idea created by the owner, the company management came up with the following analysis column by column:

1. *Increased market share as the business target:* The company's business target is to increase the market share in North America in four years from 10 percent to 40 percent.
2. *Performance required:* According to the management's estimate, the number of new products developed per year has to be doubled, from one to two products. To achieve this, the product development process cycle time has to be halved from two years to one.
3. *Process to be developed:* The management identified the product development process as the development topic to achieve set performance targets.
4. *Competency to be developed:* The needed special competencies to be developed are the knowledge of customer needs at the North American market and the use of process management approaches in order to speed up the process.

1 Strategic Goal			2 Performance Required			3 Process to be Developed	4 Capability to be Improved
	Current	Target		Current	Target		
Market share	10	40	New products	1/year	2/year	Product development process	Customer process know-how Process management
			Development cycle time	2/year	1/year		
Working capital turnover	1	2	Manufacturing cycle time	4 weeks	1 week	Manufacturing process	JIT
			Inventory turnover	2	10		Removing overlaps

The capital cycle time increase from one to two has been analyzed in a similar way.

2. Create Commitment

At this stage, the commitment to the development plans has to be consciously planned and included in every step. Even the best strategic plans are useless if they are not realized. The way the plans are prepared has a great influence on the implementation commitment.

Case 1: In Rauma's P500 Program, the aim was to achieve the set profitability by the end of 1993 through internal development (capability strategy). As in the Customer Focus Program, used as an example, the responsibilities and tasks in the program were presented and agreed upon by corporate management, the Rauma technology group, division management, business units, and division boards.

Organization	Responsibility
Rauma board	Ignition
Rauma technology group	Support/dissemination
Division management	Pace setting/leadership
Business unit management	Making it happen
Division board	Approval and follow-up

When top management shows its commitment, it is easy for others also to commit, as the following example demonstrates.

Case 2: In a one-day seminar, the company management introduced the preliminary development topics, goals, and development projects to the department managers and other key persons. Union representatives were also involved. With the Double Team Group Working Method, the benefits and flaws were gathered from management's proposal. Proposals for solutions of the detected weaknesses were created in groups.

During the following week, management changed its proposal according to the improvements found. The plan was introduced once more to the same group, which collected the benefits and the remaining weaknesses. After a week a third meeting was held, in which the development topics, goals, and development projects were approved. The project managers appointed the project groups, which planned the employee involvement for each phase of the program.

3. Turn Targets into Measurable Objects

At this point, before approval of the final strategic plan, it must be ensured that it is achievable in practice. The concrete and measurable projects must be defined, the needed development compe-tence must be available, the projects must be organized, and the schedules, goals, metrics, and follow-up must be defined.

A company analyzed the strategic goals, determined in the first stage, and came up with the following development projects:

Business Target	Development Project	Responsible
Market share in North America from 10 to 40%	Determining customer needs	Susan Sales
	Developing product development process	Paul Product
Capital turnover from one to two	Developing JIT production	Pat Production
	Global product distribution	Dave Development

A preliminary schedule, a profitability estimate, and a resource require-ment plan was prepared for every project:

Schedule						Financial Impacts				
Project Phases	200a	200b	200c	200d		Financial Impacts	200a	200b	200c	200d
1	xxxxx					Sales				
2		xxxxx				Costs				
3			xxxxx			Capital				
4		xxxxx	xxxxx			Break even				
5				xxxxx		Profitability				

4. Evaluate the Program

At the same time, the plan has to fulfill the market, financial, and competence requirements and has to be achievable. Depending on the company's situation, the compilation of development plans can start from four requirements:

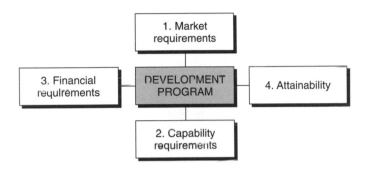

The development program planning can start from various points, according to the numbering in the diagram. Find out which alternative applies in your program:

1. **Market Requirements Approach**

   In a "textbook case," proceed as follows:

   1. Start the planning by identifying market requirements and opportunities, taking competition into consideration.
   2. Determine the competencies required to meet the market requirements or to use opportunities.
   3. Ensure that the competency to be improved also leads to cost efficiency and fulfillment of the financial requirements.
   4. When the first three conditions have been filled, evaluate the attainability of the project.

In the other approaches, the steps will be fulfilled in a different order from the "textbook case" 1-2-3-4 order.

2. Capability Requirement Approach

If your organization has innovations to be exploited, take these steps:

2. Start the process by identifying a competitive capability (innovation)—for example, a new technology.
1. Search the market and customers for the innovation.
4. Ensure your ability to realize and exploit the innovation.
3. Calculate that solutions meet the financial requirements—that is, payback time.

3. Financial Requirements Approach

A company has fallen into deep financial problems. The planning starts, then, from financial requirements:

3. First set the financial requirements, such as cash flow.
2. Define the competency that leads to the desired cost level. The competency requirements can be related to reorganizing and cuttings cost.
4. Ensure that the plan can be realized.
1. Ensure that implementation of the plan does not disturb the market.

4. Attainability-Based Approach

The company knows capabilities to be improved, but it has difficulties in implementation. The company is in deep financial trouble, and it realizes the need to reduce its product range and a radical number of employees. The sales division resists reduction of the product range, and personnel department is against downsizing. Follow these steps:

4. Prepare the plan so that it can be accepted and realized. i.e. To sell the company to its current operating management (MBO). The company concentrates on profitable products and markets and eliminates everything else.
2. Determine the competencies required, such as how to realize MBO operation and reduce the product range and number of employees.
3. Ensure that financial requirements are met—that the first three years will be without major financial problems.
1. Safeguard the markets. In the case of MBO, you provide a positive impression of the arrangement for the market.

In the following sections, an evaluation of each requirement and a real-life case study are presented.

Meeting the Market Requirements

Primarily, change must meet customer requirements or support exploiting new market opportunities. Success in the market decisively influences the company's growing possibilities and the income. The market requirements and possibilities come from outside the company—for instance, from clients, the competition situation, and market cycles. Ensure  *that these requirements and opportunities are agreed on in the company. It is insufficient to set the goal in order to be only better than before. The objective has to be set according to the external demands and opportunities.*

Rosenlew Household Appliances developed a new refrigerator and freezer product series and modernized its plant (a more detailed description on the development program can be found in chapter 5, page 199). The goal was "To develop products and production exceeding the world class standards and competition for the next 10 years." The market requirements set for the development program were as follows:

Market Requirements
1. Product range, design, and cooling technology that meet customer requirements and are competitive
2. Marketing through several trademarks and sales channels
3. Restoration of the market share in Finland
4. Significant increase in exports

When completed, the project met all the set market requirements. As a result of product development, a very competitive line of refrigerators and freezers were developed. The products were manufactured under several trademarks and marketed through several sales channels. In Finland, the market share exceeded the former level, and exports were increased significantly.

Meeting the Competency Requirements

Competency is connected to the business processes, technology, and skills, with which the market requirements are met. You can buy competencies, but competencies that lead to a lasting significant competitive edge are created through learning. The learning requirement is aimed at individuals or the whole staff.

Rosenlew Household Appliances

Market Requirements	Competency Requirements
1. Product range, design, and cooling technology meeting customer requirements and being competitive	1. Leading-edge product and manufacturing technology
2. Marketing through several trademarks and sales channels	2. Product management/modularization
3. Restoration of market share in Finland	3. Quality, speed, reliability, and flexibility through JIT production
4. Significant increase in exports	4. BSHG's market channels and improved exporting skills

The product and manufacturing technology was learned from Bosch Siemens Hausgeraete (BSHG), a Germany company, (benchmarking). The products were modulated to enable a wide product range and product variety, products with several trademarks and production in short series. The production was reorganized according to the JIT production philosophy. Scandinavian exports were multiplied by using the BSHG sales organization. The company's own sales resources were attached to other export markets. The fulfillment of the competency requirements led to the meeting of the market requirements, with the aid of the following performance improvements:

- Competitive products
- Doubled capacity
- Doubled productivity
- Reduced cycle time to a quarter
- Doubled product variety

Meeting the Financial Requirements

The competency must meet the market require-ments, but in an economical way, so that the prof-itability requirements are also fulfilled. With a bet-ter competency the income can be increased and the expenses decreased, and the decrease, in capi-tal used is achieved. All that can lead to improved return on assets, better cash flow, a lower break-even point, and improved solidity.

Usually, different financial requirements call for different kinds of com-petency. Requirements can even be in conflict with each other. Low costs could lead to heavy investments and a long production chain within the com-pany. A low critical point of profitability could lead to the concentration on assembly and use of subcontractors. The increase in profits would require a focus on product development, and better cash flow could require a decrease in product development investments.

Rosenlew Household Appliances

Market Requirements	Competency Requirements
1. 2. 3. 4.	1. 2. 3. 4.
Financial Requirements	**Attainability**
• Turning heavy losses into profit • Radical increase in capital turnover	

The competency needed to fulfill the market requirements also met the financial requirements when measured by the following improvements:

- The sales were doubled.
- Productivity was doubled.
- There was a significant decrease in the capital used.
- Profitability was excellent.

Meeting the Attainability

A development plan may fulfill the first three requirements and be the best possible, but it is not necessarily achievable, at least not at a sufficient speed. Check that the following prerequisites have been met: permanent demand, management's will, aspiration and inspiring vision, management com- 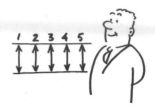 mitment, *involvement of personnel, development professionals, the right timing, project orientation, and the project finalizing ability.*

Rosenlew Household Appliances

Market Requirements	Competency Requirements
1.	1.
2.	2.
3.	3.
4.	4.
Financial Requirements	**Attainability**
• Turning heavy losses into profit • Radical increase in capital turnover	• Major change • The extensive project • Simultaneous product and manufacturing development • Speed requirements • Learning from others (benchmarking) • Sufficient development resources • Holistic view, to the most minute details

The household appliance development project was carried out, achieving the goals set in the planned three-year schedule. Crucial for the plan to achieve was the benchmarking partnership with BSHG, which is described more fully in chapter 5, page 200. Other factors to consider are presented in Part 3, page 199.

5. Launch the Development Projects

The management has to ensure that projects start. The typical reason for an unfulfilled development project is that it never actually got started. Projects are always delayed at the beginning, not at the end: in the beginning, the goals, responsibilities, and task distribution can still be vague. It is hard to arrange time and assign resources to a  *new project. The commitment can be questionable, and the development competency, is still small.*

In the *ABB Customer Focus Program,* the management ensured that all the development programs were started on all the areas that substantially influence success, that the plans were made, and that sufficient development competency for the project was available. The program's essential goal was to halve the total cycle times of all the *business processes.* The application of effective, proven development models made the project's beginning easier and faster.

ABB Sweden, T50 Business Cycle Coverage				
Number of Companies	**R&D Cycle**	**Offer Cycle**	**Order Cycle**	**T50 Impact on Marketing**
Have project	14	27	37	14
Have no project	14	7	0	22
Not relevant	10	4	1	2

6. Execute the Program and Follow Up

Ultimately, the program implementation shows up in the measured results. A development project without possibilities for measurement does not lead to significant results. With a perceivable measurement, the company's important information is transmitted to everyone. Measurement provides feedback from the learning. Measurement can ensure that the company is on the right development path. Measurement is the tool of supervision, feedback, and reward.

The measurements can focus on schedule, resources used, investments made, and goals achieved. Traditional measurement targets are quality, time, cost efficiency, and flexibility. The "new" targets can be the product variability to fulfill specific customer needs, the rate of employee involvement, reactivity to customer demands, innovativeness, internal customer satisfaction, learning from errors, and so on.

The development projects must be organized and carried out in such a way that the improvements planned are achieved and the organization development competency increases. Therefore, the progress of development competencies should also be measured.

Corporate T50 Objectives				
	Current Status	**Dec. 1991**	**Dec. 1992**	**Dec. 1993**
TCT-reduction	7%	20%	35%	50%
On-time delivery rate	85%	90%	95%	97%
Companies 100% engaged in T50	55%	70%	95%	100%
Weighed poll among employees	62%	70%	80%	95%

One of the major program goals at ABB was to radically increase employee involvement in development activities. An external research institute interviewed 600 randomly chosen ABB employees by telephone about their extent of participation in the development program (weighed poll among employees).

7. Exchange Development Experiences

Company management must organize occasions in which development experiences are transferred and internalized within the company. This can occur by various means, such as by organizing experience exchange meetings, by encouraging open dissemination of development results and experiences, and by moving and educating the developers. Management has to create an atmosphere in which the bad experiences can also be shared with the same enthusiasm as the good ones.

A year after the start of ABB's Customer Focus Program, a one-day experience exchange seminar was organized, divided into eight subject areas. Each unit's manager and project manager presented his or her own project, as well as the results achieved. Five hundred ABB employees from Sweden participated. Well-documented project descriptions and achievements were distributed to participants. The first internal success stories originated in this manner and are constantly gathered and announced with internal bulletins.

The experience exchange seminar schedule can be found on the next page.

Seminar Schedule

Time	Session 1	Session 2	Session 3	Session 4	Session 5	Session 6	Session 7	Session 8
09:30–10:15	T50 molds ABB Sweden Bert Olof Svanholm							
10:30–11:10	Power Systems, Delivery of HVDC	T50 and the R&D cycle	Coordination with suppliers	ABB Automation and time-out	Goal-oriented groups—how do they operate?	ABB Switchgear/ instrument transformers	To make use of T50 on the market	
11:20–12:00	Network Control	CEWE's project BRYT 90	T50: The economical system and product calculation	ABB Relays present plus	ABB Distribution, low voltage switchers	Switchgear/ B manual of components	Organization assignment of tasks and the salary system	
12:00–1:00	Lunch							
1:00–1:40	Goal-oriented groups—how do they operate?	To make use of T50 on the market	T50 and the R&D cycle	ABB Switchgear/ instrument transformers	ABB Distribution, low-voltage switchers	ABB Switchgear division A	ABB Service	Organization assignment of tasks and the salary system
1:50–2:30	Coordination with suppliers	Organization assignment of tasks and the salary systems	T50: The economical system and product calculation	Switchgear/ B manual of components	Network control	ABB Components	ABB Scandia's distribution center	Goal-oriented groups—how do they operate?
2:30–3:00	Break							
	CEWE's project BRYT 90	ABB Components	ABB Automation and time-out	ABB Switchgear division A	ABB Scandia's distribution center	Power systems, delivery of HVDC	ABB Relays present plus	ABB Service
	Panel discussion, obstacles and threats							

8. Finalize the Program

The development project can be finalized only after it has been successfully brought to the path of continuous improvement. Most projects are ended too soon. The resources and attention are diverted to the more serious problems. Aim at early results. Often, the results are achieved only when all the building blocks are positioned correctly. The measurements must continue to the end.

Case: A significant development step was in question. The change included the acquisition and introduction of a new technology. Because core technology was in question, the company wanted to ensure that continuous development would start at an early stage and would never end:

- A 10-person team, including all the necessary resources to plan, carry out, maintain, and develop the tasks, was created.
- The team members were chosen considering their development talents.
- Entrepreneurship and development training was given to the group.
- The whole group was present at the technology acquisition and received technology training by the supplier.
- A reward system was created for the group to support continuous improvement.
- The benchmarking process, which the machine supplier wanted to start, was crucial to the success. The skill of continuous technology development was learned during the process from two clearly more experienced companies.

A continuous benchmarking partnership was established with a company, which was later expanded to four partners. These companies, including the technology supplier, are committed to exchanging development experiences.

9. Continue Management Commitment

Management's continuous interest is the basic requirement for the success of strategic management. Every signal management sends has a great significance. Managers are not evaluated according to what they say but what they do. "What is held in respect is taken an interest in" (Plato).

Case 1: Signs of management's interests in the Customer Focus program.

Signals by Management What Makes the Employees Feel Management's Commitment	
Attention	**Time**
How often do they ask employees about the program? Are they interested in news? Do they give information? Are they passionate about the projects?	Do they come to the meeting? How often/For how long? Do they come to working group meetings? Do they have the latest information? How do they spend their time?
Do they really care?	**How much do they invest personally?**

Case 2: It is said that CEO Percy Barnevik called in one ABB unit and had the following conversation:

Hello, Laura. In my last presentation, I used the parameters from your development project. It is an excellently implemented project. I would like to use it as an example again in my next presentation. Could you send me the performance parameters from the last two quarters? I suppose that lately the figures have been even better.

SELF-EVALUATION QUESTIONS

Evaluation Criteria Business Strategy	Priority	Current and Target Performance				
		1	2	3	4	5
Market Opportunity Analyses						
1. Do you know the progress of the total market, in the past and the forecast?						
2. Do you know current and future customer expectations?						
Competency Analyses						
3. Do you know your own and your competitors' market shares?						
4. Do you know your capabilities to meet customer requirements, compared with your competitors?						
5. Have you determined the capabilities needed to meet customer requirements?						
6. Do you know your current capabilities?						
Alignment						
7. How well do current market opportunities align with your current capabilities?						
8. How well do future market opportunities align with your current capabilities?						
9. Have you planned how to improve exploitation of market opportunities?						
10. Have you identified capabilities to be acquired?						
11. Have you conducted benchmarking in strategic planning?						
12. Is involvement of personnel sufficient in strategic planning?						
Overall Grade						

(continued)

Evaluation Criteria Competence Strategy	Priority	Current and Target Performance				
		1	2	3	4	5
1. Have you set your business targets, are they well known, and is everyone committed to them?						
2. Have you defined your current business idea, is it well known, and is everyone committed to it?						
3. Have you defined your target business idea (3–5 year), is it well known, and is everyone committed to it?						
4. Does everyone understand interactions between financial performance, process performance, capabilities, and development projects?						
5. Have you turned business plans into measurable and challenging development projects?						
6. Have you specified responsibilities of achieving set development targets?						
7. Have you evaluated how well your development projects meet market requirements, capability requirements, financial requirements, and attainability?						
8. Are development projects monitored by management, is measuring sufficient, and does management show its commitment?						
9. Does management organize possibilities for exchanging development experiences?						
10. Are development projects finalized?						
Overall Grade						

x Your evaluation of the current performance level o Your target	Priority 1 Not significant 2 Significant 3 Important 4 Very important 5 Competitive advantage	Current and Target Performance 1 Poor 2 Adequate 3 Good 4 Very Good 5 Exceptional

Chapter 3

PRODUCT MANAGEMENT

Strategic management

Product management	Process management
Competitiveness, manufacturability, and flexibility	

Development management

Content Summary

This section illustrates the importance of mass-customized products and the manageability of operations in competition. It also explains what mass customization and modularization are and the benefits that can be achieved by implementing them.

Aquamaster-Rauma is a globally significant manufacturer of propulsion units and marine winches. This case describes how in 1990–1994, the company was able to totally change its operating principles, expand into global markets, and radically improve its profitability. The company identified its new business idea and systematically implemented it through mass customization and process management. As a result of the program, Aquamaster-Rauma was able to shorten its lead times from months to weeks, from weeks to days, and from days to hours.

This company case describes how business ideas, mass customization, process management, and continuous improvement are linked. The project set an example for other companies and is benchmarked by many. This case begins with the launch of the development program and continues through the development of both the business idea and mass customization. At the end of the case, benchmarking visitors tell how they interpreted and applied the development process to fit their own environment.

This section describes and illustrates the stages of mass customization. The model is an application of a development concept and technology developed by Innomat. The technology is based on its configuration technology domain expertise and innovations. Innomat (acquired by i2 Technologies, USA, 1998) acted as a consultant. In connection with the project, Innomat continued developing a plus-modular mass customization software program, which was awarded Best Software in Finland 1995. I was involved in this project as the internal consultant for Rauma and gained my experience in this way.

Kalle Välimaa, the founder of Innomat, has decisively influenced the success of this case and the development of the plus-modular mass customization model (Kalle is not related to Kari Välimaa, the manager at Aquamaster-Rauma). He has personally been involved with the development of this chapter.

The list of questions in this chapter will help you evaluate your own organization's current and future position and will form a basis for discussion on the differences among personal evaluations. It will also give advice on how to plan your improvement actions.

INTRODUCTION TO PRODUCT MANAGEMENT

QUICK NOTES	
Page 64:	Read the complete text.
66–71:	Read headings, illustrations, text boxes, and tables.
72–73:	Read the complete text.
74–96:	Read headings, illustrations, text boxes, and tables.
97–99:	Read the complete text.
100–131:	Read headings, illustrations, text boxes, tables, and the text In *italics*.

Why Mass Customization?

Controllability is Lost Early in the Selling Stage

It happens quite often that the manager gives subordinates the following speech: "Things aren't looking very good. We haven't made our numbers, and wc promised the board we would. Everyone remembers the lay-offs last time. Now we really have to concentrate on selling and BRING EVERY SALE HOME."

The controllability of the business process creates prerequisites for internal efficiency. The controllability of the production process, however, is often lost early in the selling stage. The deal is made, but the salesperson is not exactly sure what was sold, and the customer is not exactly sure what was purchased. "The order justifies the means." It often seems that at this stage everything else is of secondary importance to the sales department and management.

The fact is, controllability was already lost when the *product range* and related *extent* and *variability* were being defined. The product range evolves little by little, according to customer requirements. Product sales, engineering, development, and manufacturing often lead their own lives.

Many managers eagerly begin business process development but forget that it leads to only a marginal profit improvement unless the product range has first been mastered and product structures changed.

Many cases require that the product range be defined and the products developed *at the same* time as the business processes (even networks) are being developed. The production process must be treated as if it were a product, because it often has the same life span as the product it generates.

Customers Have Individual Needs

In traditional competition, the customer expects a fairly priced, good-quality product with fast availability and good service. Companies compete by offering either inexpensive *standard* products or tailored (but more expensive) product *applications.*

Particularly in global competition, the customer has numerous alternatives to choose from. There is great pressure on companies to offer tailored applications at the same price as standard products.

Tailoring Has Eliminated the Controllability of Operations

In many companies, an expanding product range, an increase in tailoring, and diminishing quantities have caused big controllability and financial problems. The number of product variations has grown to meet the acute needs of customers. To meet these needs, it is necessary to develop specific products and product variations. Fulfilling all customer needs has, therefore, *multiplied* the number of products, materials, components, and methods to be managed.

The company product system was designed to meet only individual *customer needs.* The system does not take into account the needs of *internal customers.* The sales department sells what the customer wants, and the product engineers design the customer-specified product. The purchasing and production departments have always worked on different products.

It has not been possible to create *repetition* at any stage, which inevitably leads to poor controllability, inconsistent quality, and high costs.

Competitive Factors Change Constantly

The customer is interested primarily in the company's product or service that meets his or her needs and expectations better than the competition. The product or service is, therefore, the core of the company. Companies usually are founded because the founder has a product idea.

In competition, the role of the product can vary for different reasons:

- Product innovation can cause revolutionary changes in the market.
- If competing products are comparable, the price may become the decisive factor.
- Certain product features are not always enough; rather, the competitive factor is a combination of features.
- Products are technically the same, so the competition is about the services connected to the deal.
- Instead of standard products, the competition is about customized applications.

The company must identify how competitive factors change. Through product development, the company actively changes the competing factors of its line of business to be favorable. At the very least, the company must be able to adapt rapidly to changes.

The company must continuously develop its capabilities to do the following:

- Identify customer needs
- Determine the level of competition
- Determine the products and product qualities
- Design favorable product structures
- Run fast product development processes

These are long-term processes in which the company cannot afford to fail. From the beginning, it must ensure that the development process will reach the set objectives. A good way to do this is through benchmarking and applying the development models.

Modulated Mass-Customized Products as a Solution

When the product has been mass-customized, it is easy to choose variations to meet the needs of the customer. Product structures are also designed and modularized according the needs of internal customers.

The basic idea of mass customization is to simultaneously identify and take into account the requirements of both external and internal customers. These requirements must be carefully considered when determining the following:

- Product range
- Amount of product variations
- Extent of customer application
- Product structures

The goals in modulating the products are to achieve the following:

*A wide range of products
with the smallest possible number of modules.*

*The ability to meet customer requirements
quickly and cost-effectively.*

The modules are *primarily product features* that fulfill customer needs. The modules created from individual customers' needs make up a product that fulfills the customer needs. The modularized product family may contain no traditional products at all or any so-called basic products from which variations are developed. The principle is to put the product together case-by-case from the modules designed beforehand, according to the customer's needs. It is also possible to assemble standard products from the modules to fulfill the requirements of various customer segments. In this case, the company has normal product catalogs. The benefit of the modularization is, therefore, cost-effectiveness. The product must be modularized so that the entire process, from customer requirements to customer satisfaction, can be managed as module wholes.

How the Number of Variants Affects Profitability

The following interdependencies are typical for a traditionally designed, non-modularized standard product and related production.

Variety Index	Productivity	Unit Costs	Break-Even Percent of Capacity
1	100	100	46
2	76	120	61
4	57	145	80

Source: Stalk, George, Jr., and Thomas M. Hout. 1990. *Competing Against Time.* The Free Press, New York.

This study shows that, as the number of variants increase, the following occur:

- *Productivity decreases.* The number of parts, work stages, and methods increases, and lot sizes decrease. As controllability becomes more difficult, the queues and waiting time become longer, and quality becomes inconsistent.
- *Unit costs increase.* The number of materials and components increases, smaller quantities can be bought at a time, and purchasing costs rise. Inventory and warehousing costs increase. Lower productivity drives up costs.
- *The break-even point increases.* As controllability becomes more difficult, the number of "controlling" staff increases, causing fixed costs to rise. Different products require different manufacturing methods, which increases the number of machines and capital used.

With modular products, a rise in customer applications does not increase the number of components, materials, and modules to be managed. Thus, increasing customer applications does not have the same negative effect.

Simultaneous Doubling

Company	Product	Factory Labor Productivity	Net Asset Productivity	Product Line Variety
Yanmar	Diesel engines	1.9 ×	2.0 ×	3.7 ×
Hitachi	Refrigerators	18	17	13
Komatsu	Construction equipment	18	17	18
Toyo Kogyo	Cars, trucks	24	15	16
Isuzu	Cars, trucks	25	15	n.a.
Jidosha Kiki	Brakes, etc.	19	n.a.	n.a.
Simple average		20	18	21

Source: Stalk, George, Jr., and Thomas M. Hout. 1990. *Competing Against Time.* The Free Press, New York.

Since the Second World War, the Japanese have often changed their competitive advantage. The first competitive advantage was based on low wage costs. The next was customization and large production lots, through which high and uniform quality was achieved.

Today, the Japanese competitive advantage is gained through customizable products and small lot sizes while still maintaining high quality and low costs. In the 1980s, the Japanese car industry significantly increased the amount of alternative car models and extra features. The basic factors enabling this were product modularity and the JIT philosophy, in which a model range could be increased without increasing the size of in-process inventory. The American car industry was forced to manufacture cars in long series for dealers, or then deliver the cars through long delivery times. This resulted in an increase of employed capital, which caused the American car industry to lose its competitiveness in the market.

Through the five-year project, Japanese companies (see table) were able to double the productivity of labor and capital. At the same time, they also doubled the number of different products while increasing their income flow, raising cost-effectiveness, and decreasing employed capital. Therefore, all profitability factors were affected.

CASE STUDY: AQUAMASTER-RAUMA

Case Study Summary

Aquamaster-Rauma is a prominent maker of propulsion units and winches for marine purposes worldwide. In the years 1990 to 1994, the company multiplied its most important economic and operative indicators and significantly reduced its dependency on the economic trends of the shipbuilding industry.

Deck Machinery Works of Rauma-Repola and Hollming Engineering, the manufacturer of Aquamaster propulsion units, merged in 1988 to form one company. The merger brought about significant cost benefits, which was, of course, the main purpose. Profitability, however, was not high enough to have ensured continuous renewal of the company. Also, the company's profitability fluctuated significantly according to industry trends. The initiative to launch the development program was taken by the managing director at that time.

The main objectives of the development programs were substantial growth, profitability improvements, and smaller fluctuations due to economic trends. These objectives required expansion into global markets, development of the customer base, and significant growth in internal efficiency.

New customer requirements came along with the new markets. To satisfy them, the company needed new competencies. Competitor analyses and market research were conducted, with the intent of selecting and developing the most important competitive advantage: *the ability to fulfill customer needs quickly and economically in all selected markets and segments.*

The development program was launched by conducting a preliminary study, which showed that it was possible to halve lead times and working capital, while simultaneously doubling productivity. The target could be reached by putting the propulsion units and winches into their own product lines, plus-modularizing the products and organizing the production of module factories by JIT principles.

The board of directors approved the final development program, with the strategic target of expanding the customer base, thus diminishing dependency on trends in the shipbuilding industry. The target called for tripling the number of quotes, orders, and product variants. This objective would have called for multiplying the number of engineers, which could not be done. The only possibility was to decrease radically the lead times of quotes and orders to be processed, as well as product design and production.

The company reached its development targets on the upswing of the shipbuilding industry. The plus-modularized products, which varied according to the customer, as well as the short lead times, enabled the company to benefit from the growth and significantly increase its sales.

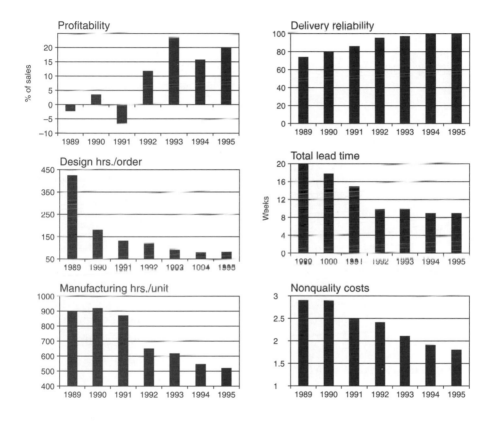

Having clearly the shortest lead times in the market, Aquamaster-Rauma succeeded well in bidding situations and was able to price its products more freely. The company's profitability rose to an all time high and remains there to this day.

Description of Case Study

What We Used to Do

> We sold what the customer wanted. We tailored the products according to customer wishes. We offered the product properties the customer wanted, without knowing how this would affect product structure. We gave the customers inaccurate budget quotes, which they considered binding. As the orders came in, we wondered what we had actually sold. We engineered the products every time from scratch. There were no set rules for customizing. Production had to manufacture a different product every time. You could go on and on about our stupidities. A great deal of them were caused by the fact that our product was not engineered to vary according to the customer.

This is how Kari Välimaa, present site director of Aquamaster-Rauma, explained the situation to benchmarking guests from another company that was just launching its own development program. The people were visiting Aquamaster-Rauma in Rauma, Finland, to learn about the company's development program called the Lead Time Program.

The delivery process of the visiting company was currently being developed. Indefinite product structures turned out to be the source of the problems in the delivery process. The visiting development group recognized in its organization the same issues Mr. Välimaa described. The visitors made a list of questions that Aquamaster-Rauma would answer. The following sections feature a selection of the discussions held during this benchmarking visit.

A Program Launch and Management

What originally brought about your Lead Time Program?

Significant cost benefits were gained as a result of the 1988 merger. Profitability, however, was not high enough to ensure the continuous renewal of the company and the development of its competitiveness. Profitability also fluctuated greatly according to economic trends in the shipbuilding industry.

The managing director at the time was of the opinion that something needed to be done but was not quite sure what it should be. Under the direction of Rauma Group management, he initiated a preliminary study leading to the launch of the Lead Time Program.

What were the objectives of the preliminary study and how was it made?
Our (Aquamaster-Rauma's) managing director and the preliminary study group agreed on the following objectives:

- Identify development requirements for reaching strategic targets.
- Identify weaknesses and strengths of each operation.
- Estimate potential improvements of the major performance indicators.
- Set main targets for the program.

The preliminary study lasted for approximately two months. Key people in the company were interviewed, and their views of the present state and development opportunities were gathered into a report. The product system was analyzed, and its modularity and manufacturability were studied. The production flow from quote-to-order-to-delivery was simulated on a computer software program, which enabled us to set the lead times, turnover speeds and productivity targets.

What were the objectives of your Lead Time Program?

Based on the preliminary study, we set the following initial targets:
1. Cut product lead times by at least half.
2. Raise delivery reliability to 100 percent.
3. At least double labor productivity.
4. Decrease costs of quality defects by at least half.

At a later date, we specified the initial targets for each separate product. The following table is an example of lead times (in weeks) from order to delivery:

Product	1989	1993
Aquamaster US 381	14	6
Aquamaster US 1401	16	8

How did you convince the management that the investment would pay off?
The managing director launched the program within the limits of his authority. About 20 people took part in defining the development objectives and planning. This was how we got middle management interested and even enthusiastic about the development program.

The plan and objectives were presented to the board of directors in a way they could easily understand. We used the following economic indicators to convince the board of the program. Based on our presentation, the board accepted our proposal. We also succeeded in surpassing the set targets.

Financial Indicators	Target in 1989	Realized in 1993
Reduction in inventory	FIM 10 million	FIM 14.9 million
Increase in profit	FIM 9.5 million	FIM 25.7 million

Project costs were estimated to be approximately FIM 10 million. We did a portion of the work ourselves, which was worth about FIM 6 million. Consultant services cost approximately FIM 4 million. The costs did not exceed the estimate. In fact, we financed the program by money allocated from reduced inventory. The actual problem was how we could allocate 20,000 of our own working hours for the approximately three-year-long program.

We could convince the board that competitiveness and profitability could be achieved through mass customization based on the plus-modularization methodology. Mass customization is the basis for process management, and shorter lead times are an important competitive factor. I believe that our own enthusiasm helped convince the board to accept our proposal.

How did you manage to clearly exceed the financial results?
When we launched our program, demand was already declining, and half a year later it hit bottom. We had to stop the program for a while and lay off staff to adjust our production capacity to the declined demand. We then continued with the program and executed it while demand was still low.

We had just finished with the development work when demand began to grow. The Lead Time Program not only increased our effectiveness but also enabled us to benefit fully from the growing demand. Without the Lead Time Program, it would never have been possible.

> Had we been operating the old way, we would have had to triple the amount of competent product engineers, which would not have been possible. Experienced engineers are not easy to find on short notice. Even if we would have been able to find new people, their skills would not have matched that of an experienced engineer.

Plus-modularized products enabled us to allocate product engineering resources and move them to product development. As a result, our new successful product, the Contaz propulsion unit, was created. Through the Contaz, we made our way into a new customer segment, which in turn influenced our excellent success.

How has management followed up the results after the program?

By profitability follow-up. However, profitability tells only about the past, not about future competitiveness. Today, management is also interested in performance that measures the development of future competitiveness. The most important factors are lead and turnover times, delivery reliability, and productivity of design and manufacturing, as well as quality costs.

What development issues were included in the Lead Time Program?

We had experience in developing products and manufacturing. Developing plus-modular mass customization was something totally new to us. Luckily, we realized what plus-modular mass customization was all about. It became partially clear right after the preliminary study and entirely obvious before our presentation to the board. Nevertheless, our ideas on plus-modular mass customization changed later many times. The crucial thing was that, right from the beginning, we were convinced of the benefits we could achieve.

Innomat consultants helped us understand that plus-modular mass customization is not the only thing that can make dreams come true. Many other things are needed. In addition to PRODUCT SYSTEM development, we started 13 other projects:

1. Customer requirement system
2. Sales support system
3. PRODUCT SYSTEM
4. Production planning system
5. Material handling of the factory
6. Production system
7. Quality control system
8. Salary and bonus system
9. Financial control system
10. After-sales system
11. Maintenance system
12. Culture and training
13. International purchasing system
14. Transportation and forwarding

The word *system* was used for the development areas to emphasize their processlike nature. (The words *process* and *mass customization* were not buzz words at that time.)

Each project had its own development group with its own targets and plans. We proceeded in all fields simultaneously. Many things were interdependent and, because the work was done simultaneously, the whole program proceeded more quickly. This motivated everyone to take part in the development process.

> The critical part of the program was developing the PRODUCT SYSTEM, which included product plus-modularization because other projects were timed according to it. Almost everything else depended on the new opportunities provided by plus-modularization product assortment.

How did you get enough resources for everything?
We were in a hurry and eager to develop. We had just gone through a severe reorganization and knew what it meant to lack competitiveness. At the same time, we compared our own manufacturing costs with other subcontractor quotes. The results were really against us.

I stopped working as sales manager to focus on managing the program *full-time*. My background as sales and product development manager was a lot of help in the new job. We succeeded in taking the product development manager—off his normal duties, to come and work as a *full-time plus-modularization professional*. Also, some other managers of the various projects worked full-time.

We understood that we did not have enough experience of our own to implement a development program of such proportion, so we hired experts from Innomat to consult in project management, plus-modularization, and production management.

> Product plus-modularization contributed most in the allocation of resources. After the plus-modularization, considerably less working hours were needed for quote making, project management, product design, production planning, and manufacturing. Through product plus-modulation, we were able to allocate resources for development work. *The first breakthroughs were the most important.* After that, time savings really increased.

At first, propulsion unit and winch production took place in separate workshops. Later, the products got their own business lines. This reorganization facilitated the sharing of responsibilities and tasks, while making it easier to manage and run the program.

How did you get the whole organization to participate in your program?
As I said, we had just cut costs and made cost comparisons of various subcontractor quotes. People had their doubts, but they understood the financial facts.

We conducted an attitude survey of the whole staff Above all, we wanted to know what, in their opinion, were the most important areas to develop. This gave us further information and motivated the entire staff to participate in the program.

We compiled a 130-page, easy-to-understand, illustrated handbook for the staff. It contained information on what required development and why, who would be doing it and how, what the objectives were, and how they would be measured.

As much as we could, we involved the staff in the program. We also trained, communicated, and kept them informed during the entire program.

Developing a Business Idea

You said that the profitability of your company fluctuates significantly according to economic trends in the shipbuilding industry. What have you done about it?
Yes, it was our biggest problem. We depended on a market area and a certain number of customers, which limited us a great deal. *We set a target to raise the number of customers from 20 to 150.* We set yearly targets to raise the number.

It is usually up to sales to win new customers. Sell more, get new customers. We spent a lot of time defining what it would take to achieve this. It turned out that we couldn't expect the sales department do it alone, because it simply did not have the resources. Bidding for quotes was troublesome, the quotes were inaccurate, product structures were confusing, product specifications defective, and so on. *We had to set prerequisites first.*

Through *plus-modularization,* we were able to achieve this and arrived at the following results:

Expanding the Customer Base				
Performance		1989	1993	Target
New potential customers	Pcs.	20	150	150
Orders from new customers	Pcs.	3	8	10
Number of offers	Pcs.	500	650	800
By the following improvements				
Lead time of offers	Hours	8	4	1
Accuracy of offers	FIM	50,000	1000	1000
Deviation from planned cost	%	30	5	1

"New potential customers" indicates the growth of the market area. A specially founded marketing organization was responsible for selling to new customers. It was not possible to get orders unless the number of quotes could be increased considerably. Through shortening lead times and improving the accuracy of the quote preparation phase, we were able to increase the number of quotes without hiring more staff.

What other industry-specific characteristics did you take into account?
When we started the program, both the winch and propulsion unit businesses were lumped together as one single, comprehensive organization. At an early stage in the program, we saw that these businesses were totally different, as the table below indicates.

Characteristics of Business	Propulsion Unit	Winch
Customer requirement	Moving and controlling of the vessel	Mooring of the vessel
Customer expectations	Overall economy Operation reliability	Meet the requirements of the classification organization Space saving on deck
Sales arguments	Paying back of investment Load transportation ability Controllability of the vessel	Price Manning requirement
Required core competency	Product technology Varied, customer-specified products Understanding of customer business	Power transmission techniques Materials

Based on these arguments, two separate divisions were established as their own profit-centers with their own product lines. Production was also separated.

From this point on in this case, my answers apply to propulsion units only.

We defined the characteristics of the propulsion unit business at that time and forecasted its development. Based on this information, we listed our *competitive advantages.*

Characteristics of Business in 1989	Forecasted Development	Competitive Advantages to Be Developed
1. Large demand fluctuations.	Will continue.	Increasing the number of potential customers.
2. The prevailing, conventional product was a propeller at the back of the shaft line, which ran the length of the ship.	In tugboats and in coastal vessels, the need for a controllable propulsion unit was recognized.	Product innovations.
3. All manufacturers had long delivery times.	The lead times of shipyards were getting shorter.	Cutting the delivery time in half and increasing flexibility.
4. Propulsion units were tailor-made. The delivered product was always different.	The need for customer-specific applications would continue to exist.	Modulated customer-specific products.

As we analyzed the characteristics of the industry, the issues came up in the above order.

In practice, the order of the above table was reversed. It was necessary to begin the development program by plus-modularization in order to create prerequisites for individual customer applications, short lead times, and flexibility and to allocate design resources from custom design to product development. We were able to increase our potential customer base and become a market leader through our product innovations and plus-modular products, as well as through fast delivery times.

How did you define your markets and what was your definition based on?

The main markets were Scandinavia and the former Soviet Union. Our target was to expand into the global market. This was based on the board of directors' strategic target: to double sales and the financial result before the year 2000 and decrease dependence on the economic trends in the industry.

Growth was achieved by the following:

- Use our tugboat know-how in the global market
- Customer-applied and plus-modularized products for fulfilling customer requirements
- New propulsion unit types and applications for new vessel categories

> The prerequisite for becoming a global player was a solid understanding of customer requirements, which we did not have. However, we understood that only plus-modularized, variable, and customer-specified products could fulfill the requirements of global customers.

How did you segment markets and what reasons can you give for the division?

The markets were segmented according to customer needs and the required technological skill, into the following table:

Customer Segment	Customer Need	Required Technological Core Competency
1. Coastal vessels	Economical operation Navigation capability Fast maneuvering in and out of harbor Safety	Multipropulsion system
2. Tugboats	Maneuverability Bollard pull	Propeller with nozzle
3. Container vessels and tankers	Effective use of cargo space Reliability	Two propulsion units Placing equipment properly
4. River cruisers and ferries	Traveling comfort No vibration	Shape of stern CRP-type propulsion units Flexible mounting
5. Cruise ships	No vibration	As above

How did you choose the products for each segment?

The products for each segment consisted of *different combinations of plus-modules,* always individually chosen for each order. Thus, we do not have traditional products but always pre-engineered, connectable plus-modules.

The number of common plus-modules can vary considerably in different segments, as the following examples show:

Segment	Common Modules
Tugboats Container vessels	0%
Tugboats Ferries	100%
Tugboats River cruisers	50%

How did you define customers' expectations?

The customer invites only those suppliers that *fulfill his or her basic needs* to compete in the final round of price negotiations. If each supplier offers products that meet the customer's basic needs, the winner is the one who can best meet the customer's *expectations*.

The following numbers indicate the relative importance of customer expectations according to segment. The evaluation was conducted by our own employees and by customer interviews.

Segment	Customer Expectations			
	Delivery Time	Price	Reliability	After-Sales
1. Coastal vessels	1	1	3	3
2. Tugboats	3	3	1	3
3. Container vessels and tankers	1	1	3	3
4. River cruisers and ferries	1	2	2	3
5. Cruise ships	1	2	3	3

1 Extremely important
2 Very important
3 Important

The customers in each segment form a chain. The needs and expectations of each link in the chain must be considered. The following example illustrates how we defined the customer needs and expectations in each segment's customer chain.

Customer Chain	Customer Needs and Expectations
Ship owner	Suitability for operation, right performance, reliability, economical operation, delivery speed, after-sales service
Shipyard	Easy installation, low price, fast delivery
Tanker to be assisted	Sufficient towing capacity/thrust, safety
Harbor	Environmental factors

What are your competitive advantages and how did you define them?
Based on the analyses, we identified the *competitive advantages,* which we distinctly wanted to improve and which differentiated us from our competitors in each segment. (See the following table.) The number shows the relative order of importance (1 = extremely important; 2 = very important; 3 = important).

Segment	Competitive Advantages				
	Understanding of Customer Business	Local Presence	Concept for Variable Customer Needs	Short Delivery Time	Product Features
1. Coastal vessels	1	2	2	3	1
2. Tugboats	1	1	3	1	2
3. Container vessels and tankers	1	3	1	3	1
4. River cruisers and ferries	1	2	2	1	3
5. Cruise ships	1	3	1	3	2

The competitive advantages that were chosen for development were based on customer needs and expectations, regardless of whether they were identified or not.

How did you arrive at your present product range?
As I said earlier, we did not have standardized products in the traditional sense, only *plus-modular combinations applied to customer requirements.*

The products that are put together using pre-engineered variants are called *standard variants*. Products that require additional customer-specified design are called *customer variants*. The propulsion unit is made up of parts, which typically require *tailoring* of such areas as the shape of the propeller (according to the power of the main engine,) the length of the shaft (according to the size of the ship), and the connections/interfaces to the ship according to its form.

How did you define internal customer expectations for mass customization?

Our biggest problem was to tailor the product to each customer, which increased both costs and lead times. Every product was engineered from scratch. From production's point of view, it was always a different product. We could not create any repetition. The products had to be plus-modularized, so that they met the requirements of both external and internal customers.

We divided our business into four processes: product development, sales, customer applications engineering, and production. We defined future operating principles for each process, of which the most essential are mentioned below. Plus-modular mass customization gave us the opportunities to realize them.

Product Development	Sales	Customer Application	Production
Customer requirements to the operating process, with fast and correctly measurable quantities Fast development cycles through self-organizing cross-functional teams, concurrent engineering, early supplier involvement, and sense of urgency	Modulated sales documentation leading to: - Modulated products - Fast and accurate offers - Clear orders	A wide range of products out of a small number of modules Meeting specific customer requirements superior to the competition	Modulated JIT manufacturing: –In small series –Without inventory –With no defects –According to customer demand

How did you define your organization and production strategy?

Although both winch and propulsion unit customers often bought both products, their needs were so different that, early in the program, the two products were separated into their own business units. Winch management, marketing, and product development remained in Finland, but production was moved to South Korea to take advantage of cheaper production costs.

The reorganization of the propulsion unit business unit went hand-in-hand with our objective to *organize according to business processes.* Instead of the earlier division by market areas, the propulsion unit business was divided into business segments driven by customer segments, as described earlier. The production facilities are common to all the business segments. All operations relating to the propulsion units are concentrated in Rauma, except for sales and service functions, which are located worldwide.

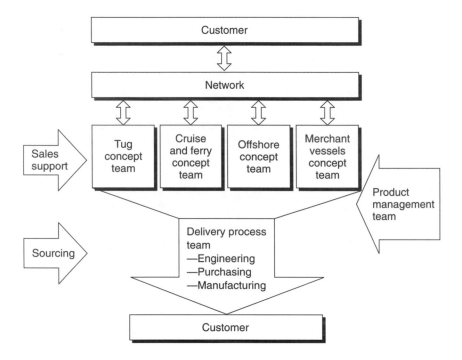

Plus-Modularization of Products

How was product plus-modularization carried out in practice?

The ultimate target of the development program was to improve profitability. It was reached by increasing income and cutting costs. The sequence is presented in the following model. We started from the middle, with plus-modularization. It had *positive effects in both directions.* Plus-modularization allowed us to vary the product according to the customer, which led to better sales and additional income. Another result of plus-modularization was better controllability, which also resulted in better cost effectiveness of the operations.

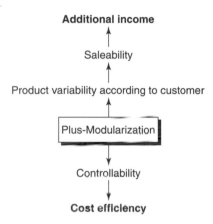

Plus-modularization began by defining the customer's *basic need:* moving and steering the vessel. To reach this definition, we used sales maintenance and modeling tool technology. This gave us the *idea for the function* of our product: the controllable propulsion unit. It is a product that fulfills the customer's basic need.

The customer's basic need was further divided into *secondary needs.* One *basic plus-module* corresponds to each secondary need.

Secondary Customer Need	Basic Module
Thrust	**Propeller**
Placing of thrust element	Lower shaft
Installation into the vessel	Middle part, bottom well cover
Synchronizing the rotation speed	Upper shaft

The secondary needs of the customer were further broken down into product features, from which the customer selected. A corresponding plus-module was determined for every feature. If **thrust** from the previous table were taken as an example, the basic plus-module to go with it would be **propeller.** Thrust is further divided into product features, such as vessel speed. The plus-module that corresponds to that feature is an open, right-, or left-handed propeller.

Secondary Customer Need	Basic Module
Thrust	**Propeller**
Product Feature	Module
Speed of the vessel	Open propeller, right-handed and left-handed
Operating in ice	Ice-strengthened
Thrust	Propeller with nozzle, right-handed and left-handed
Efficiency	Contra-rotating

We plus-modulated all our products according to this principle and made them extremely variable.

How did you turn customer requirements into product features?
As I said, the customer's basic need, which is moving and navigating the vessel, was divided into secondary needs, such as thrust. Product features were determined for the secondary needs—for example, speed to thrust.

Performance measures and values were determined for each product feature. Since we had these performance values as alternative choices for the customer, we were able to ensure that our products fulfilled customer expectations in various situations. The competitive advantages, which we defined at an earlier phase, were also included in these product features and performance values.

How did the program benefit the sales department?

Previously, the sales department sold propulsion units, which were then altered to customer requirements. Today, sales identifies the customer's needs. Every need has its own product plus-module, which the sales department puts together to form a product. Alternative product features, from which the customer can select what he or she needs, are determined for each module.

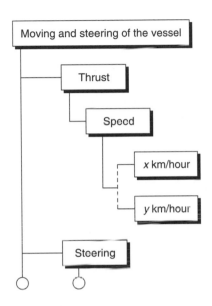

When a standard price has been set for each plus-module and related part, quote preparation is faster and the quotes more accurate.

What were the benefits of this program for product engineering?

It is no longer necessary to engineer each module from scratch every time, because the standard plus-modules pass the engineering department. This has had a dramatic effect on both product engineering and production lead times.

Performance Criteria	Measure	1990	1993	Realized
Lead Time Reduction in the Entire Delivery Chain				
Quotation preparation	Hours	8	4	1
Order handling	Days	10	3	1
Product engineering	Days	40	20	1
Total lead time	Weeks	18	10	6
Improving Productivity of Customer Application Design				
Product engineering	Hrs./order	330	100	80
Project management	Hrs./order	100	45	30
Number of drawings	Pcs./order	45	12	10

However, it is not possible to satisfy the needs and expectations of every customer only through standard product plus-modules. Tailoring is still necessary. We made clear *rules for tailoring;* we tried to predict and set parameters (only certain dimensions are allowed). Now that every product does not need to be engineered from scratch, more time and effort can be put into focusing on the customer's special needs, which, in turn, helps us beat the competition.

What were the benefits for the production department?
Sales has a *support system,* which guides the customer to the modulated solutions and enables effective product engineering, acquisition, and manufacturing, so every need and feature has a pre-engineered matching product plus-module. Each plus-module has its own documents for controlling, manufacturing, and ordering the necessary materials and components. Behind each plus-module code are the following:

- Prepared pricing system
- Prepared product specification
- Prepared product description
- Prepared drawings and part lists
- Prepared purchasing routine to obtain materials and components
- Prepared work stage chain and manufacturing methods

The product itself, together with the materials needed to manufacture it, as well as the components and subcontracting, is consistent. As the product range became uniform, quality problems decreased, and quality costs were subsequently reduced by nearly half. The following changes in material management became possible:

Measure	1989	1994
Percentage of items with long-term purchase contracts	25%	91%
Items that can be "called home" automatically	0	1973
Items that can be "called home" by workers	0	712

How did you prioritize the products to be plus-modularized?
We started with the product that had the largest sales volume, which was the small propulsion machinery. It was also technically the easiest. It gave us the biggest benefits and quickly budgeted resources from product engineering.

We carried out the plus-modularization in two stages. The principles for so-called quick plus-modularization are the following:

- Create product structure by regrouping the existing drawings and combinations.
- Use existing production entities as much as possible.
- Implement necessary technical changes in order to accomplish the plus-modularization principle—that is, the possibility of adding modules without affecting other parts of the product.
- Eliminate everything unnecessary and define the customer's real needs.

Quick plus-modularization helped get fast results without big investments and quickly allocated resources for actual product engineering. The principles for full plus-modularization, which follow quick plus-modularization, are the following:

- Develop a new product or significantly redesign the existing product.
- The construction principle is the same as in quick modularization.
- Engineering product and production methods are developed closely together.
- Consider objectives of standardization.

In the case of a totally new product, only full plus-modularization applies.

What competencies did you develop?

To gain the competitive advantage, we knew we would have to develop the following core competencies:

Core Competencies	Statement of Reason
Production of large body parts	Quality—for example, consistency
Assembly	Quality—for example, installation accuracy
Test drives and quality control	The propulsion unit and control equipment assembled at the plant (competitors do it only at the shipyard)
Close cooperation between R&D engineering and production	Fast handling of feedback
Global service	A competitive advantage on the market
Delivery speed	An advantage in pricing

What advice would you give us now in retrospect?
The most important issues usually come up in the context of our failures. In addition, my advice would be the following:

- *Inform and communicate.* No matter how much you inform and communicate, it's never enough, or else the timing or subject is wrong.
- *Don't do all the development alone.* Rather, use development professionals. Someone always has more expertise; find out who. In our case, it was Innomat.
- *Proceed in several areas simultaneously.* It speeds up the program. Things depend on each other. The problems and solutions can be found more easily when the issues are seen from different angles.
- *Ensure the whole staff's involvement from the very beginning.* Development is everyone's responsibility.
- *Organize the program.* The areas of responsibility should be clear.
- *Allocate development resources from their normal duties.* Development does not happen by itself but requires resources. Use the best people.
- *Don't try to start out with a perfect plan.* Test different things and make corrections as you go along.
- *Make a division between routine work and development work.* Development work should be done either full-time or in at least one-day blocks.
- ***Come up with an idea for how to involve the sales department from the very beginning.*** It is difficult to get salespeople to commit because of different customers and market areas, and they are busy making sales.

Meeting of Benchmarking Visitors

The visitors asked questions, which both benchmarking parties had carefully prepared. The answers were accurate and concrete, and the achieved results, in particular, were interesting and prompted the visitors to present more questions.

It was 2 P.M. The visit had been in progress since 8 A.M. After a brief tour of the factory, the visitors gathered to review their notes, digest what they had heard, and think about additional questions.

Most people in the group were enthusiastic. Pam Personnel (personnel manager) and Peter Product (product engineer) were in charge of planning and organizing the program. At first, they appeared to be somewhat frustrated. Here is a short take on the group discussion:

Peter Product: For this company, the program worked well, but our company is different. Mr. Keen [president] should be here; this belongs to top-level management.

Pam Personnel: In our company, as far as I can remember, two full-time development project managers were appointed in the past 10 years. One was transferred to do something more urgent, and the other one left the company after only six months, because he was completely unsupported on the project. And, yes, there was a third one, but he wasn't given anything "demanding" to do.

Peter Product: Mr. Vael [sales manager] was supposed to participate today.

Pam Personnel: Yes, so we agreed. But then he couldn't come because he has a sales negotiation today.

Peter Product: The customer is, of course, important. It's just that in our company the customer is an easy excuse for neglecting other work.

The leader of the group, Dave Development, wanted to diffuse the situation and said:

Dave Development: Everything you've said is true. This is the way our development culture works. However, I believe that Mr. Keen [president] will change it. We, too, have been through some tough times lately. But now, for the first time after the cutbacks, we are starting to see the light again. Mr. Keen understands that the program should be launched immediately. It was his idea to start training and using benchmarking processes in plus-modular mass customization and process development.

Pam Personnel: I'm sure benchmarking will help speed things up, but it will take time to get these kinds of results. We just have to arrange it so that he can come here.

Dave Development: Yes, I believe we can arrange it. During this visit, we'll ask if we can come again. The purpose of a benchmarking visit is not to just listen and look around but also to learn. We can't copy anything from here directly. We need to understand why they did the things they did, in order to apply them to our company.

Program Launch and Management

Pam Personnel: We especially tried to take notes on things relating to project organization and management, where their methods differs from ours.

We don't use consultants, for example. Actually, our management decided not to use any. Plus-modular mass customization used to be totally unknown to Aquamaster-Rauma. Without Innomat's expertise, this company could not have been able to develop plus-modular mass customization. We should also have the courage to let somebody from outside evaluate our operations [refer to page 75].

Peter Product: The targets were really challenging. They believed in the opportunities of plus-modular mass customization, got motivated, and pushed their
proposal through. We may have targets to develop production, but, as for product
development, we have only estimates and intentions for sales [page 75].

Pam Personnel: Their main target, to shorten the lead time, was easy for
everyone to understand, accept, and measure. It also had to do with their
important strategic goal of expanding the customer base, which made them
less vulnerable to economic fluctuations. It was a program for the top management level.

Peter Product: They also knew how to turn their target into money. And
money talk is easy for management to understand [page 76].

Pam Personnel: They had to stop the program and reduce the staff. How in the
world did they manage to go through with it? We still have to ask them about
that.

Peter Product: When we are not doing well, savings and cutbacks take
place. They, on the contrary, invested FIM 10 million and 20,000 working
hours, so they were ready for the boom when it started [page 76].

Pam Personnel: "The measures of future competitiveness" was a good idea.
It sounds sensible. In our company, results tell about success, so profitability
is the way to measure it [page 73].

Peter Product: Obviously, there is no single, sure-fire solution. They also
launched 13 other projects simultaneously. We have to ask more in order to
find out which ones would apply to us. We could learn a lot from this company. It was an excellent idea to base everything on plus-modularization,
which then set the pace [page 77].

Pam Personnel: How did they allocate all the necessary development
resources? They used the very best ones. The best people may well be three
times better than the average, which triples the resources. Establishing two
separate divisions made things clearer, which helped motivate people. Often,
it is a question of motivation, not of time [page 78].

Peter Product: The best idea was to start the plus-modularization from the
best-selling product, plus-modularize it fast, and allocate resources for development. Fast results also increased the faith in the project. We could do the
same thing. We are really short on product development and engineering
resources. All our engineers are tied up in tailoring customer applications. On
the other hand, our best-selling product may be one of the most complicated
to plus-modularize. We should ask some more questions about this.

Pam Personnel: We often use lack of time as an excuse for not doing something. In reality, though, we don't always know what we should be doing or how. Trying hard and achieving little just consumes energy. The Innomat consultants brought know-how with them. We should ask in which form they gave it, whether it was given as advice, guidance, or training.

Peter Product: They made a 130-page publication and distributed it to all employees. Sounds like too much. The pages were not full, however; there were a lot of pictures, and the text was easy to understand [page 79].

Pam Personnel: The real benefit was obviously the fact that management was forced to think about its goal and how to reach it. The management usually has visions but is seldom able to convey them to the whole staff.

Peter Product: We could still ask how they would do the things they considered to be the most crucial.

Dave Development: We received good answers to all our questions. Peter Product and Pam Personnel will prepare to ask more questions.

Product Modularization
The subjects relating to organization and management were handled, and questions concerning plus-modular mass customization followed.

Dave Development: Danny Design and Diana Design were to concentrate on questions relating to mass customization.

Danny Design: We find that the business is good if we have a good enough sales force. They were able to really define the necessary means for winning new customers [page 80].

Diana Design: Usually, we don't have time to discuss these things. The sales-people travel around the world, and we stay here, doing our thing. But we have to sit down and discuss these matters together. We have to find the means. Let's ask how they managed that.

Diana Design: We've only paid attention to our immediate customers. In fact, our customer chain is longer than theirs. How little do we actually know about the other customers?

Danny Design: Our problem is poor production management. There is a tremendous amount of different components and different products. We just invested in a new production planning system. How has it helped us? We should have done it by ERP mass customization. The process cannot be managed if mass customization is not realized first.

Diana Design: This trip didn't teach me how to modulate yet, but it was easy to understand how to identify product features from the customer needs, in order to benefit the customer. The salesperson can concentrate on understanding customer needs and the product features she needs most. She just fills out the form on a computer and the quote is ready. It can be easily configured according to the customer's needs.

Danny Design: Each product feature has its own plus-module, price, and documents needed for selling, procurement, and manufacturing.

Diana Design: Now it's easy to concentrate on selling. Being between sales and production, we spend half the time trying to figure out just what was sold.

Danny Design: I would like to see all the documents related to a couple of plus-modules.

Diana Design: It's not easy to control the product structure. I want to ask what software they use.

Danny Design: In our company, the product development process is the same as research concerning the prototype. The work is then passed over to engineering, manufacturing, and sales. We launched the development of the delivery process. We need to include the improvement of the product development process in it. We could ask a couple of question about that.

Dave Development: Plus-modularization seems to be a very demanding task. We can ask some additional questions in order to understand it better. It would be worth another benchmarking visit to come and learn about technical realization. When we get back to our office, let's think how we could benefit from this visit and create a better benchmarking partnership.

Pam Personnel: In my opinion, the most important thing we learned was that this company started from the same difficult position as ours. We have all the chances to succeed. It takes time, and for that reason we are in a hurry to get our developing program started.

DEVELOPMENT MODEL FOR PLUS-MODULAR MASS CUSTOMIZATION

The following is a presentation of the 10-stage model for developing plus-modular mass customization. The model was applied from a plus-modular mass customization development model developed by Innomat. The technology is based on its configuration technology domain expertise and innovations and has developed further through similar projects that Innomat has consulted.

Mass Customization Development Model

1. Recognizing the Need for Change	2. Determining the Customer Requirements
Business objectives Business idea Strategic projects	Management requirements External customer requirements Sales requirements Product engineering requirements Production requirements Cost calculation requirements
3. Planning the Program and Setting the Targets	**4. Defining and Modeling External Customer Requirements**
Financial performance targets Operative performance targets Operational targets Time targets Organizing project and resources	Customer requirements will be modeled to ensure that the requirements of all customer groups and markets have been considered.
5. Product Engineering	**6. Sales Design**
Defining the product policy Modifying customer needs into plus-module construction Part lists Drawings Work stages and costs	Sales structure Pricing structure Sales material Training material After-sales material
7. Defining the Organization and Production Strategy	**8. Developing the Process**
Markets Production units Subcontracting Organization	Product development process Quote-order-delivery process
9. Continuous Capability Improvement	**10. Establishing Improvement and Continuous Development**
Competitive advantages Core capability The sources of capabilities Continuous learning	**Changing the Mind Set**

Summary

Stage 1: Recognizing the Need for Change
The company's business objectives, business plan, and required development projects are the basis for change.

Stage 2: Determining Customer Requirements
The objective of defining external and internal customer requirements is to identify them and estimate how they could be fulfilled through the product and mass customization.

Stage 3: Planning the Program and Setting the Targets
Projects do not implement themselves. Their feasibility, launch, and implementation must be ensured. The projects must be planned and organized, and their development process controlled.

Stage 4: Defining and Modeling External Customer Requirements
Customer requirements are modeled in graphic tree form to ensure that the requirements of all customer groups and markets have been thoroughly considered.

Stage 5: Product Engineering
Customer requirements are changed into plus-module construction according to the defined product policy.

Stage 6: Sales Design
The sales structure created at this stage forms the basis of a tool that is used by sales during customer discussions on choices based on product features and quote preparation.

Stage 7: Defining the Organization and Production Strategy
The market and product structure are decisive factors, which provide the opportunities to organize the operation and on which production strategy should be selected.

Stage 8: Developing the Processes
The products enter the market only as a result of the company's business processes. Plus-modular mass customization creates significant new opportunities to develop these business processes.

Stage 9: Continuous Capability Improvement
Competitiveness comes from the required capabilities, which must be identified and constantly improved.

Stage 10: Establishing Improvement and Continuous Development
The results of the development project should motivate new work methods and rationale. It requires changes in the entire business culture.

Stage 1: Recognizing the Need for Change

Business Objectives

The *business objectives* set by the company are the starting point for recognizing change. These business objectives are related primarily to growth, profitability, and market position.

The main business objective of Aquamaster-Rauma was to expand into global markets in order to double its turnover, improve profitability, and diminish dependency on industry-specific economic trends.

When preparing strategic plans and setting business objectives, it is essential to understand the line of business as well as any past and future changes. Any increase or decrease of market demand, or changes in economic trends, competitive situation, customer needs, environmental requirements, and product and manufacturing technology must be taken into account. It is important to understand the special characteristics inherent in the line of business, including the competition. The competitive situation may have changed or be changing. You can influence it to change. You need to know your own competencies and whether there is a need to improve them. You should also have an understanding of the present and future importance of your products in the competitive situation, because all of these factors determine how much you should invest in your products and plus-modular mass customization. Aquamaster-Rauma defined the main characteristics of its line of business, evaluated its future development, and chose which competitive advantages should be developed (see pages 81–84).

Aquamaster-Rauma's intent was to grow its marketing area worldwide. Its marketing area was divided into five customer segments: coastal vessels, tugboats, container ships, river cruisers, and cruise ships. The segments were defined by distinctly different customer needs and technological core know-how. It is not enough just to define customer needs. It is also necessary to possess (or develop) the competencies that satisfy customer needs better than the competition. Only after the needs and required competency match can the customer segment be selected as an objective of the company operations (see page 84).

Business Idea

> The company creates its *business idea* based on its business objectives, market-
> ing opportunities, competitive situation, and required competency. Through the
> business idea, the company determines which products and services can fulfill
> the needs of certain customers in certain markets, and what the competitive
> advantages the company competes with are.

Aquamaster-Rauma chose marine winches and propulsion units to be its
products and related after-sales service to be its service. The markets were
identified to be global and the customer segments to be the following: coastal
vessels, tugboats, container ships, river cruisers, and cruise ships. Each segment had its own specific requirements. Company lead times and the ability
to find a solution to customer needs through customer-specific and highly
developed products were considered to be the company's most important competitive advantages.

Strategic Projects

> The business idea chosen as the objective is implemented by strategic projects.
> Developing *plus-modular mass customization* can become a vehicle for imple-
> menting the new business idea. Successful plus-modular mass customization
> can also give new opportunities for developing the business idea. It is, therefore,
> a question of matching the marketing opportunities with the opportunities cre-
> ated by plus-modular mass customization.

It is a significant decision to apply large-scale plus-modular mass customization in the scope presented in this book. It should be based on carefully
considered business objectives and business ideas (chapter 2). Because plus-
modular mass customization provides the company with significantly better
chances in the global market, the business objectives and idea must be reviewed
at this point and the new opportunities carefully considered. The following
trends related to plus-modular mass customization are important and generally
agreed upon and should be taken into account:

- Businesses become global and competition gets tougher.
- Product life span decreases and product management becomes difficult.
- Time as a competitive factor continues to increase.
- Machines develop into systems, the alternatives increase, and product
  scope expands.
- Data become a commodity. You have to know how to handle it.
- Machine and system intelligence grows, and there is an explosive
  increase in product R&D costs.

- Networks and cooperation with subcontractors increase, and the importance of plus-modular mass customization increases.
- Manufacturing becomes decentralized and spreads throughout various countries. This requires that product data be handled precisely and independently from languages and time zones.
- Quality demands and cost pressures increase.
- Business processes and information systems are revived, and processes are streamlined.

Stage 2: Determining Customer Requirements

> Products and plus-modular mass customization should be run in such a way that market competitiveness improves together with internal cost-effectiveness. Understanding customer requirements is crucial when developing an adaptable product. It is not possible to develop product controllability without first knowing what requirements the product and plus-modular mass customization are expected to fulfill.

A large number of internal and external customers, each with different requirements, present the challenge that the product should meet an almost endless number of requirements. For this reason, it is not possible to control the requirements of the entire concept. A customer requirement analysis, in which customer requirements for the product and plus-modular mass customization are analyzed, is necessary.

The objective of defining customer requirements is to estimate how they can be fulfilled by the product and plus-modular mass customization. Other objectives are to point out the advantages and to prepare the project plan. In the following text, customers are grouped accordingly: management, external customer, sales, product R&D engineering, production, and cost accounting.

Management Requirements

> The responsibility of management is to set the business objectives, prepare the business idea, and define how these goals will be reached. Management will also lead the necessary change.

Means to reach the business targets. Management expects that the products and plus-modular mass customization will support the implementation of the chosen business idea. Management expects products that not only fulfill customer requirements but are also economical to manufacture and suitable for successful competition in global markets.

Defining the product policy. Management expects a clear rationale, identified customer needs, and manufacturing feasibility for defining the product policy. It also expects a tool that ensures the compatibility of the chosen markets, the company's own capabilities, and product policy.

Development leaps and continuous improvement. Management expects to achieve a significant, sustainable improvement leap in addition to a competitive advantage. This calls for plus-modular mass customization, which not only allows but also activates continuous development in product management, as well as in all business processes.

External Customer Requirements

The product must meet customer needs and expectations better than the competition. It is possible to compete in the market with product features, service factors, and price. The customer buys what he or she feels offers the best combination of these factors.

Product Features	Service Factor	Price Factor
Performance	Easy to buy	Purchase price
Reliability	Customer service	Installation costs
Safety	Put into service	Operation costs
Flexibility	After-sales service	Maintenance and repair costs
Ease of use	Maintenance and repair service	Service costs
Durability	Flexibility	Payment terms
Design	Delivery reliability	Warrantee
Environmentally friendly	Delivery time	

It is not enough simply to understand the customer's needs and expectations. It is also important to know how satisfied the customer is with the products and those of the competition. This is the basis of our own competitive advantage and customer satisfaction objectives. It is also not enough to merely understand the requirements of the customer who buys the product, but it is also essential to know the needs of each link in the customer chain. Our customers tend to give extra value to their own customers. We can create an important competitive advantage if we are able to bring some value added to the businesses of the entire chain of customers.

In Aquamaster-Rauma's customer chain, the *owner* values suitability to his or her operations, the *shipyard* values short delivery times, the *tanker* (to be assisted) values sufficient towing capacity, and the *harbor authorities* value environmental factors. The requirements of all customers have been included in the product, plus-modular mass customization, and process management.

Sales Requirements

> The main responsibility of the sales department is to sell products based on the *product policy* and customer requirements in certain markets. Other responsibilities include informing the rest of the organization about orders, order book developments, and future needs of the customers.

The adaptable product. The product that is configured according to customer needs enables sales to compete successfully against a standard product or an expensive tailor-made product.

Extensive product support. Sales needs a relatively simple product selection structure to allow for additions and changes in real time as the customer asks questions. This calls for extensive product support, the ability to provide the salesperson with product data on request. Other forms of this support are engineer data, sales margins and profitability data, availability data, and sales data. The speed of sales is a very valuable competitive factor. The following are the three main tasks of product support:

- Describe the product in the customer's desired language.
- Prevent combinations that would not work and that have not been engineered.
- Reduce the need for contact between sales and engineering while sales negotiations are underway.

The customer often finds the buying situation more pleasant when product properties can be discussed rather than sitting through a difficult-to-understand technical presentation.

Sufficient market potential. Sales needs a sufficient amount of potential purchasing candidates with needs that can be fulfilled by the selected product policy. Having market potential basically means doing business in the global market, which makes it possible to adhere to the chosen product policy and still reach sufficient volumes. As for product variations, it is necessary to compete with local tailor-made products. Compared with these products, customer requirements can be fulfilled better. Sales requires a system to transfer quote and order data in accurate form in real time and in the requested language, which in turn eliminates the need to travel around the world to confirm that the data were received correctly.

Real-time quote and order configuration. Immediately after the customer has chosen the product, he or she should be given a clear and accurate quote with comprehensive information concerning what was ordered, such as contact information and delivery terms. It is necessary to describe the quoted product explicitly in a specification that matches the customer's requirements. Prices must be provided in the agreed-upon currency and must include all related tax and customs duties information. All information concerning this deal must be easily available.

It must be possible to modify the quote in real time according to the customer's wishes. It must also be possible for sales to keep production and materials management up-to-date in real time on any development and changes concerning quotes and orders. One key task for shortening total lead time is to handle the orders in real time. (When all aspects are computerized, more human resources can be allocated for product development.)

Flexible pricing. The salesperson must be allowed to change the price of the adaptable product by changing its scope. Product configuration enables the salesperson to quote a product that meets customer requirements at a competitive price. This, in turn, enables the salesperson to have an outstanding competitive advantage over someone selling a standard product.

Chance to present the product. Sales should be able to present the selected individual product to the customer before he or she agrees to purchase it. It must be possible to present the customer with alternatives, in which configuration can be done by configuring plus-modules.

Customer follow-up application. The salesperson must have the opportunity to record the customer's future needs and visions on a customer need database, which can be used for product, service, and business process development.

Product Engineering Requirements

> Product engineering is responsible for creating products that fulfill customer requirements in the area defined by product policy. Additionally, when engineering the product, product engineering must remember the requirements of the company's internal customers.

The real-time transfer of customer requirements data for product engineering. The successful use of customer data requires that customer requirement analysis be conducted before the engineering phase. It also must be possible to review and update the analysis during the engineering phase. The best way to handle the real-time transfer of data on changes in customer requirements is to integrate the follow-up application of customer requirements as part of the sales data processing system. The sales system is used every day by the sales staff. It is not necessary to use a separate tool for entering the customer requirement data into the system.

Achieving economy of scale. The general practice was to engineer a product for a certain customer from beginning to end and then repeat the process for the next customer, according to that customer's requirements. Although there was an effort to use the previous engineering solutions, economy of scale could not be attained. When defining adaptable products, all global customer requirement modules are engineered at one time. This enables a shorter total engineering time. Through a simultaneous product R&D process, it is possible to enter all markets at the same time, which ensures that marketing can also gain economy of scale.

Creating parallel product development processes. Dividing the product to be engineered into plus-modules facilitates the product development of variant modules in parallel processes. This enables significantly shorter total lead times for engineering the entire global product range and entering the markets simultaneously.

Pre-design of tailor-made parts. About 80 percent to 90 percent of customer requirements should be satisfied by converting customer needs into product features. The remaining 10 percent to 20 percent can be individual. These customer requirements should be put into their final form separately each time according to the parameters and/or other customer data. The tailor-made sections must be predetermined with connecting interface.

Production Requirements

> Production is responsible for manufacturing the products, which are sold by sales and designed by the engineering department. The products must correspond with the product policy, must be manufactured within the time and quality agreed upon with the customer, and must meet the cost budget.

Accurate processing of the order. Accurate configuration-based orders and order processing accelerate production start-up by several weeks, compared with manually processing the order. Production, therefore, has enough time to carry out the manufacturing process. Accurate order processing activates the work processes of plus-modules mentioned in the factory order.

Cell manufacturing. Production controllability has a crucial impact on lead times. The best way to achieve controllability is to create self-controlled production units, or so-called production cells. Typically, a cell manufactures a product or section of a product from the beginning and is responsible for the control of the work and materials processes. Total operation control is achieved by controlling the cells where the number of load points is only a fraction of the control points in a functional plant.

Through standardized work processes and materials purchasing, it is possible to gain economy of scale for modules, although the final outcome is a customer-specified product. Because the production and materials purchasing phases are planned well in advance, things can be expected to run smoothly.

When producing standardized plus-modules, the use of subcontractor capacity becomes more effective. The subcontractor may receive data on the customer requirement-based plus-module even before the need surfaces. Standardized work processes and materials purchases enable very effective capacity control. When controlling the pre-engineered plus-modules, it is possible to use very precise capacity control, because the exact work time and materials availability can be predicted. This enables production of nearly 100 percent and accurate delivery. Standardized work processes are also a precondition for using automation and modern production technology. Both NC machine tools and automatic materials handling equipment require work process repetition to enable economical use.

Cost Accounting Requirements

Cost accounting is responsible for determining product costs according to the product policy. The job of cost accounting becomes difficult if products are different in every order.

Accurate cost accounting. Cost accounting is expected to handle the adaptable product as accurately as it handles the standardized product.

Moving resources from cost accounting to pre calculation. To secure better profits, it is far more important for the company to do cost accounting before the deal is closed than after it. The need for subsequent accounting decreases if product costs can be accurately calculated early in the quote stage.

Automatic cost accounting of additional costs. Additional costs consist of, for example, customs duties, taxes, and other payments. To achieve effective cost accounting, it must be possible to calculate these additional payments automatically into the total cost.

Stage 3: Planning the Program and Setting the Targets

If stages 1 and 2 prove that there is a need and potential for development, it is time to launch the development program. The targets, program manager, development organization, internal and external resources, and schedule must be defined.

Results include a product range with customer-adaptable products for global markets along with economical manufacturing and precise quote preparation and order handling practices, including prepared support materials for procurement and manufacturing.

Example of Financial Performance Targets

Measure	Current	Target	Change
Turnover	FIM 112 million	FIM 112 million	+− 0
Costs	FIM 101 million	FIM 90 million	−FIM 14 million
Profit	FIM 11 million	FIM 22 million	+ FIM 11 million
Gross margin %	10%	20%	10% units
Capital, employed	FIM 100 million	FIM 98 million	FIM 2 million
Return on capital employed	11%	22%	11% units
Market share	9%	9%	0

If the improved competitiveness enables additional sales of 100 units, it could nearly double the market share, savings, and free capital.

Improvements in financial performance are based on the following time and capital savings. The costs of the development project are not included in these calculations.

Time and Cost Savings	Expected Savings
Sales	36,500 hrs.
Product development	9,450 hrs.
Production control	750 hrs.
Material management	1,500 hrs.
Manufacturing	750 hrs.
Total	48,950 hrs FIM 14.0 million

Measurements of Capital	Capital Savings
WIP	FIM 1 million
Sales stock	FIM 1 million
Total	FIM 2 million
Interest %	25%
Interest costs	FIM 0.5 million

Operative Performance Targets

Aquamaster-Rauma set its operative development targets according to the following table.

Performance	Measure	1990	1993	Target
Performance Requirements for Customer Satisfaction and Overall Efficiency				
Delivery reliability	%	75	95	100
Warrantee costs	%	20	18	below 1
Total lead time	Weeks	18	10	6
Inventory turnover	FIM million	25	17	15
Value-added per person	FIM million	17	38	50
Lead Time Reduction in the Entire Delivery Chain				
Quote preparation	Hours	8	4	1
Order handling	Days	10	3	1
Engineering/design	Days	40	20	1
Total lead time	Weeks	18	10	6
Improved Effectiveness of Customer Application Design				
Engineering/design	Hrs./order	330	100	80
Project management	Hrs./order	100	45	30
Number of drawings	Pcs./order	45	12	10
Simplified Materials Management				
Long-term agreements	%	25	60	75
Order given by an operator	Component	0	449	700
Manufacturing planning done by an operator	Component	0	63	100
Increased Customer Base				
Potential new customers	Pieces	20	150	150
Orders from new customers	Pieces	3	8	10
By the following improvements:				
–Number of offers	Pieces	500	650	800
–Lead time of offers	Hours	8	4	1
–Accuracy of orders	FIM	50,000	1000	1000
–Deviation from planned cost	%	30	5	1

Operational Targets

Financial and operational performance improvements are results of changes in operating practices. The planned changes in operational practices are described at this stage of the project. The operational targets to fulfill external and internal customer requirements at stage 2 could be described as follows.

1. *Management.* Products and plus-modular mass customization enable expansion into global markets, a planned growth in the company strategy, and a decreased dependency on economic trends. Management, therefore, has a solid basis for defining and controlling the product policy. Products, which are varied according to customer requirements, offer more value-added than do the competitors' products, which in turn motivates the customer to pay more for the product. The cost-effectiveness of the whole organization continues to improve.

   • Global markets become possible.
   • There is a solid basis for defining and controlling product and service policy.
   • It decreases dependency on economic trends.
   • It enables better and continuously improving profitability.

2. *External customer.* The customer receives an individualized product that fulfills his or her requirements at a competitive price. Additionally, the lead time from customer inquiry to taking the product into use is shorter than that of the competitors. The purchasing situation is also pleasant for the customer, because he or she can discuss the product from his or her practical point of view and can concentrate on defining the product features.

   • The customer receives a fast and reliable quote.
   • Local conditions and individual requirements of the customer are taken into account.
   • The product delivery time is short and reliable.
   • The product, spare parts, and service documents are accurate and clear.

3. *Sales.* Sales can immediately provide a product quote, which can have up to hundreds of variations. The quote contains accurate product specifications, and the price is set immediately.

   • Quote preparation is faster.
   • The customer gets an individual product based on standardized solutions.

- Fast and reliable delivery is a significant competitive advantage.
- Factory orders are more accurate and handled more quickly.
- Agreed-upon deliveries times hold.

4. *Product design.* All products and product variations are designed into plus-modules before the sale is made. By maintaining the sales structure, the engineering department can give product support to sales in an effective and easy-to-use form.

- Engineering work is minimized for each order.
- There are fewer item names.
- Routines are clear.
- Resources can be moved to more innovative work.
- Designs are used repeatedly.

5. *Manufacturing.* Accurate orders are transferred to production. The work processes of required pre-engineered plus-modules are activated. The production cells manufacture the whole or partial product from beginning to end and are in charge of work processes and materials control. The standardized work processes and materials acquisition in modules provide repetition, better productivity, and more uniform quality. The subcontractor is delivered the data for manufacturing the customer requirement–based plus module even before the need surfaces. Repetition is achieved through plus-modules, enabling more economical use of NC machine tools.

- Lead times are shortened.
- Flexibility, productivity, and quality are better.
- Inventory turnover is faster.
- Order processing is accurate, control and supervision are simpler.
- Work processes and materials acquisition are standardized.

6. *Cost accounting.* Plus-modules can be combined in all permissible ways to set an exact price on all combinations.

- Plus-Modular cost accounting.
- Directing resources in advance cost accounting.
- Automatic cost accounting of public costs.

7. *After-sales Service.*

- There are fewer spare part items and quicker turnover of stock.
- Spare parts and service instruction documents are accurate.

Time Targets

A study made by McKinsey & Co. shows that, if a product is late to the market by six months, its lifetime return is reduced by one-third. This study, like many other studies, shows the importance of development time in competition. It takes time to run a strategic development project; therefore, it should be started without delay.

The schedule of a plus-modular mass customization development program could look like this:

Phase	20xx				20xy			
	I	II	III	IV	I	II	III	IV
1.–3. Launch of project	x							
4. Modeling of customer requirements		x	x			x	x	
5. Product engineering			x	x	x			
6. Sales design				x	x	x		
7. Organization and production strategy	x			x				
8. Development of the processes		x			x	x	x	x
9. Continuous capability improvement						x	x	x
10. Establishment as a total system					x	x	x	x

Organizing the Project

The project must have a full-time project manager who has experience and a clear understanding of customers, product development, and the quote and delivery processes. He or she should also have experience in the systematic developing of operations, as well as the ability to use both internal and external know-how. To support the project manager, it is necessary to name a management group from within the organization comprised of members from the process areas. The chairperson of the committee should come from top management. The investment required to develop plus-modular mass customization is significant, but the new opportunities it affords are huge. It will significantly change the company's operating principles and practices.

The actual work is done by the project group, with the project manager acting as group leader. At least one member of the group must be an expert on plus-modular mass customization and modularization. This person must work full-time. If the company wants to run the project so that it is competitive in terms of speed and quality, an external plus-modular mass customization consultant must also be included in the project group. Other resources depend on the extent of the project.

The task of **management** is to define the product policy according to the business idea and to ensure the availability of resources. Management makes sure that the new operating practices will be put into use and gets the business process owners to develop their own processes and use the opportunities of plus-modular mass customization.

Sales is in charge of defining the customer requirements and participates actively in developing the product and product structure. The use of plus-modular mass customization starts from the sales operations. Sales is responsible for taking the sales systems into use according to plus-modular mass customization and is in charge of using the new global opportunities.

Product development is responsible for developing the technology when required. It participates in defining the plus-modular mass customization principles and uses them in product engineering.

Product engineering participates actively in defining product structures and is in charge of the customer-applicable engineering according to the developed plus-modular mass customization principles. Product engineering is in charge of transferring allocated resources to, for example, product development.

Production participates actively in product structure development and adds its own requirements to it. It develops its own processes using the opportunities of plus-modular mass customization.

Financial management defines its own needs and is in charge of using the new possibilities in cost accounting.

Information technology participates in choosing and developing the information systems required and brought about by plus-modular mass customization.

After-sales service defines its own needs and is in charge of using the new opportunities in its own functions.

Stage 4: Defining and Modeling External Customer Requirements

> When defining customer needs, it is necessary to create a simple and fast method for finding the most important requirements from the vast number of less important needs. The basis of successful plus-modular mass customization is to model customer needs in graphic form. To outline the graph in tree form, customer needs must be completely understood.

First, all customer needs identified through a customer requirement analysis are modeled. This step helps create a basis for product and production policy decisions, which are based on the actual market situation, taking into consideration all customer groups and market areas.

The customer requirement structure merely describes the customer requirements. When creating the structure, the technical specification of product features and application requirements are not included. Product-specific technical solutions are handled in stage 5 in connection with defining the plus-module construction.

Following is an example of how to define external customer needs for a trailer. At the concept level, the customer need is to transport goods. On this level, the customer may choose from several alternatives, such as a truck, van, ski box, or rented trailer. This is where the first decision concerning product policy is made.

The need is specified as the transportation of goods by pulling them behind a vehicle. The most essential customer needs are the payload, cubic measurement of the load, protection of the load, and ease of loading. In the example, each need has been given as a measurable quantity, determining the limits of the need and the offered alternatives. For example, the payload varies between 50 and 1500 kg. Thus, 1500 kg and 900 kg were offered as alternatives.

This principle can also be used for defining and analyzing other customer needs and alternatives.

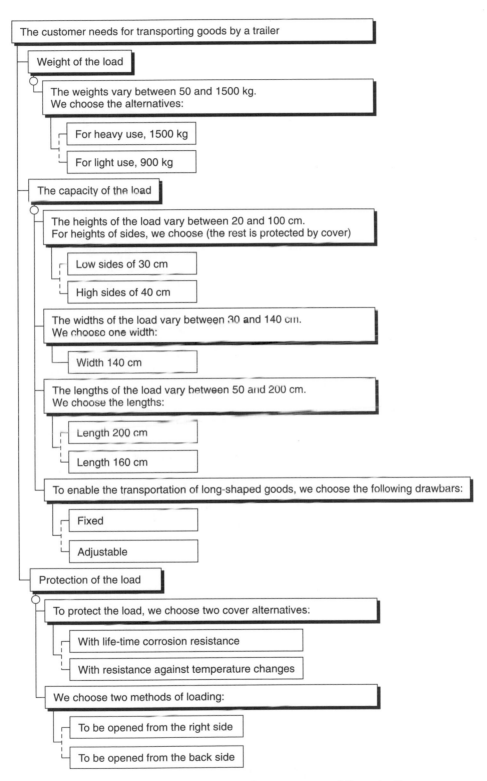

The customer needs for transporting goods by a trailer

Weight of the load

The weights vary between 50 and 1500 kg.
We choose the alternatives:

For heavy use, 1500 kg

For light use, 900 kg

The capacity of the load

The heights of the load vary between 20 and 100 cm.
For heights of sides, we choose (the rest is protected by cover)

Low sides of 30 cm

High sides of 40 cm

The widths of the load vary between 30 and 140 cm.
We choose one width:

Width 140 cm

The lengths of the load vary between 50 and 200 cm.
We choose the lengths:

Length 200 cm

Length 160 cm

To enable the transportation of long-shaped goods, we choose the following drawbars:

Fixed

Adjustable

Protection of the load

To protect the load, we choose two cover alternatives:

With life-time corrosion resistance

With resistance against temperature changes

We choose two methods of loading:

To be opened from the right side

To be opened from the back side

Example for modeling external customer need for a trailer

Stage 5: Product Engineering
Defining Product Policy

In this case, the term *product policy* means the decision whether or not to fulfill a certain customer need. When product policy decisions are made, the primary consideration is the customer requirement structure. The product policy determines which customer needs will be fulfilled and to which customers sales will be directed.

When the customers have been selected, the necessary customer expectations are defined (modelled) in the customer requirement structure. Thus, to define (model) the product policy means to find the optimum compromise between the best short-term and/or long-term economical result. Other facts that affect product policy are manufacturing possibilities and any ideas sales has for market development.

Modifying Customer Requirements into Plus-Modular Construction

The selected customer needs will be constructed into plus-modular technical solutions.

The goal is to model the minimum amount of plus-modules that satisfy all selected customer needs. Plus-modularization means that, if a certain customer need is added to the product, it must be possible to do so without removing anything. For example, if alternative hooks are fastened to the trailer, it must be possible to change them without modifying the construction of the rest of the trailer.

The objective is to meet customer requirements through technical innovations and solutions, as well as flexible product structure.

In plus-modularization, there is no fixed basic product to which individual customer-specified needs are added. Many modularization techniques fail because the basic product was considered to be a fixed product. Later, however, there are always variation pressures on the basic product.

According to the software, customer requirements are processed into the plus-modular construction. There are six levels involved. The following illustration shows three levels. The additional three would be work methods, materials, and components.

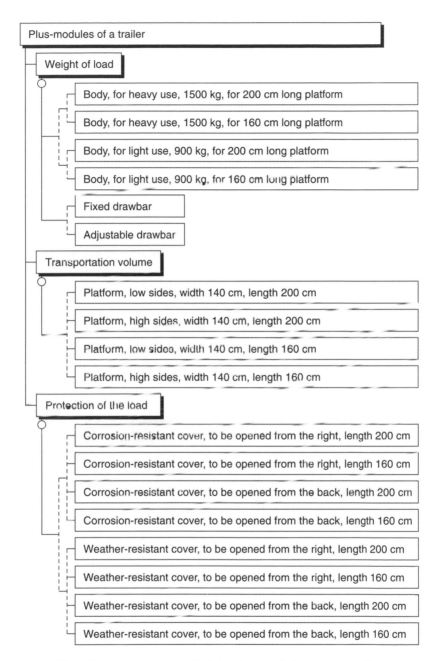

Changing customer needs into plus-modular construction

Connecting interfaces are internal features built into plus-module construction. They determine which plus-modules can be connected and which cannot.

Stage 6: Sales Design

Creating the Sales Structure

> Based on the customer requirement structure and plus-module construction, sales structure is created by the salesperson and customer. It consists of a sales scene and built-in intelligence. The sales scene is the external appearance of the sales structure; it is from the sales scene that the customer and salesperson select features according to the customer's requirements.

The technical choices do not require attention because they are built in as internal intelligence. Eliminating technical details simplifies the visual appearance and focuses customer interest on the opportunities that the adaptable product offers. The following illustration further describes the adaptable customer-applicable product and its benefits.

> When we buy a trailer, the salesman undoubtedly makes the sale. We make our choice either by comparing all the trailers at one dealer or by comparing several dealers' trailers.

I used to do the same thing. The available models were in the product catalog. Ten percent of the models were in stock, the rest had a delivery time of four weeks. In fact, I did not necessarily even need a trailer. What I needed was a way to transport goods. Most important, I needed weight and capacity. I also needed to protect the goods I was transporting. I also wanted easy loading and unloading. It was not easy to make the purchase. The salespeople were constantly trying to sell me trailers in their selection. Not one dealer met all my requirements. And, even if they were able to, they suggested models with features I didn't need and wasn't willing to pay for. Finally, I found the right dealer. He didn't immediately push his catalog on me but asked me about my transportation requirements according to the following steps:

- He first asked about the payload. I selected the maximum weight allowed for my car. The dealer found the weight in my registration book. We chose 900 kg from the available alternatives.
- Next, he asked me how much space my load would require. I told him it would be about 130 cm wide, 180 cm long, and 30 cm high. The alternative 140 × 180 × 30 cm was then selected.
- "What about the drawbar? Should it be fixed or adjustable?" asked the dealer. I did not know what to answer. "Do you want to carry wood or other long goods?" he asked. "No," I answered. "Then the fixed drawbar will be OK," he then replied. That was a sensible suggestion, because it was also much cheaper.
- "Do you need protection for the goods?" he then asked. I answered, "Yes, it should tolerate some rough handling." I chose a cover made of weather-proofed sheet metal.
- "Which side do you want to use for loading and unloading?" he continued asking. "The back," I answered.

He seemed to find the questions easy. He even promised a delivery time of just one week. I got exactly what I needed without paying for anything extra. When I wondered about the reliability and flexibility of their delivery, I got to know their order-delivery-process. There is more about that in stage 8.

> I also learned that the dealer would have had to stock 64 model variations in order to fulfill all alternative requirements.

The following figure shows how the dealer changed my requirements into product properties.

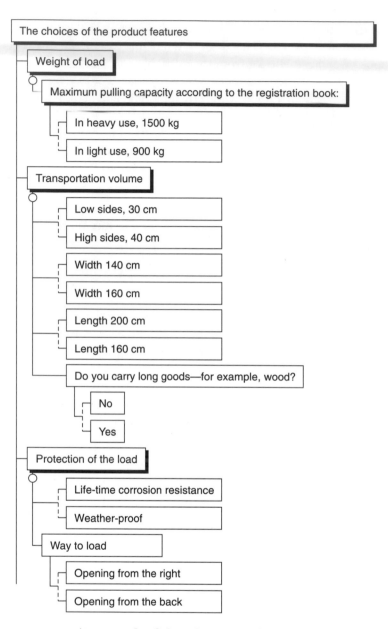

The choices of the product features

Weight of load

Maximum pulling capacity according to the registration book:

In heavy use, 1500 kg

In light use, 900 kg

Transportation volume

Low sides, 30 cm

High sides, 40 cm

Width 140 cm

Width 160 cm

Length 200 cm

Length 160 cm

Do you carry long goods—for example, wood?

No

Yes

Protection of the load

Life-time corrosion resistance

Weather-proof

Way to load

Opening from the right

Opening from the back

An example of the sales scene of a trailer

Stage 7: Defining the Organization and Production Strategy

> Successful lines of business are usually based on global operations. Finnish companies go global mainly through company acquisitions. In most cases, the immediate solution is to organize the company so that it has independent business units with their own products and business processes, without using the total size and competencies.

During the previous recession, companies were forced to eliminate overlapping products, production, assets, and organization. This happened by eliminating seemingly overlapping products from the product range and by dividing product responsibilities among units. The actions were taken under pressure and in a hurry. Decisions were made and carried out quickly; even so, some important results were achieved.

Because of the rush, defining global customer requirements was overlooked, as were the synergistic opportunities of the divided product families. The products were developed for certain markets. To meet the requirements of the new markets and production units, companies tailored and added features to their products. But, as the businesses expanded, new problems surfaced because the products, sales, manufacturing, and service were not designed for worldwide markets and because the vast opportunities afforded by plus-modular mass customization were not used.

There is a choice of several alternatives, centralized, decentralized, matrix solutions, and so on. Different demands call for different solutions:

- To bring the development engineering and manufacturing close to the customer, support a decentralized organization.
- To be globally effective in product development and manufacturing as well as have low fixed costs, support centralization.
- Fast growth and reductions when necessary support light structure, concentration on core competencies, and use of subcontractors.
- Changing demand and currency fluctuations support flexible production strategy.

> As environmental factors and the company competencies change constantly, there must be ongoing testing of the organizational structure and production strategy. Changes must be made as needed.

In the following example, a company has determined the requirements for plus-modular mass customization in order to implement global competitiveness and production strategy.

---

1. The product family to be developed must beat the competitors that will enter the markets with copies of our products.
2. The product family must be engineered for global markets and decentralized manufacturing and should contain following features:
   - It must be easy to apply to local standards and requirements.
   - Product modules should be easily configured according to local needs.
   - It must be designed for modular manufacturing and be independent from the manufacturing place.
   - It must be modularized in such a way that production can be moved easily to another country, and manufacturing on our own premises can be increased easily as volume grows.
3. The product family has been engineered for effective production processes. This requires, among other things:
   - A small number of parts
   - Standardized parts
   - Constructions suitable for mechanization and automation
4. The product family has been modularized to fulfill the requirements of every stage of the business process from quote calculation to spare parts delivery.
5. Simultaneous product design, product management planning, and a global production system are prerequisites for achieving high efficiency and a competitive advantage in the global marketplace.

Stage 8: Developing the Processes

> Process control without plus-modular mass customization is an illusion. Many companies start large business process development programs but often with only marginal benefits. The product range, variation principles, and imperfect plus-modular mass customization prevent any significant changes in the processes. One of the most important advantages of plus-modular mass customization is product engineering and the allocation of product engineering resources for product and process improvement.

Product Development Process Development

A great product idea is not enough. It must be introduced to the market quickly and economically. Beginning with the first delivery, quality and cost efficiency must be achieved as planned. Products are also subject to continuous development, in order to keep meeting changing customer requirements. These often contradictory requirements surface in the product development processes, which must be effectively supported by other business processes. The competitive factors are quality and speed.

> Therefore, the product development process has two targets:
>
> 1. To produce new competitive products and services to fulfill customer requirements quickly and economically
> 2. To run the product development process faster each time with improved quality

The product development process can be divided into parts. Its quality can be improved, and it can be made faster in many ways. Through plus-modular mass customization, the following steps significantly affect the quality and speed of product development:

1. When defining customer needs, the needs are identified and the customer need structure for global markets created. Modeling ensures that the needs of all customer groups and market areas are taken into consideration.
2. In product engineering, the customer need structure is changed into plus-modular construction—that is, the chosen customer requirements are constructed into plus-modules and technical solutions. The customer requirements and technical solutions are combined in a distinct way to make product policy decisions easier.

3. The *sales design* creates preconditions for the sales of goods. The sales structure is created in this stage. From this structure, the salesperson, together with the customer, makes product feature choices that fulfill customer needs. At this stage, other sales support materials are also created, such as written documentation, prices, and brochures. Another part of the sales design process is to train the salespeople on the new product and its sales structure. This ensures proper product application.

4. Sales and distribution can focus on global markets because customer needs are included in the customer needs analysis and included in the product without changes to product quantity. The various customer needs increase only the number of plus-modules.

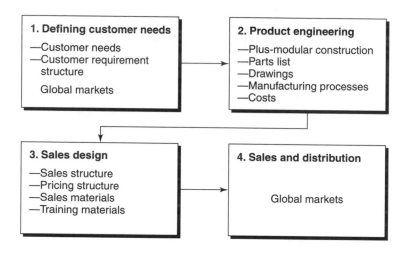

When developing products already in the product range, product development mostly consists of designing plus-modules that fulfill new customer needs or are more economical to manufacture. The intention is to have product supremacy in the markets while developing plus-modular mass customization. Practice shows that lead times of a new product is cut almost in half and, in some cases, to only a fraction through plus-modular mass customization.

Developing the Quote-Order-Delivery Process
The process can be divided into parts, and its quality and speed improve in several ways, as presented in the following example.

The ordinary course of the quote-order-delivery process may be as follows:

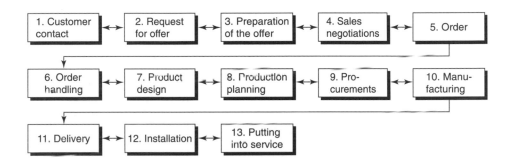

The traditionally engineered product and process have long lead times because of continuous contact with the next process stage (for studying and defining various possibilities), as well as contact with the previous stage (for validating matters):

---

1. *The customer contact* presents his or her needs, and the salesperson returns home to prepare for the next sales trip.
2. The salesperson receives the *inquiry.*
3. The salesperson returns to his or her office to *make a quote.*
4. *Sales negotiations* lead to a new inquiry, and the salesperson returns to the office to answer it. There will be several rounds of negotiations and trips with several contacts. The competitors are also out with their own quotes. It is possible that all this is so time-consuming and pushes the delivery time so far back that the customer can no longer even consider the quotes.

5. The customer has big problems with *placing the order* because of the large number of defective quotes with variable contents.

6. If the *order is received,* the receiver must start validating what actually was sold, to whom, where, and on what terms. Those who receive the order at the factory must contact the salesperson, who in turn contacts the customer, which may even result in new price negotiations.

7. The order is then forwarded to *product engineering,* who may also wonder what exactly was sold (the person who originally received the order concentrated only on the delivery terms). This causes more contact between sales and the customer. The product is engineered by configuring solutions of the previous orders, and it is tailored according to customer needs. Combining old solutions often takes more time and causes more quality errors than engineering a completely new product.

8. *Production planning* receives the parts lists and product drawings, which again leads to clarifications with product engineering, because, every time a new product is in question, the parts purchasing, subcontracting, staging of work, and contracting must be done from the beginning, with an effort to use the old data.

9. Certain *components* cannot be *obtained.* Changes require customer approval. The delivery time must be renegotiated because the original information the capacity planner received was defective.

10. *Manufacturing, installing, and training* at start-up run into similar problems. New designs, products, and parts require different solutions than previous stages because there is no repetition of results to learn from. The same problems are experienced by the technical writers as well as the product's service organization.

The principles of process management help eliminate these problems. There are descriptions made on work processes and operating practices. Project teams, sales teams and corresponding teams are formed to ensure the required capabilities and improve the flow of information.

In successful development programs, improvements are significant. Lead times are shorter and nonquality costs diminish. Generally, however, the results are not always so significant. An extensive product range, the construction of products, and numerous customer requirements prevent any noticeable improvement in process controllability.

Even in successful development programs, not enough value is added for the customer to greatly improve the company's competitive advantage and pricing possibilities. Only after plus-modular mass customization is combined with process management can radical results be achieved.

> The problems previously described either disappear completely or decrease considerably with a customer-need-based plus-modular product assortment.

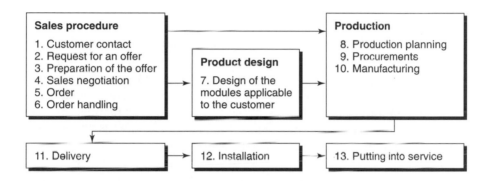

In the example of the trailer purchasing process, I came to understand the quote-order-delivery process of the trailer manufacturer. You cannot talk about a process in the traditional sense, because many things belonging to the traditional process have diminished to only a few.

At the beginning of the customer contact, my needs were identified. Based on the outcome, I asked for a quote. The dealer also gave me a printout of the quote right there. Pricing was based on my exact needs, so I was immediately able to make my decision to buy.

The salesman passed on my order right away as an internal factory order. Thus, the buying event consisted of selection of the product, a request for a quote, the pricing of the quote, the order, and the internal order all in one. However, the salesman had a great deal of alternatives to quote. (In this case, there were 64. In reality, some products may have hundreds of millions of alternatives.)

A week later, when I went to pick up my trailer, I learned how the factory processed my order when it got it. I was astonished! Since the salesman used a computer program early in the selling stage, he made the quote according to my requirements and changed it into an internal order by pressing a button.

At the factory, the order was lined up with other orders to be manufactured by modules. The required modules were specified in the internal order given by the salesperson, so, during the selling stage, it was clear what modules to make. The salesperson and I did not have to concern ourselves with technical details.

The manufacturing of all modules began simultaneously; finally, the modules were put together at the final assembly stage. This was why the order not only was handled effectively but also enabled a short lead time; no time was wasted on clarifications. The product modules were manufactured side-by-side, and, if the factory would not have had a capacity load, production of my unit would have started five minutes after I signed the order!

Because the modules were previously engineered standard modules, all parts lists and purchase structures existed. The maker of the chassis knew exactly which parts to get from stock. Without leaving the factory, she could order just the right wiring harness and electrical parts for my trailer from suppliers.

The subcontractor was provided in advance with the data on wire harnesses suitable for each module. The contractor worked under a long-term business contract. Thus, the actual purchasing was just "calling home" the parts, which made the whole process run smoothly.

At delivery, the trailer was inspected and the applicable documents supplied. My order and the internal order with a list of manufactured modules were also included. It contained a concise instruction booklet with information on only the features I had ordered. Additionally, every module had a corresponding spare parts list and codes.

It was just as simple as it sounds, but the important thing was that, of all the alternatives, I got exactly the trailer I wanted, and I got it quickly.

Stage 9: Continuous Capability Improvement

Ideas turn into competitive products only if the company has the required capabilities. Capabilities can be related to the product, plus-modular mass customization, or product development process. They may also consist of a deep customer knowledge or product expertise and manufacturing techniques. Core knowledge of the company products and production processes must be continuously identified and developed. Continuous learning, in turn, calls for personal learning agreements.

For example, to achieve better competitiveness, the core know-how of a forest machinery manufacturer could be the following:

Product-Related Core Capabilities

- Cutting techniques
- Ergonomics of the mobile working machine
- Measuring techniques
- Capabilities to develop modular and customer-applicable products

Product Development Process–Related Core Capabilities

- Global plus-modular mass customization and global product development processes
- Continuous identification of customer needs
- Continuous competitive benchmarking
- Customer needs passed quickly to product engineering process
- The speed of product development process
- Meeting development plans and targets

Quote-Order-Delivery Process–Related Core Capabilities

- Fast quotes according to customer needs
- Superior lead times enabling customer-applicable production
- High productivity

As time is an important competitive factor, even the learning phase may be too long. Repetition helps speed up the learning phase. Plus-modulated products offer repetition throughout the entire organization, thus making the learning phase faster.

Stage 10: Establishing Improvement and Continuous Development

> The benefits of plus-modular mass customization are established in stage 10. The precondition is learning the developed operating principles and practices, applying them strictly and developing them continuously.

Plus-modular mass customization consists of a number of useful and practical tools and operating principles. But it is also a new rationale that takes time to root. The customer-applicable product is a way of thinking. This way can be more holistic than before. Previously, the idea was let's sell what we have. We will expand into new markets and add new features to our basic product to fulfill the needs of the new markets. Earlier, product families were created almost unintentionally. In plus-modular mass customizing customer-applicable products, the product family is engineered at one time for global markets.

The customer's opinion is essential when considering the applicable plus-modulated product. The customer has certain needs, which certain plus-modules or their combinations can fulfill. Plus-modules are pre-engineered to ensure that the organization operates effectively and makes faster deliveries. Earlier, products, business processes, and related development led their own lives. Plus-modular mass customization enables simultaneous development. Additionally, plus-modular mass customization enables significant changes in the processes, not merely minor ones.

Learning a new rationale is not a fast process, and it does not happen by itself. It happens through understanding, participation, and gained benefits. A change in rationale shows in people's attitudes and values throughout the entire business culture.

> *Who is responsible for changing and developing*
> *the business culture of an organization?*
>
> ### It is the director's task.
>
> *The task begins from stage 1 and ends at stage 10.*
> *Then it starts again from the beginning.*
> *It is a never-ending process.*

SELF-EVALUATION QUESTIONS

Evaluation Criteria	Priority	Current and Target Performance				
		1	2	3	4	5
1. Is the lead time for order handling before manufacturing short enough?						
2. Is delivery reliability good enough to satisfy the customer?						
3. Are the internal business processes clear?						
4. Does the product engineering of each order require resources?						
5. Does product development correspond with customer requirements?						
6. Is it easy for the customer to interpret the product specifications?						
7. In addition to the product engineering required by each order, does the engineering department have any time left for developing new products?						
8. Are the orders of dealers clear and can they be passed on to production as they are without additional work?						
9. Would the present sales force be able to sell more and get a better sales margin?						
10. Does the company have a clearly defined product policy?						
11. Is there unambiguous documentation for the whole range of products?						
12. Are the lead times short enough?						
13. Is it easy enough to control the purchasing and subcontracting?						
14. Is it possible to create customer-specified products for global markets quickly and economically?						
Overall Grade						

x Your evaluation of the current performance level o Your target	Priority 1 Not significant 2 Significant 3 Important 4 Very important 5 Competitive advantage	Current and Target Performance 1 Poor 2 Adequate 3 Good 4 Very Good 5 Exceptional

Chapter 4

PROCESS MANAGEMENT

Strategic management

Product management	Process management
	Quality, efficiency flexibility, enthusiasm

Development management

Content Summary

This section illustrates how *process development* and *process management* can be used to create competitive advantage. The book reviews the theory of process management briefly and examines why process development produces better results than developing functions.

Ahlstrom Machinery in Finland is a leading supplier of equipment and processes for the pulp industry internationally. The Pump Division is a leading supplier of pumps for the pulp industry globally. Ahlstrom Pumps manufactures products both in the United States and Europe.

The case study illustrates how a development project was launched at Ahlstrom Pumps from 1993 to 1994. It shows how process development was defined as a strategic project, aiming at becoming a world-class company in all of its business processes. The objective was to repeat the same success the company had already achieved in developing the production process for its pumps, of which the Mänttä production plant was an example known all over the world.

The case study shows how the *process management model* was created, how the pilot processes were selected, and how they were put into effect. I was the Development Manager at Ahlstrom Machinery and was responsible for activating the development programs and acted as an internal process development consultant.

The book presents a model for an *eight-phase development program*. Each phase is illustrated via the improvement of R&D processes at Prostec. The model was developed on the basis of personal experience and certain examples. One such example is the development model used by Ahlstrom Pumps Product Line. Its developer claims it is based on 300 successful process management projects.

The questions will enable you to evaluate your own organization's *present and target levels* of development, to examine the reasons for differences in individual evaluations, and to plan development measures.

Introduction to Process Management

QUICK NOTES	
Page 133:	Read the complete text.
135–143:	Read headings, illustrations, text boxes, and tables.
144–147:	Read the complete text.
148–170:	Read headings, illustrations, text boxes, and tables.
171–173:	Read the complete text.
174–188:	Read headings, illustrations, text boxes, tables and the text in *italics*.

Why Process Management?

You can still gain competitive advantage!
JIT production philosophy completely changed both our way of thinking and our way of operating. In the 1980s, a company could still gain competitive advantage with a *JIT production philosophy*. By the 1990s, moving to JIT was playing "catch-up" with everyone else.

In the same way, companies can still gain competitive advantage in the 1990s from *process management*. However, by the next decade the competitive advantage aspect will have been lost, and they will just be trying to catch up.

The critical tasks of management have been planning the structures and organization of the company, staffing it, setting goals, delegating, and monitoring profitability. As difficulties arose, it has been the organization that was changed first. It has been decentralized or centralized, completely functional or product-oriented. Solutions to problems have been sought through organizational change.

Nothing has necessarily changed, though. The same people have been there in different boxes, but with the same thoughts, and companies have carried on operating according to their old principles and practices. The result has been to change from a spring organization to a fall organization, but the way of operating has remained the same. Each department head has looked after his or her own patch, maximizing his or her own power base. The next quarterly report has been more important than customer satisfaction, and departments would rather compete or quarrel than work together.

Many companies have recognized that traditional methods of measuring results in an organization restrict rather than promote the exploitation of people's skills.

In many companies, the shortcomings of the traditional organization have been recognized, and they have given up organization charts. Others have drawn their organizations as overlapping circles, emphasizing cooperation and flexibility. Still others have decided that, from now on, they will work in processes and teams. Hierarchical and inflexible organizations are not needed.

In spite of these drawing exercises and formal training, there has been no real action taken—no real change. In the worst cases, programs of management by objectives and other traditional systems for managing organizations that have been developed over some decades have been thrown out but not replaced.

Organizations live in a state of great uncertainty. Traditional management systems have been forgotten in the name of new "isms." New management systems have not been developed to replace the old.

> However we describe the organization, customers' impressions arise, and have always arisen, from processes that transcend departments and companies.
>
> Every process and its *outputs*—products, delivery, maintenance, service, and so on—have their own customers with their own needs and expectations.

Profitability is a consequence of how well the outputs of the process meet the customers' needs and expectations, as well as how cost-effectively they are provided. Our *marketing process* must awaken the customer's interest in our products. Our *sales process* must create the impression in the customer's mind that our products are better than those of our competitors, in order to achieve a profitable sale. Our *delivery process* must keep the promises made in our contract. Our *product development process* must bring more added value to the customer.

> We have, however, constructed efficient corporate, profit center, and departmental boundaries and measurement systems, which set effective limits on the operation of processes.

As well as making the process operate smoothly, product and manufacturing technology as well as other skills must also be competitive. The development of products and technology has been the responsibility of the departments in the organization: product development, sales, manufacturing, and so on.

The key question is how to organize process development so as to maximize process quality and efficiency and to develop the capabilities needed at a speed that is competitive. This chapter will seek to answer this question with the help of case studies and process development models.

Business Processes—Core and Support Processes

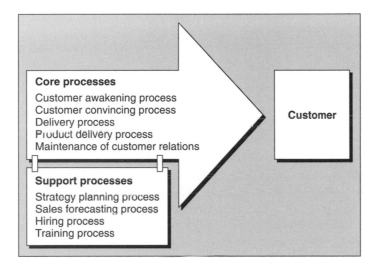

The *core processes* are the processes that produce *added value for the customer* and from which customer satisfaction is derived. Core processes are central to the business operation and are linked directly to the services provided by external customers. They are the processes that generate the income stream. They are set in motion by the customer (placing the order) and end with the customer (receiving goods). *They are set in motion by customer expectations and end with customer satisfaction.* This process occurs irrespective of changes in ownership boundaries. Crossing these boundaries makes process development more demanding. But it also creates opportunities to generate additional added value for the customer.

The customer-directed core processes need *support processes* in order to work. *The core processes are the customers for the output of these support processes.*

Process development is set in motion by analyzing the core process customers' expectations and satisfaction. The effectiveness of the core process, and thus the customer's satisfaction, may depend on the quality of the core process itself or on the quality of the support processes it depends on.

Processes Extend Across Departments, Business Units, and Enterprises

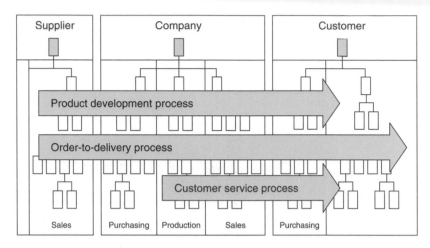

Source: Hannus, Jouko. 1993. *Prosessijohtaminen.* HM&V Research Oy, Jyväskylä, Finland.

> Companies do not compete only on their products but also on the whole chain with which their production cycle is associated with. Processes must thus be seen as a whole, and it is the "whole" with which companies or "chains of companies" compete.

The can chain competes with the bottle chain. Shipyards and their subcontractors compete among themselves. We are used to transferring costs to another member of the chain because it does not belong to us. We assign development funds in accordance with the limits of ownership. Transfer of costs or other problems within the chain do not advance the competitiveness of the chain as a whole.

The development of processes over departmental and even ownership boundaries is a new, significant challenge for corporate managers. The problem can be resolved with the aid of the owners of the processes. They are responsible for the efficient operation of the whole process, as well as for the continuous development of the process in cooperation with the departments according to an agreed-upon division of work.

> As long as process owners are appointed just as an experiment, as usually happens, process management will never achieve the results expected of it.

Locate Yourself as a Part of Your Customers' Processes

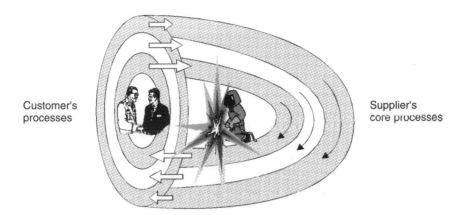

Customer's
processes

Supplier's
core processes

A *spare parts delivery process* was developed within a company. The objective was to halve the delivery time for spare parts. The spare parts process was triggered by receipt of an order, and it ended with the dispatch of the parts.

The development group realized that a customer in Indonesia usually took several days, and many calls and Faxes needed to be exchanged with the Finnish supplier, to get the spare parts numbers correct. The spare parts deliv ery itself took only three days. Repair of the production line using the spare part took a few hours. Bringing the line back to full capacity could take days.

> Process owner: "We treated it as part of the process that we owned. From the customer's point of view, the boundaries between processes were totally different. From his point of view, there was no such thing even as a spare parts delivery process. From his perspective, it was a process of repair and maintenance. Shortening the delivery time affected only a small part of the customer's maintenance process. We changed the name and boundaries of the process. The name was changed to the maintenance process. The process was triggered when a fault was found, and it ended when the production line was back at full capacity."

In another example, one company tried to solve its problem by developing its sales process. The company forgot that the customer's buying decision is part of his or her buying process. The first stage of the sales process is to learn about the customer's buying process. In a third example, a company developed a dispatch process. From the customer's viewpoint, however, it is a goods inward process.

Determining Process Targets from Customers' and Suppliers' Points of View

---

Major Process Measurements

- **Effectiveness:** how well customer expectations are met—customer satisfaction
- **Efficiency:** how well resources are used to produce output—costs and time
- **Adaptability:** how well current and future requirements are satisfied—flexibility

---

Effectiveness—Quality from Customer's Point of View

The customer's quality measures are concerned with our products, services, and way of working. For example, they may be concerned with fault levels in our products, the ways in which our products meet customer expectations, and the reliability of our deliveries.

Efficiency through the Entire Process

The overall efficiency of a process can be measured by throughput time, number of faults, waste, amount of handling, and cost. Processes overlap department, profit center, or ownership boundaries. The efficiency of the process must be measured without taking the boundaries into consideration.

Adaptability for Competition

Quality and efficiency do not always resolve competitive issues. They are regarded as given. Competition is often about the ability to meet the customer's conflicting needs and expectations without compromising on quality and efficiency.

The principles of performance evaluation have to be radically changed. Without these changes, process management is just a collection of fine thoughts, pilot projects, and maybe some success, but without lasting influence. *As long as performance evaluation is carried out by profit center and department, we will also operate in those terms.* It is not enough that process measures are used alongside our present measures. They must become the main measures. Only then will they also change our way of thinking. That is what process management is about.

Process Performance Results from Internal Customer Relationships

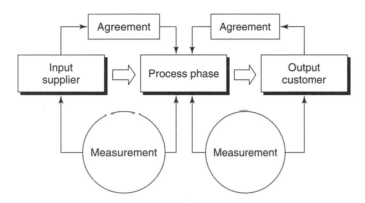

The production manager complains: "There is not enough basic information for the bidding process. Work orders to the delivery process are incomplete and change during manufacturing. The worksheets for salary calculations are badly written. Customer requirements for the product development process are poorly defined. Work instructions to the shop floor are wrong or incomplete. . . ."

The output of a previous phase in the process forms an input to the following phase. The following phase of the project has to be executed completely. *Problems with the quality or efficiency of a process are almost without exception the result of faults in the input to the process.* The accuracy of a tender will be no better than the information provided by the accounting department. Checking the accuracy of the basic data while preparing a tender often reduces the efficiency of the process. Significant and rapid improvements in the process can be achieved by improving the quality of these inputs.

Continuous process development is the recognition of the external and internal supplier-customer relationship, the joint drawing up of quality agreements, and then the observation of those agreements. When the quality of all the inputs is improved, efficiency increases almost automatically. If it is a question of wholesale renewal of the process, the process and its phases must first be examined, and the number of internal supplier-customer relationships must be kept as low as possible.

Characteristics of Well-Managed Process Management

The following features can be identified in process management:

1. The company's outputs and the processes needed to produce them are named and described.
2. The expectations and satisfaction of the customer of each output are measured, and the skills needed have been identified.
3. Process owners and development groups have been appointed to be responsible for the process and its continuous development.
4. Targets have been set for process quality and efficiency, feedback systems for continuous measurement are in place, and the organization is learning from the best.
5. A system of certification of the level of the process is in place to raise the level of the process by increments.
6. A compensation system is in place that supports the quality and efficiency of the whole process and its continuous improvement.
7. The process owners are responsible for operations as line managers would be. The department heads are in charge of resource centers that support the processes.

When the company's holiday party is organized in terms of processes, then we know we have come a long way in process management.

Why Process Improvement Pays Off

One does not get to process management by drawing process flow charts, but via a process development program. Process management represents a new way of thinking and new development principles. It means new ways of setting targets and monitoring them. It demands from all of us a new way of looking at our own work, colleagues, and customers. It is a rare company that is ready to apply the principles of process management without considerable development work.

An efficient whole does not arise
by optimizing its parts individually.

If you dissect any process into
its individual activities and
then optimize the individual activities,
the process as a whole will
not operate as well as it could.

Process development creates the preconditions needed to apply the principles of process management. Process development can generally happen in two ways:

- *Radical change approach.* Significant changes are made to the boundaries and routing of the process. Whole phases or even departments are excluded from the process. Information technology may replace a large number of stages or reduce the throughput time to a fraction.
- *Continuous and incremental improvement approach.* There are no significant changes made to the boundaries or routing of the process. Development is concentrated on the internal customer-supplier relationship, improving quality and efficiency of the process by developing the skill base and cooperation between people.

CASE STUDY: AHLSTROM PUMPS—PROCESS IMPROVEMENT PROGRAM

Case Study Summary

Turning Strategies into Measurable Development Projects

In 1993, the board of Ahlstrom Machinery decided to instigate a joint development program for all four product lines. (The precedents were ABB's Customer Focus and Rauma's P500 corporate-level programs.)

A working group was formed. The group carried out interviews throughout the organization and, on the basis of these, identified an area of interest to everyone: *implementation of strategic plans.*

It was generally felt that strategic planning was well directed; they were able to formulate plans, and the content was good. However, there were serious shortcomings in implementation. Many of the points of the strategic plan were bullet points with no explanation, most of the issues covered by the plan were never even started, the financial effect of the plans was not calculated, the development resources needed were not planned for, development resources were only a fraction of the plans that were drawn up, and so on.

> The following objective was set: to turn the strategic plans into development projects and to implement the projects.

The program was started. A simple instruction for planning strategic projects was drawn up. The product lines analyzed their strategy, prioritized their development targets, and drew up a two- to three-page project plan for each target.

The areas covered by the plans were project organization, resources, timetables, strategic effects of projects, financial calculations, risks and fall back plans, and positive surprises. The implementation of the plans was monitored at monthly meetings.

One of these development programs was *Business Process Management Program in Ahlstrom Pumps' Global Business.* The following case study describes this improvement program. (Ahlstrom Pumps was one of Ahlstrom Machinery's product lines.)

Planning Strategic Projects

Product Line Summary

Development Projects	Investment (mFIM)	Responsible	Involved	Profitability Impacts (mFIM)		
				1993	1994	1995
Growth 1. 2.						
Cost Cutting 3. 4.						
Development 5. 6. 7.						
Total						

Initial Schedule and Financial Impacts for Each Project

Project Phases	1993	1994	1995	1996
1.	xxxxxx			
2.	xxxxx			
3.		xxxxxxxxxxxx		
4.		xxxxxxx	xxxxxxxxxxxxxx	
5.			xxxxxx	xxxxxx

Financial Impacts	1993	1994	1995	1996
Sales				
Costs				
Working capital				
Break-even point				
Profitability				

Ahlstrom Pumps' total turnover was about FIM 500 million. There were production plants in Finland and the United States of America. By the mid-1980s, the Mänttä Pump Factory had reduced its throughput times from four weeks to five days through a program of investment and the introduction of JIT production philosophies. It acted as the benchmark company for the other pump manufacturing units.

As the product line had expanded internationally, its operating principles were also to be applied globally. The global operating principles had been drawn up and documented, using Hewlett-Packard as an example.

The product line management group decided to start up the next phase of the improvement program. This time improvement must include other business processes as well as manufacturing and at a local and global level.

A working group was set up to examine how best to exploit the principles of process management in Ahlstrom Pumps business operations. The group examined the philosophy of process management in depth by reading the literature on the subject and inviting leading Finnish and American consultants to make presentations of their process improvement and process management models.

The working group developed a process management model that was applicable to its circumstances. The management group decided to use this model and start up three process improvement projects as pilot projects. The pilot processes were *the Customer Convincing Process, the Impeller Delivery Process,* and *the Customer Complaint Process.*

At the same time as the pilot projects proceeded, the pump product line's international management group (30 people) were given two days of training in process management. The management group selected one of the process improvement models that had been presented earlier. Two internal consultants were appointed to work full-time on this project and received one week's training in the Unites States.

One of the pilot projects, the improvement of the impeller delivery process, was later expanded to cover the delivery of the whole pump, and this then included the sales operation.

The objective of the improvement of these processes was to reach world class in other processes as well as production.

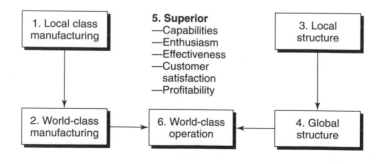

Schedule for the Initial Phase of the Program

Phase	| 1993														1994			
	September				October				November				December					January			
	36	37	38	39	40	41	42	43	44	45	46	47	48	49	50	51	52	1	2	3	4
Strategic planning	O	O	O	O																	
Establishing the prestudy team	X																				
Developing a business process model		O	O	O																	
Developing BPI model		O	O	O																	
Presenting the model to management					O	O															
Distributing articles and books			O				O	O													
Organizing for the BPI program											X										
Executing prepilots												O	O	O	O	O	O	O	O	O	O
Selecting the consultants												O	O	O	O						
Management training decision																	X				
Management training																				O	
Selecting the BPI model																					X
Training two champions in the United States																					O
Organizing the full-scale BPI program																					O

Description of the Case Study

The Management Initiated Prestudy Program

We sat opposite the director of Ahlstrom Pumps' product line. He wanted to talk to us about the start-up of the business process improvement program:

In the three-year plan of spring 1993, business processes improvement was defined as one of the strategic development areas. It now has to be put into motion.

We formed a working group which drew up a plan to start up the process improvement program in Ahlstrom Pumps' international business operations. The group included Ahlstrom Pumps' IT manager, human resources manager, one line manager, and an internal consultant. The board also insisted that the marketing manager, production manager, finance manager, and product development manager were closely involved with the production of the plan.

Our plan was to be presented to the management group of Ahlstrom Pumps by the end of October. The initial research objectives and methodology were agreed as follows:

---

1. To provide answers for the following questions:

   a. What are the core processes of the Pump Business?
   b. What are the development needs and targets?
   c. What are appropriate improvement models?

2. To conduct the prestudy of the program:

   a. To create the business process management model for Pumps
   b. To execute the pilots to test the model

Getting into the Idea of Business Process Management

The prestudy group held its first meeting. Each of us had some understanding of what process management was all about, and everyone had experience in developing manufacturing according to the principles of JIT production philosophy. We understood that, for us, it was not a question of process management being something new and very different.

However, we had a feeling that there must be something new that we were not yet aware of. We decided to go into the whole matter very thoroughly. Our first task was to exchange our experiences, course materials, and articles to bring together all the information we had gathered on the subject. We acquired more literature and articles on the subject, and of these the most inspiring was Michael Hammer and James Champy's book *Reengineering Corporation.* H. James Harrington's *Business Process Improvement* gave the best description of the process improvement technique. At a later stage, we also distributed articles for other people to read.

We frequently asked ourselves the question "Is there a company in Finland from which we could learn about this?" We acquired process flow charts and some other information from three Finnish companies. Unfortunately, our attempt at benchmarking did not get past the stage of being a good idea.

Identifying and Mapping the Core Processes

Core Process	Purpose of the Process
Sales process	To convince the customer
Delivery process	To deliver customer satisfaction
Product development process	To create value-added for customers
After-sales processes	To maintain customer relations

We tried to define the purpose of the process from the customer's point of view, not of the process itself. We tried to find a name for the process that would encapsulate what it would achieve from the customer's point of view. In this way, the sales process became the *customer convincing process.*

Creating the Model for Business Process Management
The prestudy group drew up a model that described new insights into process management for us. Our model included the following observations concerning the content of process management and how to move to process management.

Functional Organization and Profitability Dictate Our Actions
Initially, we thought about the shortcomings in the present management and measurement system. We concluded that the following was the company's most important management principle: to be a functional organization whose operations are directed and evaluated on the basis of profitability. Once a year, the CEO declares the financial targets for the following budgetary year. The target is further divided to the various divisions, product centers, and front line management.

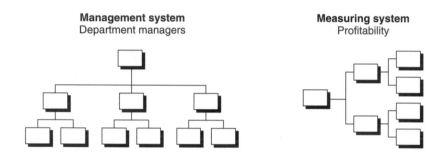

Every one of us had our responsibilities and authority defined and our own particular tasks. In the organization, we all knew exactly who our boss was and who our subordinates were. We knew our rights and responsibilities. Each of us had targets derived from the profitability model. The major measures were related to sales, costs, and working capital depending on function. Our performance was evaluated against budget.

The organization and management for profitability had achieved what they were originally set up to achieve. The organization is to administer people and profitability calculations are to monitor the interests of the owners. However, there is one critical issue missing from the picture: customers and their expectations. Another point is that measuring profitability shows how we have succeeded in the past. It says nothing about our abilities to compete in the future. It gives only a limited indication of our strengths and weaknesses. It is difficult to learn and improve from the feedback it gives so as to become more competitive in the future.

Turning Functional Thinking into Process Thinking
Next we began to think about how to rectify the shortcomings we had identi-fied. Instead of a hierarchical and functional organization, we should divide our operation into processes. The outputs our customers experience are gen-erated by processes. We had constructed strong departmental boundaries and measurement systems geared toward profit centers and departments, and these prevented the organization from overall functioning efficiently.

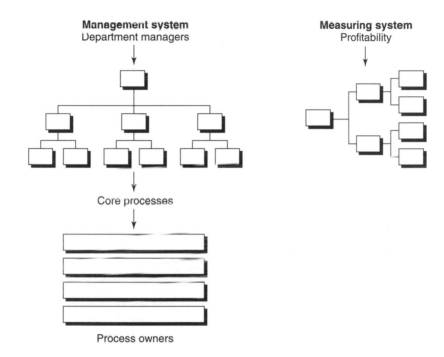

Department Heads versus Process Owners
In order to get processes to work and develop, we needed process owners who would be responsible for their operation and its improvement across depart-ment, profit center, and ownership boundaries.

Profitability through Customer Satisfaction
How could we measure the performance capability of processes? Profitability measures would not be suitable. We had to find new ways of measuring. Each process has its own customers with their own expectations. The purchasing manager expects a low price and reliability in the customer convincing process, the maintenance manager expects continuity of operation and speed in the after-sales process, and so on.

A new measure of customer satisfaction must be selected for each process and used to direct the operation of that process. Customer satisfaction must be the guiding force. Profitability is the result of customer satisfaction.

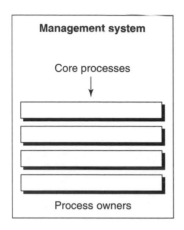 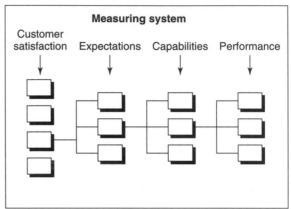

Customer Satisfaction Is the Result of Meeting Customer Expectations
Customer satisfaction is generated when we are able to meet customer expectations. Expectations are usually directed toward products, services, and our way of working.

Customer Expectations Are Met through Capabilities
To fulfill customer expectations, we need capabilities, which can be either product or process technology that fulfills customer expectations. Capabilities can also be such issues as quality, reliability, speed, flexibility, and costs.

Performance Measures for Customer Satisfaction
and Capabilities Are Required
Customer satisfaction and our capabilities must be measured. We measure their present levels, their target levels, our competitors' levels, and the benchmark level (the best, irrespective of business sector).

Network of Process Owners and Functional Heads

Our thoughts about required capabilities gave rise to our concept of the division of labor between the process owners and department heads. The process owner is responsible for the development of the capabilities needed in the process. Quality, reliability, and so on are the result of the operation of the whole process. Department managers are responsible for developing the product and process technologies. The process owner's role corresponds to that of a line manager, while the department manager has a staff position.

Process Management through the Transformation Process

We understood that we would not move to process management just by drawing process flow charts. The question was one of a fundamental change in our way of thinking, not an organizational change. We would move to process management only through a process of change that would take time.

The following are some observations we made, which we felt would apply generally to any company:

- "We look after customer complaints well as far as the customer is concerned. The internal handling of complaints, though, ends as soon as a cost center is found."
- "Our sales companies around the world are evaluated on the basis of their profitability. Their profitability, though, is affected more by internal transfer pricing than by customer satisfaction."
- "If machining were in a different building than assembly, it would be a separate profit center."
- "The foundry does not get money for investment because of its poor profitability, however, its profitability is based on internal transfer prices."
- "In accounting terms, the foundry is loss-making. It is an important part of the pump delivery process. Its losses, though, have no effect on the profitability of other production units."
- "We are really organized by buildings. Each building has to have its own president."

The need for change seemed so great that we began to ask the question "Is it possible at all in a large company?" The following were some of our thoughts:

1. *Process owners have to be responsible for matters that they have never had traditional managerial authority over.* If the process owners regard their jobs as a trial, they will not have the attitude toward it that they need. As one person who had been involved in product development projects put it:

   > There are representatives from different departments in project teams. The representatives of the departments make good decisions. However, these are often ignored. Departments make their own decisions in their own interests. The official organization will always prevail over the unofficial one.

2. *Process owners have to manage the process as a whole.* Where do we find people who can do that? How long will it take to train them?

3. *Process owners need sponsors to support them.* Sponsors are the people in the organization who have profit accountability. An example of a sponsor is the production Manager who is responsible for all the manufacturing units through which the delivery process passes. The process owner in this example is the production manager in the last stage but one, assembly. The manufacturing units may be separate profit centers in various locations. The conventional way to manage them would be to set profit targets for each profit center, delegate, and evaluate the results on the basis of the profitability of each center.

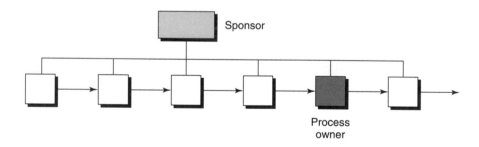

The worst problems, though, were found between the different stages or profit centers. The greatest gains from process improvement were to be had from precisely these "in-between" areas. These were the issues over which the profit centers or departments argued or, in the worst cases, did not discuss with each other at all. The process sponsor actively develops the process by supporting the process owner. How could we get the sponsors to give up their "comfortable" profit center management and support the process owners as process sponsors?

4. *Measurement must correspond to process boundaries.* Alongside the traditional profit center and departmental accounting may come process specific measures. The official measurement system will always prevail over unofficial ones. Official figures are reported to the board. Management's compensation packages are tied into them. It is the official figures that the organization's managers ask about on a daily basis. Unofficial figures are asked for only when dealing specifically with the project.

   Unofficial measures do not lead to permanent changes in ways of thinking, but that is what process management requires. If objectives and performance evaluations do not follow project boundaries, then process management will remain a set of fine ideas.

5. *Process management is customer-driven.* Process management does not diminish the importance of profit forecasting and monitoring. It is a question of what comes first. Almost without exception, development has been instigated by the objective of reducing costs.

   The starting point for improvement work in process management is customer expectations and their fulfillment. Look for areas that will improve competitiveness in the market. Look for improvements that will increase sales or allow you to increase prices. Look for areas that will increase income. When improvement in these areas also reduces costs, then the effect on profitability is at its maximum.

   Managers look for rapid results and concrete savings they can achieve quickly. Those are cuts or savings programs. In the best cases, they are improvement projects, but they are usually just cost-saving exercises.

   We recognized that low costs are of no use if we have no income. The amount of goods sold and the price level achieved have an overwhelming significance for the profitability of the company.

   How does one turn the heads of managers, and the whole organization, away from cost reports and toward customer expectations and satisfaction?

Presenting the Business Process Management Model to Key Staff

We presented the process management model we had developed to seven key people in the company. We discussed it with each of them separately for about two hours. We particularly emphasized the importance of the customer in process improvement. Following, please find a letter we wrote for potential interviewees.

Dear Interviewee,

We have been commissioned to map out the development needs and opportunities for our product line. We are testing to see if the principles of business process improvement can be used to improve the business operation of our product line.

In order to do this we need your help. We would like to interview you and hear your opinions about customer expectations and the capabilities we need to satisfy them. We would also like to know what you think their present level is and what their development needs are.

We will be using an information collection model which requires no preparation on your part.

The Working Group, 9/27/93

We received a positive response from everyone to our thoughts on what process management is and how it would be sensible to start up process improvement. As the sales manager put it,

> I am not motivated by the profitability of the whole product line. It is a function of so many things over which I have no influence—for example, company acquisitions. Identifying customers' expectations and working together to satisfy them, that I understand. That is concrete. That is what sales has always tried to do. It would be great if we could get the whole organization to try to do the same.

Launching the Business Process Improvement Program

The Objectives of the Program

The improvement program was started up at a meeting of the company's management group. Opening the meeting, the director of the product line observed:

> We have three pump plants: in Mänttä, Karhula, and in Easley in the United States. Using the principles of JIT, they have reduced their throughput times from weeks to days and have significantly improved the quality of their production. They have improved and reached world-class level.
>
> Over the past few years, we have also moved from a local organization to a global organization with global strategy and division of responsibilities.
>
> Quality and speed in production alone are not a sufficient competitive advantage. We must achieve the same quality and speed in all our business processes. We must be world-class throughout our global operation, not just in production.
>
> We will achieve that by adding to our capabilities, and that will add to our enthusiasm. We will use those capabilities and that enthusiasm to improve our efficiency and deliver customer satisfaction; from that comes improved profitability.

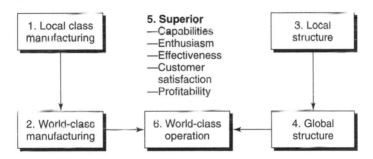

Never Ending Journey toward World-Class Operation

Business Process Management Model

The prestudy group presented the model it had developed and had presented earlier to the key personnel.

Phases of the Program

The prestudy group presented H. James Harrington's five-stage process management model along with the tasks for stage 1.

Phase I.   Organizing for the BPI program

Objective: To ensure success by building leadership, understanding, and commitment

Activities: 1. Establish an executive committee.
               2. Appoint a BPI champion.
               3. Provide executive training.
               4. Develop an improvement model.
               5. Communicate goals to employees.
               6. Review business strategies and customer requirements.
               7. Select critical processes.
               8. Appoint process owners.
               9. Select the process improvement team members.

Phase II.   Understanding the process
Phase III.   Streamlining
Phase IV.   Measurements and controls
Phase V.   Continuous improvement

Program Pilots

The prestudy group made a proposal for pilot projects to be started up:

1. Customer convincing process
2. Impeller delivery process
3. Customer complaint process

The objective was to test the model created by the group, to develop the training material that would be needed, and to assess the need for consultants. After the pilot projects, a real process would be selected. It would be a complete core process from customer need to customer satisfaction.

Internal Consultant for the Program
The prestudy group proposed that a full-time internal consultant be appointed within the pumps product line. The position and tasks were defined as follows:

- The appointment is for at least two years and reports to the top management.
- It is a full time appointment.
- The consultant will activate the whole organization to undertake far-reaching process improvement.
- The consultant will draw up instructions for process improvement methodologies and the responsibilities and tasks of the process owners and development groups.
- The consultant will act as an internal consultant on process improvement methodologies.

Testing and Selecting the Improvement Model
Bearing in mind the breadth of Ahlstrom Pumps' operations and the demands of process improvement, we believed we needed external assistance. We decided to select a consulting firm that had a lot of process improvement experience and capabilities in international training and consulting. We justified the use of external and experienced consultants as follows:

1. High aspirations require high-level improvement capabilities, both internally and externally.
2. A rapid, reliable start would be ensured by using proven improvement methodologies.
3. Using external consultants would give us access to benchmark companies from whom we could learn.
4. External consultants would help us avoid the worst mistakes.
5. External consultants could coach the internal consultant we had selected.

During December 1993, we invited five Finnish and two American leading consultancies to present their process management models. Several members of the company's management team attended these two-hour presentations, thus obtaining good training in the subject.

The board selected an American consultancy and the process improvement approach they took. Two full-time internal process consultants received a week of process management training in the United States. One of them worked in Finland, the other in the United States. During training, they were given manuals on all aspects of process improvement, and it was decided to apply these in our process improvement.

Training the Global Management Team

The management team decided to arrange two days of training for an enlarged, international management team. The prestudy group was charged with finding a suitable trainer. The training took place in March 1994. Thirty managers from Finland and the United States took part. The training was run by a well-known Finnish process management consultant. The training lasted two days and covered the following main areas:

- Basics of business process management and improvement
- Business process management and improvement in practice
- Process management
- Defining customer satisfaction and customer expectations
- Case studies
- Group work

Obstacles to Overcome in the Initial Phase

The management team worked in groups to predict the obstacles we might come up against:

Difficulty in identifying suitable processes	Resistance from external interests (repair workshops, unions)
Difficulty in choosing suitable pilots	Short-term profit objectives
The pilot could be too difficult	Acute, major issues steam rollered over
Different cultures in the different units	Insufficient resources
Protection of territory and way of working	Resignation of internal consultant
Remaining a prisoner to the past	Not enough time
Achieving mutual trust	No investment in improvement systems
Geographic distance	No investment in training
Overcoming various boundaries (national, legal, corporate, profit center, departmental)	Let's improve without measurable objectives
Complicated internal organization	Lack of committed process owners
Achieving commitment	Process driven from outside—not as concrete and functionally driven
Identifying commitment	Management process does not reach the practical level
Lack of real desire	

Starting and Executing the Pilots

The management team decided to start up three pilot projects. Two of them are presented on the following pages.

Customer Convincing Process, Pilot 1

Organizing and Starting the Pilot

The operating principle behind the customer convincing process (the sales process) is "to convince the customer to make the deal." It was the process closest to the customer and so the best way of starting the process improvement program. We started with a one-day event. The key personnel from the different phases of the process, who worked for three different profit centers in different places, participated in the event.

Participants

Marketing Director	Pump Industry, Karhula
Sales Director	Pump Industry, Karhula
Sales Manager, Finland	Pump Industry, Karhula
Production Manager	Pump Factory, Mänttä
Product Engineer	Process Pumps, Mänttä
Product Line Director	Foundry, Karhula
R&D Manager	Process Pumps, Mänttä
IT Manager	Process Equipments, Karhula
Human Resource Manager	Process Equipments, Karhula
Development Manger	Ahlstrom Machinery

The event started with three hours of process theory and a one-hour introduction from the marketing director. The aim of the event was to define the customer's buying criteria—that is, the expectations to be satisfied in order to get the customer to make a buying decision in favor of the particular selling company. We selected a *process pump* as the product, the *pulp industry* as the customer, and *Finland* as the market.

We defined customer expectations and satisfaction and the required capabilities using the double team method. They were based on the group's own evaluation. This was like homework before asking customers. First, we tried to increase our understanding of customer expectations, customer satisfaction, and the required capabilities. We started up a learning process, not a customer satisfaction assessment process.

Defining Customer Satisfaction and Customer Expectations
We documented the results in the following table (the values have been changed).

Customer Expectation	Importance		Our Own Performance		Performance of the Best Competitor	
	%	Trend	Current	Target		
1. Total economy of the product	20	↗	3	4	4	Comp. A
2. Product performance and features	25	→	4	4	3	Comp. A
3. After-sales	15	→	5	5	2	Comp. B
4. Other services	5	↑	3	4	2	Comp. A
5. Easy customer-supplier contacts	20	↗	5	5	3	Comp. B
6. Quality of operation	15	↗	2	4	2	Comp. A
Total	100					

1 Poor	4 Very good	↘ Less important	↗ More important
2 Satisfactory	5 Competitive advantage	→ Same importance	↑ Significantly more important
3 Good			

The table gave insights that were new for many of us. Here are some of them:

1. ***Customer satisfaction is more than product quality.*** Points 1 and 2 in the customer expectations column of the table were concerned with products. We estimated that their combined importance from the customer's point of view was 45 percent. Points 3 and 4 were concerned with the services we provide. Their combined importance was 20 percent. Points 5 and 6 were concerned with our way of working, and their importance was 35 percent. For the first time, we had jointly observed that the product was not the only factor in customer satisfaction, and it was not even 50 percent of the overall satisfaction score.

2. ***Customer satisfaction depends on all of us.*** We also saw that the only point where sales had the sole influence was point 4, easy customer-supplier contacts. We had generally thought that the volume of sales depended on how good our sales staff was. For the first time, we had jointly observed that in our case the sales people influenced only 20 percent of the satisfaction of customer expectations. The remaining 80 percent was affected by the rest of us. Selling the product was thus an issue for the whole organization.

3. ***Each process has unique customer expectations.*** The table gave the starting point for the improvement of other core processes as well:

- Points 1 and 2 belonged to the product development process.
- Points 3 and 4 concerned the after-sales process.
- Point 5 belonged to the sales process (customer convincing process).
- Point 6 dealt with the delivery process.

Every process has its own customers. Every process has to address its own customers to determine their expectations exactly, as well as what it takes to meet them and what capabilities are required. The ideas we gathered contained plenty of material that could be used to select the target for improvement:

- What is important for the customer?
- How will expectations change in the future?
- How does the customer find us today?
- How would the customer like to find us?
- How does the customer find our major competitor?

Defining Capabilities to Meet Customer Expectations
Customer satisfaction can be increased by developing the capabilities that deliver it. The double team (work group method) continued by defining the capabilities that would fulfill customer expectations. The following is an example of customer expectations from point 5 of the previous table (easy customer-supplier contacts).

Necessary Capabilities for the Customer Expectation	Importance		Our Own Performance		Performance of the Best Competitor	
Easy Customer-Supplier Contacts	Points	Trend	Current	Target		
1. Customer process know-how	25	→	3	4	3	Comp. A
2. Compability to solve problems	25	↗	3	4	4	Comp. A
3. Availability	15	↗	4	5	3	Comp. B
4. Service-mindedness	15	→	5	5	2	Comp. A
5. Prompt service and quotation	10	↗	5	5	3	Comp. B
6. Language knowledge	5	↗	2	4	4	Comp. B
7. Know-how in other services	5	↑	3	4	N/A	
Total	100					

1 Poor	4 Very good	↘ Less important	↗ More important
2 Satisfactory	5 Competitive advantage	→ Same importance	↑ Significantly more important
3 Good			

Developing Capabilities Required to Meet Customer Expectations
The required capabilities can be developed in many ways. Quotation speed can be improved by developing the tender process. Getting hold of sales staff quickly can be resolved by buying technology. Language skills are improved by personal study. With this information, personal study programs can be drawn up and learning and improvement started up.

Identifying Customer Satisfaction and Expectations through Interviews
To identify customers' real expectations and what it took to meet them, interviews with representatives of two customer companies were carried out.

Pilot Results
Improvement of the customer convincing process started from determining and analyzing customer expectations. By analyzing them, we picked particular points for improvement. For example, the European sales manager used a similar model to identify customer expectations for other products and markets.

The pilot project ended here. The following phase—actually describing, measuring, and developing the sales process—was not started up. The pilot had not produced any measurable improvement. In accordance with its objective, it gave valuable experience about developing a process from the customer's standpoint. This experience was put to good use in the second pilot project, the impeller delivery process.

Impeller Delivery Process, Pilot 2

The impeller delivery process involved nearly 100 people in three profit centers. An impeller is an important part of a pump; it is a single part and can be defined quite clearly. It runs over departmental and profit center boundaries and so is a typical situation in which the principles of process management and improvement apply perfectly. With the customer convincing process, we had practiced customer-driven work. In this pilot, the main focus of attention was on describing, measuring, understanding, and developing the process.

Starting the Pilot and Pilot Targets

The improvement process was started in the fall of 1993. At first, it affected only the foundry's role in the process. In January 1994, it was clear that we would not achieve any significant improvements if we developed the foundry's role alone. We had to develop the whole delivery process. The impeller delivery process was selected as the pilot because it was felt that the whole pump delivery would be too demanding.

The improvement process was officially started up in April 1994 by the parent company's director of production. The objective was to achieve significant improvements in reliability of deliveries, through-put times, and quality. The pump product line management also expected major improvements in customer satisfaction and profitability.

Improvement was to occur according to the principles of process improvement. It was decided to use the corresponding process at the Easley (USA) plant as a benchmark process for comparison and learning.

Defining the Process

To make the pilot easier, the process neither started nor finished with the customer. It was triggered by the arrival of an order in Mänttä, and it ended after assembly when it left Mänttä for the customer.

The process was divided into five subprocesses:

1. Order handling process
2. Manufacturing process
3. Machining process
4. Assembly process
5. Delivery process

Process Improvement Approaches
Improvement was to occur in two phases:

> Phase 1: Examining the need for, and possibility of, radical change and implementation where possible
> Phase 2: Participative improvement using continuous development methodologies

Schedule
The timetable for the major milestones was as follows:

1. Decisions on the investments needed to be taken by September 30, 1994.
2. Significant improvements were needed by the summer of 1995.
3. The project was to continue to the end of 1995 so as to get it on track for continuous improvement.

Responsibilities of the Pilot Team
The primary objective was to achieve the improvement targets that had been set. The secondary objective was to develop and apply systematic process improvement methodologies and the results of benchmarking research. Third, the pilot had an obligation to document the progress of the improvement program and methodologies. Finally, the pilot group was responsible for the transfer of the capabilities and experience acquired to other process improvement projects within Ahlstrom Machinery.

Improvement Team for the Pilot

The members selected for the process improvement group were the following:

- Director of production as sponsor
- Production manager at Mänttä as process owner
- Owners of each of the subprocesses
- Time and motion analyst as an improvement resource
- Internal consultant as the director of the improvement process

---

A development group was appointed for each of the subprocesses.

Training

The improvement project started with two days of process improvement and benchmarking training. The development groups for the process and all the subprocesses took part. A total of 20 people were trained, 14 white-collar and 6 blue-collar workers.

Process Improvement Action Steps

The following steps were taken:

1. The internal and external customers of the process were identified.
2. Their expectations and what was required to satisfy them were defined.
3. The inputs, outputs, and stages of every subprocess were described.
4. Measurements were taken in each subprocess:

   - Operations
   - Number of times handled
   - Storage transactions
   - Inspections
   - Transport between stages
   - People involved
   - Documents involved

5. The cycle time and value-added time for the process and each subprocess were measured.
6. Points 4 and 5 were repeated at Easley for comparison purposes (benchmarking).
7. A comparison between Finland and Easley was made.

Performance Measure	Finland	Easley	Reason for Differences in Performance Ability
Operations			
Number of times handled			
Storage transactions			
Inspections			
Transport between stages			
People involved			
Documents involved			

8. The results of the benchmarking process and improvement opportunities that had been identified in other ways were used to define the improvement objectives more precisely.

Performance Measure	Current	Target
Delivery reliability	60 / 90%	100%
Cycle time	16 days	8 days
Quality costs		−50%
Number of operations in the process	390	210

9. A description of the work involved for each phase was drawn up and compared with those from Easley so as to analyze the reasons for the differences in performance capabilities.
10. Improvement measures were planned and an implementation timetable produced.
11. Performance capability objectives were set and the schedule produced for their improvement throughout the process.

Performance Measure	Owner	Progress						Target
		−94	12/94	6/95	12/95	6/96	12/96	12/96
1. Delivery reliability								
3 measures								
2. Lead Time								
10 measures								
3. Costs								
12 measures								

12. The first investment proposal following process rather than profit center boundaries was produced.

What Did We Learn about the Pilot?
The main focus in developing the impeller delivery process was on process description, understanding, measuring, and comparison with the corresponding process at Easley (benchmarking).

We learned a number of things:

- How to put boundaries to the process and organize improvement
- The significance of the pilot in developing the improvement model
- The importance of documentation when transferring experience to others
- How to describe the process and its methodologies
- How to measure the performance capability of the process
- How to set improvement objectives
- How to produce implementation and progress plans
- The importance of the director of the improvement process
- The importance of improvement resources
- The importance of process-specific measurements
- How to combine process improvement and the benchmarking process

We also made the following observations about our chosen way of working:

- Profit centers optimize their own operations on the basis of profitability.
- Every profit center has its own management system, order book, and billing. Managing for profit includes the right to select one's own management system.
- Different compensation systems set different priorities for operations.
- Distance permits difference.
- As long as official measurements support profit centers, then profit center thinking is almost impossible to eradicate.
- Subprocess owners find it "childishly" easy to identify the main problems in the process, as long as they get together and look at things from the point of view of the overall measurement of the process.
- The solutions are also obvious.
- Radical improvement does not come without radical change.
- Up to now, everything has been "easy." Real change in management skills will be needed to go forward.

Pilot Results

In the pilot process, we learned the techniques of process improvement. Also, major decisions were taken and implementation plans produced in the pilot. It confirmed that the targets of improving delivery reliability and halving throughput times could be achieved.

Launching the Full-Scale Program in May 1994

On the basis of training and the experience gained from the pilot, the management team of the Pumps product line decided to implement the first full-blown process improvement project. The process was the "pump delivery process." The pilot impeller delivery process was broadened:

- The beginning was to be driven by the customer.
- The middle dealt with the whole pump.
- The end was the acceptance of the pump by the customer.

In the early stages of the project, the process customers were limited to those in Germany and the manufacturing was limited to Finland.

An improvement model produced in the United States on the basis of 300 successful projects was used in the process improvement project. In part, it was the same as the improvement model we had already worked with.

PROCESS MANAGEMENT DEVELOPMENT MODEL

The following pages present an eight-stage model for process development and moving over to process management. The example, Prostec Oy, is based on fact, but the name has been changed. You may use the example for practice by identifying the central issues in the stages of the account, which follow the account.

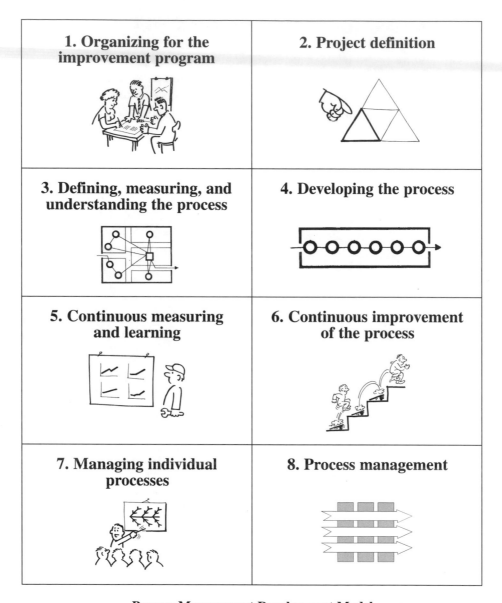

Process Management Development Model

Summary

1. **Organizing for the Improvement Program**

   The development program is planned and launched. The need for development is recognized, the management team is trained, the processes to be developed are selected, the process owners are appointed, and development goals are set.

2. **Project Definition**

   The contents of the process to be improved are defined, the project plan is drawn up, a development group is formed and trained, and its work begins.

3. **Defining, Measuring, and Understanding the Process**

   The development group describes the process using flow charts, measures its performance, and identifies problems, then draws up suggestions for immediate improvements.

4. **Developing the Process**

   The process is developed and streamlined, and the required capabilities are identified. The implementation plan is drawn up and approved.

5. **Continuous Measuring and Learning**

   Measurement systems are developed as a feedback system for continuous learning and development.

6. **Continuous Improvement of the Process**

   The continuous development methodologies and principles are developed. These will be used to improve the development level of the process incrementally.

7. **Managing Individual Processes**

   The developed processes are managed using process management principles. The process owners and development groups are responsible for both the day-to-day operation of the process and its further development. The central objectives of the process are customer satisfaction and the efficiency and flexibility of the process.

8. **Process Management**

   The management of the operation of the whole company happens through the network of processes and process development groups. The network is complemented by departments responsible for the development of technology and employees.

1. Organizing for the Improvement Program

The development objectives that will support the business objectives of the company are defined. The development model is selected. The development program organization is appointed. The management team is trained. The processes to be developed are selected. The process owners, sponsors, and development groups are appointed.

Things have gone well for Prostec. The company is a process and equipment supplier to the food processing industry and, within its own product sector, it enjoys a market share worldwide of almost 40 percent. Profitability is fair. The management group has instigated a development program that will use the principles of process management to maintain profitability and market share.

The company's internal consultant interviewed key personnel and gave the management group two days of training in the principles of process management.

The First Day	Lectures and Discussions
Morning	The Objective of the Development Program Theory and Practice of Process Management Theory and Practice of Business Process Improvement
Afternoon	Process Improvement Program Phases, Overview Presentation of the Program Phases 1–8 Benchmarking Business Process Improvement and Benchmarking
The Second Day	**Group Work**
Morning	Clarifying Strategic Targets Clarifying Business Idea Identifying Core Processes of the Organization
Afternoon	Determining Initial Development Targets Organizing the Development Program

The management group decided on the following eight-point development plan:

1. **Organization:** Prostec
2. **Manager of the program:** Mac Manager
3. **Consultant:** Internal Consultant
4. **Executive group of the program:** Management Group

5. Business Targets	6. Performance Measures	7. Processes to Be Improved
Profitability Through radical reduction of nonquality costs	Meeting technical targets Meeting budget Meeting R&D plans	Product development Customer convincing Delivery process
Customer satisfaction Through significant reduction in customer complaints	Customer complaints Corrective actions Preventive actions	Product development Customer complaint

8. **Organizing the processes to be improved.** Three process to be developed were selected, and sponsors and process owners were appointed. The worst problem was seen as the variances from the product development objectives and keeping to the plans. The first process selected for development was the *product development process,* and the objective was to improve conformity with the objectives, budgets, and plans.

Process	Sponsor	Process Owner
Customer convincing process	Mac Manager	Susan Sales
Product development process	Mac Manager	Paul Product
Delivery process	Mac Manager	Pat Production

2. Project Definition

The boundaries of the process to be developed are defined. The project plan is drawn up. The process development group members are appointed and trained. Development groups refine the development objectives. The key personnel for the project are identified. All necessary communication is carried out. The process development projects are started up.

Traditionally, product development has operated within the frames of the research department's annual budget. Research was responsible for the process or prototype until manufacture. The development project was transferred from research to departments, sales, design, manufacture, installation, and maintenance.

The interview carried out by the internal consultant brought many faults to light. The selection of product development projects was a chance affair. Starting up and ending projects was ill-defined. The transfer from one department to another resulted in confusion and wasted time. It was not possible to stick to plans and objectives (if indeed there were any plans and objectives). The consequence was significant *extraordinary expenses.*

The boundaries of the product development process were defined. The start-up was triggered by the initial research phase, and the process ended when the warranty period on the second sale expired. The following subprocesses and their owners were selected.

Subprocess	Subprocess Owner
1. Feasibility study	Paul Product
2. Research and pilot	Raul Research
3. Product design	Alice Appliance
4. The first delivery	Raul Research
5. Commercialization	Susan Sales
6. The second delivery	Susan Sales

The owners of the subprocesses and the owner of the overall process formed the development group.

The process development group received two days of process development training, during which the members gathered the following information about the process and drew up the project plan.

Process Definition	Project Definition
1. Process name	1. Project name and mission
2. Process purpose	2. Project overview
3. Process output	3. Project stakeholders
4. External customer	4. Project organization
5. External customer expectations	5. Project activity plan
6. Internal customer	6. Information plan
7. Internal customer expectations	7. Risk analysis
8. Process initiator and the initiating input	8. Groups, their responsibilities, and their tasks
9. Major process steps	
10. Primary inputs	
11. Related processes	

The development group selected reduction in *extraordinary costs* as a profit objective, as this had a significant effect on profitability. The performance measures and initial objectives were defined as follows.

Meeting Plans 2–4	Meeting Targets 4–5	Internal Transfers 1–4
1. Schedule	1. Meeting technical targets	1. Quality
2. Development costs	2. Material and labor costs	2. Timing
3. Project profitability	3. Nonquality costs	
4. Internal transfers between departments	4. Value-added for the customer	
	5. Newness for the customer	

1 Poor
2 Adequate
3 Good
4 Very good
5 Competitive advantage

3. Defining, Measuring, and Understanding the Process

The development group describes the process and obtains the process information required. It measures performance capabilities and the factors that restrict them. Immediate suggestions for improvement are approved. The main governing factors of the process are written down: inputs and who delivers them, process phases, and efficiency measures, as well as outputs, their customers, and quality measures.

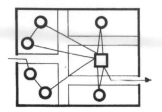

The process owner and the internal consultant interviewed the owners of the subprocesses. In the interview, they identified the most important *inputs* to the process and the most important *outputs* from it. In a joint meeting with the development group, they evaluated the quality of the inputs and outputs from the point of view of internal and external customers. The efficiency of the subprocesses was also evaluated. Problems were identified, and immediate suggestions for corrective measures were drawn *up. The following example is an analysis of the primary* input to the process.

Primary input:	Customer need
Initiator:	Customer
Customer of input:	The subprocesses of the product development process
Quality of input:	2 = Adequate
The major problem:	Targets are set based on own technical know-how.
Target:	To improve quality of input from 2 to 4
Measures:	Preparing the customer satisfaction sheet to be filled in prior to and after the project

The same principles were applied in analyzing the inputs and outputs between the subprocesses.

The product development process was defined in accordance with the following principle.

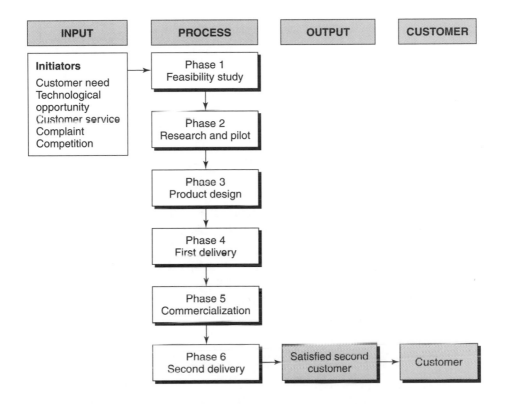

Product development had earlier been understood as new technical solutions that would interest customers. It was recognized that the process had a new objective. A new *operational idea* for the product development process was selected:

Creation of a new business activity.

Measures for the product development process that were consistent with this operational idea were selected. The most important objective was set: the total profit from the first two deliveries was to be FIM 1 million.

4. Developing the Process

The process is developed, streamlined, and described. The required skill base is identified. The implementation plan is drawn up and approved. Development is directed toward the process, phases, and tasks. Ensure that the corporate level decisions needed are taken and implemented.

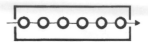

It was decided to develop the process using a real product development project. A product development project for which there was already a customer was selected as the pilot. The project manager and project group from the subprocesses were assigned to the project. It was made clear to the project team members that they were not representing their departments in the project. They were in the development team because of their own specialist skills. The team's task was to implement the project in accordance with the objectives set for it.

The process development group drew up general guidelines to define the project's schedule and objectives. The project group used them to draw up the detailed project schedule and to refine the objectives for the various areas that had been identified earlier:

1. Meeting R&D plans
2. Meeting targets
3. Internal transfers

The project owner (product development manager) was responsible for the development of the product development process, and the project manager was responsible for the implementation of the project in accordance with its objectives. The job of the process development group that had been appointed in phase 2 was to direct the activities of the project group and to develop the operating principles and practices of the process, using the experience of the project group.

As the project proceeded, the development group drew up operating models, which were documented once they had been implemented. The idea was to use them and develop them further during the following product development projects.

The significant development targets included the following:

- Improving feasibility study procedures
- Preparing instructions on how to plan and start the R&D project
- Determining decision points and criteria for the R&D process
- Clarifying the responsibilities of the project manager
- Preparing instructions for determining customer needs and expectations
- Measuring customer satisfaction
- Involving purchasing

Three of the targets were carried out using internal benchmarking and one using external benchmarking. Improvement was achieved by learning from those better and by applying what was learned.

As the development work proceeded, development targets were uncovered and documented as follows:

Initiator of the Problem	Problem and Influences	Root Causes	Solution	Priority	Responsible	Planned Date	Quality of Implementation
1.							
2.							
3.							
4.							

5. Continuous Measuring and Learning

The process measurement system was developed as a feedback system for continuous learning and development. The process team members were given an understanding of the necessity for measurement, feedback, and reward; the advantages of the process; and everyone's part in its development and application.

The project group set objectives for each of the three main areas. Examples of these were targets for the time spent on planning and for transfer of responsibility.

Meeting Product Development Plans

Meeting Schedules

Critical Points	Target	Implemented	Variance
Project decision (agreement)		9/29/94	
Project plan approval		9/29/94	
Pilot plan approval		9/29/94	
Pilot fulfilled	3/10/95		
Etc.	3/10/95		

Meeting Project Costs

Cost Type	Target	Implemented	Variance
Research and pilot	1.0 mFIM		
The first delivery	4.0 mFIM		
The second delivery	4.0 mFIM		

Meeting Project Profitability (Two First Deliveries)

Revenues and Costs	Target	Implemented	Variance
Revenues	10.0 mFIM		
Costs	9.0 mFIM		
Profitability	1.0 mFIM		

Meeting Requirements in Internal Transfers

Critical Points	Target Date	Date of Implementtation	Evaluation
1. Sales			
Clear and reliable technical and sales material			
Easy-to-get and reliable data for bid preparation			
2. Process design			
Process optimized			
Manuals prepared			
3. Technical design			
Technical documentation prepared			
Design details checked and approved			
4. Project management			
Unusual solutions documented			
Purchasing documents prepared			
5. Accounting department			
Project budget prepared			
Reliable follow-up			
6. Other corporate units			
Case by case			

The project group met at regular intervals. Its task was to compare imple-mentation with the objectives, to develop measures and methodologies that would identify variances and their causes, and to instigate corrective and pre-ventive measures.

Development of the variance process required under ISO 9000 was started as a result. It was achieved by benchmarking internally against the best unit in the company. The measurements taken showed that extraordinary costs accounted for 15 percent to 20 percent of turnover. Most of these costs arose within the product development process.

6. Continuous Improvement of the Process

The development methodologies and principles are continuously improved in an attempt to increase the level of development incrementally. At the end of each phase, development objectives are defined for every process. Everyone has received development training. Continuous development is running at full speed.

There were two objectives in the product development process:

1. To generate, quickly and economically, competitive products and services that fulfilled customer needs
2. To learn to implement the product development process faster and with better quality time after time

To achieve the first objective, the core skills needed for the process were defined, as were their development principles. Development responsibilities were defined and personal learning commitments agreed upon. External sources of technology were identified. To achieve the second objective, a special development group worked with an internal consultant and drew up an evaluation system for the development level of the process. Each level had evaluation criteria that described the degree of development of the process.

Business Process	⇨ Qualification Level ⇨					
	6	5	4	3	2	1
Product development process	x	x	x ⇨			
Customer convincing process	x					
Delivery process	x					
Supply process for special products	x					

The evaluation of the development level of the process showed that, at the end of the pilot project, the process had risen from the lowest development level, 6, to level 4. The process development group set as the next objective reaching level 3 during the next two product development projects. The main areas of the process selected for development included the following:

- Determining customer expectations and customer satisfaction measurement
- Improving the meeting of targets and plans
- Applying benchmarking for development of products and the product development process

7. Managing Individual Processes

The process owner and the development group are responsible for the continuous development of the process. The project managers and project groups are responsible for implementation of the projects. The central objectives of the process are customer satisfaction, achievement of objectives, meeting the plans, transfer of responsibility, and continuous development.

Roles

The director of product development had two roles. He was both the manager of the product development department and the owner of the product development process. The responsibilities and tasks of both roles were clarified. As department head, he was responsible for the development of product technology and the skill base required by it. He was responsible for the part played by his own department in the product development project. As the owner of the product development process, he was responsible for the continuous development of the process. He had the development group assigned to the process to help him. The members of the product development process development group were from product development, sales, the project department, and maintenance. Most of them were department heads.

A project manager was appointed for every product development project. He was responsible for implementation of the project from customer need to customer satisfaction, in accordance with the measures and objectives agreed upon for the project. The task of the project group assigned to the project was to help the project manager. The project manager and process owner worked together to continuously improve the product development process on the basis of the experience gleaned from the project.

Measurement and Reward

The work of the project managers and project groups was evaluated, and rewards were primarily linked to the results achieved and how well they had kept to the plan. The final evaluation was made when the warranty period on the second delivery had expired.

Evaluation and rewards for the results achieved by the owner and development group of the product development process were based on the results of product development projects. Another evaluation criterion was the evaluation system for the development level of the process.

8. Process Management

The management of the operation of the whole company is done through a network of processes and their development groups. The network is complemented by departments responsible for the development of technology and people. The processes and their continuous development support the attainment of the strategic objectives. The objectives are set for processes, groups, and individuals who continually keep themselves up-to-date by comparing against the best.

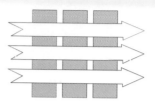

The company's management group defined the company's core and supporting processes on whose performance the success of the company critically depended. The names of the processes have also been changed (see table on page 187).

As well as the core processes, 20 support processes were defined according to the same principles. Their development happened in the stages described in this book. The development of every process was carried out as a project that gradually changed to become continuous process in phases 6 and 7. The roles presented in phase 7 are followed throughout the company, as are the principles of measurement and reward.

Annual planning of operations and the setting of development objectives are carried out for the 6 core processes and 20 support processes in terms of performance capability. The following are defined for each process:

1. Current performance
2. Identified problems and opportunities
3. Targets
4. Action plan

For each process, this is put onto one sheet of paper.

The traditional departmental organization is still used. This ensures that the necessary technical skills in the company are developed and that the resources needed for the processes and projects are available.

Roles and Process Definition	Core Processes					
	Business Planning	Customer Awakening	Customer Convincing	Delivery	Product Development	Maintenance of Customer Relations
Process owner	Mac Manager	Mats Markets	Susan Sales	Pat Production	Paul Product	Sam Service
Sponsor	Board	Mac Manager	Mac Manager	Mac Manager	Mac Manager	Mac Manager
Development team	MV, SL, JN, TY, KR	RL, KV, HL	KT, TY, JN, PK	HS, KV, SL	JV, TY, JR	OK, JN
Purpose	Developing business and capability strategies and defining programs required.	Getting customers interested in our products and services.	Getting customers to close the deal with us.	Delivering products and services meeting the deal.	Creating value-added for customer's and new business opportunities for ourselves.	Maintaining customer retention.
Output	Business idea, targets, and projects are prepared.	Feasibility study agreement is closed with the customer.	Delivery agreement is closed.	Support agreement is closed.	Support agreement is closed after the second delivery.	Next agreement is closed.
Major performance measures	Growth Market share. Solidity Profitability.	Number of feasibility studies.	Number of profitable delivery agreements.	Meeting targets, plan, and promises.	Meeting targets, plans, and promises	Customer retention.

SELF-EVALUATION QUESTIONS

Evaluation Criteria	Priority	Current and Target Performance				
		1	2	3	4	5
1. Are the process development program and its projects organized?						
2. Are the objectives consistent with the company's strategic objectives?						
3. Has management been given process development training?						
4. Is the program proceeding according to plan?						
5. Do you know your most important processes—those that affect customer satisfaction and cost efficiency?						
6. Have the process development groups received development training?						
7. Have the process owners and development groups been identified?						
8. Have process performance objectives been set?						
9. Do you know and do you measure your processes' performance capabilities regularly?						
10. Is continuous development of processes in place?						
11. Is there systematic evaluation of process development levels?						
12. Have you made visits to other companies to learn from their processes?						
13. Have other people visited you to learn from your processes?						
14. Are evaluation and reward for results carried out on a process basis?						
Overall Grade						

x Your evaluation of the current performance level	Priority	Current and Target Performance
o Your target	1 Not significant 2 Significant 3 Important 4 Very important 5 Competitive advantage	1 Poor 2 Adequate 3 Good 4 Very Good 5 Exceptional

Chapter 5

DEVELOPMENT MANAGEMENT

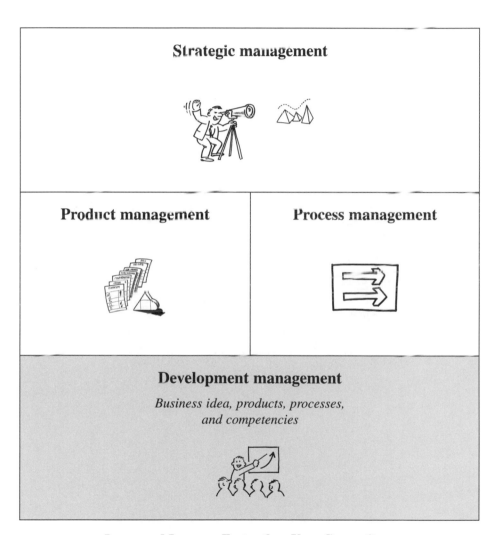

Strategic management

Product management

Process management

Development management

Business idea, products, processes, and competencies

Learn and Improve Faster than Your Competitors

Content Summary

INTRODUCTION TO THE BENCHMARKING DEVELOPMENT MODEL

QUICK NOTES
Page 190: Read the complete text.
191–198: Read headings, illustrations, text boxes, and tables.
199–200: Read the complete text.
200–206: Read headings, illustrations, text boxes, and tables.
207–209: Read the complete text
210–225: Read headings, illustrations, text boxes, tables, and text in *italics*.

Speed Up Learning: The Benchmarking Process

Taiichi Ohno, former vice president of manufacturing for Toyota, described in his book the post–World War II efforts at benchmarking:

> Following World War II, American products flowed into Japan; chewing gum and Coca-Cola, even the Jeep. The first US-style supermarket appeared in the mid-1950s. And as more and more Japanese people visited the United States, they saw the intimate relationship between the supermarket and the style of daily life in America. Consequently, this type of store became the rage in Japan due to Japanese curiosity and fondness for imitation.

Ohno further applied his observations on the supermarket by using shelf restocking as an analogy for his development of the just-in-time (JIT) inventory management method:

> From the supermarket we got the idea of viewing the earlier process in a production line as kind of an enabling process from which we developed the kanban system for inventory flow management.

In his book *Strategic Benchmarking,* Gregory H. Watson continues as follows: "Many observers have described Japanese businesspeople as 'copycats' who have excelled only in the art of imitation. This is not true—the Japanese have been applying the practice of benchmarking to their product and process developments as a means to shortcut the time it takes to implement improvement and reduce the time it takes to get products to market."

Paul Howell has observed in his book:

> The Japanese excel at benchmarking, at exhaustively analyzing the best companies in each industry, then continually improving on their performance until the Japanese products and services then become the best.

Companies have to continually develop their business idea, products, processes and the skills of their people. *What is the development of a company? It is learning.* To give some support for this answer is the following train of thought adapted from George Stalk, Jr., and Thomas M. Hout's book *Competing Against Time,* written in 1990:

1. There are constantly, in many industries, some groups of companies whose performance significantly exceeds that of the average performers, measured by customers' and owners' performance criteria.

2. Simply, they are in possession of significantly better internal capabilities, in terms of process quality and efficiency.

3. In particular, they are significantly faster than other companies in the same industry. These companies identify new market opportunities a lot earlier than the competition, react to customer requirements in half the time others do, and develop their products, services, and internal capabilities in half the time. These companies do not do things better; they just do them differently.

4. The next question to raise is this: how are capabilities created? They are created through learning. Our challenge is to create the capability for continuous learning and to apply that learning faster than our competitors. Continuous improvement is the result of continuous learning. Success, in turn, is created through applying that  learning faster than your competitors do. As matter of fact, if you want to accelerate the rate of continuous improvement, you have to accelerate the pace of learning. To speed up continuous improvement through accelerated learning is a new challenge for management—to understand the interaction between learning and business success, as well as to make it happen.

5. If we want to be included in the small group of really successful companies, we have to double the speed at which we learn. When the target is to double something, it is not enough simply to carry out development work better but, rather, to do so in a different way. To double your speed of improvement, you have to double your speed of learning. Benchmarking enables you to *learn in a different way,* making it possible to learn twice as quickly. Benchmarking complements Kolb's learning model. Learning comes from both one's own and other people's experience.

Benchmarking Definitions

Benchmarking is the continuous process of measuring products, services, and processes against the toughest competitors or the companies recognized as industry leaders.

Benchmarking is the process of identifying, understanding, and adapting outstanding practices from organizations anywhere in the world to help your organization improve its performance.

Benchmarking is the practice of being humble enough to admit that others are better at something and wise enough to try to learn how to match and even surpass them.

Benchmarking is a development model, but it also uses common sense to define the critical path for success, to look for examples of higher performance that can be applied to one's own processes. Why reinvent something that you can learn from others more quickly and with lower costs?

Benchmarking Categories

The following brief descriptions show how business ideas, products, processes, and people's skills can be developed using benchmarking. The types of benchmarking used are the following:

- Strategic benchmarking
- Product benchmarking
- Process benchmarking
- Competency benchmarking

Strategic Benchmarking

Companies' strategic choices are linked to their choice of markets and customers, their product range and core competencies, their degree of integration, their method of growth, and so on. A company's business idea is a product of these choices.

Strategic Issue	Own Company	Company A	Company B
Return on Assets	**16%**	**30%**	**60%**
Return on sales	13%	30%	12%
Capital turnover	1.2	1	5
Integration level	70%	90%	40%
Growth per year	5%	15%	0%
Growth method	New market	Acquisitions	Subcontracting
Capital invested	Marketing, R&D	Acquisitions	Assembly
Markets	Scandinavia	Global	Local
Customer segment	Large companies	Big companies	Entrepreneurs
Product mix	Mixed	Full coverage	Niche
Core competence	Product innovations	Cost efficiency	Product variety

Companies succeed with many different strategic options and combinations of them. Company B concentrates narrowly on product range, product development, and assembly. It uses subcontractors and does not tie up capital in growth. Its good profitability is generated by a high level of capital turnover.

Company A has grown by acquisition. It manufactures almost all the parts it needs itself and aims at being very cost-efficient. The result is lower capital turnover but a clearly higher percentage sales margin. Its profitability was less than Company B's that year. One year's figures are not sufficient to draw conclusions, however; the figures need to be examined over a longer time span.

Through comparing strategic choices within your own industry, you learn to understand its logic. This kind of comparison within and outside your industry can yield practical ideas not previously thought of. Development at the level of operations is useless if the strategic options selected are wrong.

Product Benchmarking

Ford's Taurus has been a success in the United States. This success is largely based on thoroughly conducted product benchmarking.

- Studied features of 50 midsized cars
- Identified 400 features as "best-in-class" (BIC)
- Made plans to "meet or exceed" BIC
- At introduction, 77 percent of features met or exceeded BIC
- Over 300 features copied from competitors
- Design process improved
- Reliability improved 10 to 15 times over previous five years
- Product was a market success.

Source: AQPC seminar manual: *Organizing and Managing Benchmarking,* 1992.

As early as the late 1970s, IBM required that all new products must have superior performance. This can be assessed only through the continuous measurement of product performance and comparison against the competition.

Manufacturing Process Parameters	Competitive Manufacturing Benchmark									
Score 20 = best vs. target 0 = worst vs. target	Base Score	IBM	A	B	C	D	E	F	IBM Position	Best of Breed
Build Process										
Min. part numbers	20	12	20	10	10	11	14	12	3	20
Min. stock levels	20	16	5	10	10	11	18	18	3	18
Min. time file	20	15	20	17	16	14	12	16	5	20
Min. order ship time	20	10	20	10	7	15	6	13	4	20
Min. number of vendors	20	15	15	18	12	13	15	16	3	18
Quality and Reliability										
Min. field defects	20	16	20	12	18	18	19	13	5	20

Technical product innovations can come from outside your own field. For example, Remington got the idea of the typewriter from a piano keyboard.

Process Benchmarking

If you measure and compare a function or a task with a corresponding one in production, sales, delivery, or billing, you find differences in multiples of three expressed with various performance measures. When you analyze the root causes of differences, you realize that, in general, 10 percent are caused by the task itself and 90 percent by the preceding or following tasks. Focusing only on benchmarking individual functions or tasks tends to result in achieving only minor improvements.

Following are the performance measures for a delivery system that are used to identify the current situation, the target, and the benchmark. Performance is measured in three areas: effectiveness, efficiency, and adaptability.

	Performance Measure	Current	Target	Benchmark
Effectiveness	Delivery reliability %	85	99	95
	Delivery time in days	7	2	3
	Product quality %	90	100	100
Efficiency	Handling costs FIM/item	100	50	40
	Throughput time	7	2	3
	Hand over/delivery	5	2	?
Adaptability	Not standard products	5%	30%	50%

> The benchmarking development model works as follows: Define your own process. Measure its performance. Identify a significantly better process in terms of the selected measures. Learn the methods and practices of that process. Adapt and implement them into your own process. Proceed with continuous improvement as an open-ended process.

Effectiveness and adaptability are measured from the customer's point of view through delivery reliability, delivery time, product quality, and product variety. The long-term objective for sales volume and price level is defined by these measures. The efficiency measures chosen influence the cost efficiency of the process and, thus, the profitability. One requirement is that nonstandard products are also supplied to the planned levels of quality and efficiency.

Competency Benchmarking

Processes can seem to be almost identical, but there are significant differences in the quality and efficiency they generate. The differences arise from differences in ability to execute the various stages, and these can be the subject of benchmarking. Consider at the following two examples:

1. *Delivery process.* The delivery processes being compared were almost identical. However, the quality generated by the benchmark process was clearly superior. This was because a particular production technology was used at a stage in production that was important for quality. Better cost efficiency resulted from a single employee operating several machines simultaneously.

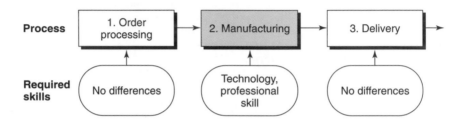

2. *Sales process.* An internal comparison of the process descriptions within different units in the group showed them to be identical. However, the sales margin of the best unit was almost double the average. It had the skill to sell products to its customers that were also economical to design and manufacture. It also got the best price for them. The most significant explanatory factor was the higher level of language skills of its salesforce, which made it possible to have close and detailed discussions with customers.

In the benchmarking process, we are interested in best practice and the methodologies, operating principles, and skills that underlay it. We are also interested in how benchmark companies have achieved their position. Where did the technology come from, how long did it take to implement it, how was acceptance of multimachine operating achieved, or how did the salesforce develop their language skills? In order to avoid learning practices that are becoming old, we also want to understand the company's plans for the future.

CASE STUDY: ROSENLEW HOUSEHOLD APPLIANCES RENEWAL OF PRODUCTS AND PRODUCTION

Summary of the Case Study

The Business Unit Had to Be Improved or Closed

"We have to invest heavily in developing products and production at our household appliances business or close it completely." That was the statement made by W. Rosenlew's directors in 1977. The company's household appliances unit produced refrigerators, freezers, and combination refrigerator-freezers. It had begun to make large losses, and its future hung in the balance.

The Changes of the 1970s Were No Longer Enough

During the 1970s, the household appliances business had undergone significant changes. A rationalization of the sector had been carried out with Upo, a household appliance business, and a sales organization had seen sales responsibility transferred entirely to the wholesale and retail outlets. The changes had a significant impact on profitability, but it had once again begun to fall sharply.

Competition became tougher as production in the sector increased. The products were no longer competitive, and our business unit lost significant market share. The structure of the products did not lend itself to streamlined production, and labor productivity was low. The result was a fall in sales and production volumes, continual reductions in the number of employees, and a loss-making operation.

> The decision by the company's directors produced a completely new range of refrigerators, freezers, and refrigerator-freezers: low energy. Their most important competitive advantage was that they used half the energy of competing products. Productivity and product variety were doubled; the throughput time was reduced to a quarter. With improved efficiencies, growth in market share, and increased export sales, big losses were turned into a good profit.

We Learned from Another Company Superior to Ourselves— We Benchmarked

When I was writing my first book about benchmarking I searched my background for benchmarking experience. I realized that the main source for our success was learning from those companies significantly better than ourselves—learning, in other words, from our masters. I realized that, in many cases, we had applied benchmarking processes without actually knowing the word *benchmarking*.

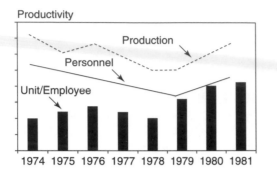
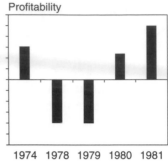

The progress of productivity and profitability of Rosenlew Household Appliances.

Selection of Improvement Objectives and the Benchmarking Partner

To use benchmarking terminology, the first step in the process "determining what to benchmark" could have been *to develop products and production exceeding world-class standards and competition for a 10-year term.* (The objective was later specified in the investment calculations. The criteria for an investment of almost FIM 30 million were an internal rate of return of 44 percent and a payback period of 5.7 years).

We did not have the faintest idea about what qualified as world-class standard in our business, so we proceeded to step two: identify a benchmark company. We found Bosch Siemens Hausgeraete in Germany (BSHG), also a producer of freezers and refrigerators, to be far ahead of us in its product and production technology. The company was willing to assist us in determining the technology we should implement and the investment we needed. For its part, it lacked products that were suitable for the Scandinavian markets. Negotiations led to a cooperation agreement. With the help of BSHG, we were able to identify the investment and time needed and to specify the profitability objectives of the investment. The following is a more detailed account of how we learned from Bosch Siemens Hausgeraete.

Description of the Case Study

We Learned How to Succeed in Benchmarking

We established a benchmarking partnership, including an agreement on the number of hours that BSHG could make available to visit its plants and ask questions on product and manufacturing technology.

Over three years, we learned many important things about benchmarking without knowing that word and concept. I will recount some of them. I will also use the vocabulary of benchmarking, which naturally we did not use then. In this description, I will concentrate only on the stages that demonstrate what benchmarking is and that taught us how to implement the benchmarking process.

> 1. Benchmarking sets standards based on external best practice.

A high internal rate of return for the investment was sufficient grounds for approving it. Benchmarking itself concerned mostly technical issues, but targets were based on competition, customer requirements, and other external best practice—including energy consumption and design, as well as product and manufacturing technology.

At that time, our calculations showed that feasible project profitability could also have been achieved through lower investments and more moderate performance improvement. But to maintain competitiveness this way for a 10-year period may not have been feasible. To ensure our competitiveness, a world-class standard was set as our target.

Incidentally, the first analysis with Bosch revealed that volume should be doubled to cover the investment required. We had to accept that goal or give up the whole plan. As you will see, we did, in fact, succeed in doubling volume.

> 2. Partnership demands mutual benefits.

At its best, benchmarking is not a one off visit but a long-term partnership from which both parties benefit. Mutual benefit may be achieved in many ways. In this case, we obtained product and production skills, and our partner obtained products suited to Scandinavian markets under its own brand name. Partnership and the exchange of information did not happen just during the project. It continued after the project, too, which allowed us to continue to learn from a benchmarking partner that was 10 times our size.

> 3. Thorough preparation by both parties is a vital requirement.

For a benchmarking visit to be successful, it is a prerequisite that both parties prepare thoroughly. You must know, describe, measure, and understand your own process before you can learn from your partner's process. However, analyzing our old products and production processes was no longer of much use to us. We concentrated on completely new developments, and we used the problems that came out of this to develop the questions we wanted to pose during our visit.

During the course of three years, we made numerous benchmarking visits to Germany. Two weeks prior to each visit, the Germans demanded a comprehensive list of the questions we needed answers to. One week prior to our trip, they sent a detailed program to us outlining, where, when, and whom we should meet to get our questions answered.

> 4. Involve the right people.

We visited them in groups of two to four people, and each visit took two to three days. It was of vital importance that the participants were those responsible for adapting what they learned. In benchmarking, experts meet each other. During a benchmarking visit, information flows in both directions. Mutual benefits can arise during the visits, too.

The most difficult part of a development program tends to be selling our own ideas to others. In benchmarking, you avoid that difficulty by taking people with you to see something they could not imagine being possible. If you have involved the right people, you can skip the idea-selling phase, or at least make it a lot easier. This feature is one of the most significant advantages of the benchmarking process.

> 5. Benchmarking is adapting, not adopting.

We learned that benchmarking is not adopting but adapting ideas into one's own environment and working culture. What works at BSHG would not necessarily work for us just as it is. Regardless of our being in the same industry, we were totally different companies. This meant adapting what we had learned and not just copying it. Following are a few examples:

1. *Manufacturing technology for small batches.* We produced 100,000 units per year, Bosch 10 times more—that is, a million a year. We could not copy BSHG's manufacturing technology directly. We took in its manufacturing technology but adapted the technology for small batches. Modular products made it possible to produce for a variety of customers and with longer manufacturing runs.
2. *From assembly lines to assembly cells.* Bosch had huge, long assembly lines with a foreign workforce. We couldn't copy that in our working culture. We took many assembly ideas, but, instead of long lines, we created assembly cells with four or five operators within each cell. Bosch used a mainly male workforce with poor ergonomics. We developed totally different ergonomic solutions for our mostly female workforce. Workbenches were designed for assembly with adjustable height and slope, depending on the work being done and the height of the workers.
3. *Energy consumption in our model to be 50 percent better.* The primary target in the whole project was to gain competitive advantage through a 50 percent lower energy consumption rating for our new products, compared with the competition's. We couldn't copy Bosch's cooling technology, so we made what was there 50 percent better.

4. ***Product appearance from Electrolux.*** Bosch design was aimed at Central Europe. Electrolux sets the design features in Scandinavia, so we could not apply Bosch's design but benchmarked the Electrolux design to our products.

5. ***Results achieved combined from various sources.*** They were as follows:
   - Bosch manufacturing technology applied to small batches
   - Bosch assembly technology applied to assembly cells
   - Bosch product technology improved 50 percent in energy consumption
   - Electrolux design
   - Designed and produced by Finns in Pori, Finland

---

6. Benchmarking is learning instead of inventing.

Benchmarking is a development tool, but it is not a case of developing from scratch. It is identifying the topic to be improved, finding out who is best in that area, learning from them, and developing further, as we did with energy consumption. In other words, you take up where others have left off.

---

7. Benchmarking is learning, not teaching, selling, or dictating.

The Bosch people hardly visited us at all. Everything we applied was taken in through visiting them and learning. In the multi-unit corporate environment, transferring best practice in the traditional way usually takes place through sending a "commando team" with experts from the parent company to teach other business units to adopt their working methods and practices and even the parent company's culture. We know what results from selling ideas in this way.

In benchmarking, we do it differently. *First,* we analyze and determine what is most important in our business, which capabilities and which performance criteria. *Second,* we determine how to measure each capability and performance. *Third,* we evaluate which of us is the best performer in those critical issues. *Finally,* instead of sending people from the best company to sell their methods and practices to others, to teach them, each of us visits that company to learn and to adapt, not to adopt, the best practices to one's own environment.

A learning approach is a better way of getting new ideas accepted than selling, and even dictating.

> 8. Benchmarking is not a traditional technology transfer.

The traditional term for this was *technology transfer* from one company to another. It was that, but it was not done in the traditional manner. At the same time, Bosch was involved in a technology transfer to Hungary. Bosch sent machine tools, drawings and training staff to Hungary, using traditional technology transfer practices. Bosch people hardly visited us at all. Everything we applied was taken in through visiting them and learning. The development process we applied was very similar to the orthodox benchmarking process.

> 9. Benchmarking fosters breakthrough performance.

By learning from the best in the world, we took a leap forward in our development. Without our learning from Bosch, this type of project would not have been feasible within the given time frame of three years.

> 10. Benchmarking accelerates continuous improvement via partnership.

The packaging for our products was made from two styrox sheets and shrink-wrap. Because of our scarce design resources, packaging design was one of the last jobs and was seen as secondary. Our partner had a designer whose main job was to improve the design of these styrox sheets to make them stronger and cheaper. All BSHG development results were at our disposal, which accelerated the continuous improvement of our products and manufacturing process.

> 11. Benchmarking is part of a total development program.

The objective of the project was to improve Rosenlew's Household Appliance business by renewing its product range and manufacturing and by focusing on exports. Benchmarking, learning from our betters, was the key methodology that led to the success of the project. However, benchmarking is not a stand-alone development tool. We used a number of other development models. We applied JIT, we purchased machines and equipment, we made innovations, and so forth. Benchmarking was one tool, albeit a vital one. It is part of a larger program, in which other development approaches and tools are also applied.

> Do not ever call your development program by a buzzword. Use the name that indicates the target of the program: "to renew the entire business through development of new competitive products and manufacturing facilities, as well as exploiting new marketing opportunities," as in our case.

We Achieved Results

We improved our products and plant and achieved excellent profitability. The improvement made our Household Appliances operation attractive to Electrolux. We signed a sector rationalization agreement by which the Pori Household Appliance business became part of Electrolux, and Electrolux's combine harvester company in Sweden was transferred to Rosenlew.

> This and other examples demonstrate that benchmarking can be used to make significant changes in an organization. Benchmarking is a methodology for fostering improvement and even for realizing something that might otherwise be totally unachievable within a reasonable timeframe.

Improvement Continues

> We created a strong competitive foundation for the unit, and it is still being improved. The benchmarking process described also created skills in Electrolux's internal benchmarking processes, which have, in turn, influenced the internal behavior of the group.

Within the Electrolux group, the management supports the units learning from one another in different ways (internal benchmarking). The following are a few examples:

1. Group management wanted the European manufacturing units to improve the use of visual material in its operations, communications, and management. Group management gave them encouragement to organize joint benchmarking visits to the group's units in North America, where they had well-developed visual solutions, which had been applied to these issues.

   Ten senior managers from various business units which manufacture refrigeration equipment formed a benchmarking group, which spent a week visiting nine group companies in North America. During the trip, each participant took photographs of things they thought important. The pictures were distributed to all the participants, and each of them made up a file of pictures as an appendix to his or her report on the trip, which the participants then took back to their own units. The files contained more than 100 pictures, which showed how the units illustrate their products, manufacturing, production control, costs, quality, health and safety, continuous improvement, payment of employees and suppliers, customer feedback, and locations of tools on the shelves.

Example 1: One unit hung a big poster over the machine or production point that was a bottleneck for the plant. Once the problem was resolved, the bottleneck poster was placed above the next bottleneck in the process. Everyone in the company knew where the bottleneck was and that it had to be eliminated.

Example 2: The product development managers from the various units in the group got together for a quality conference. Instead of the traditional cost and quality statistics graphs, the issue was illustrated with the worst disasters of the past years. They were prominently placed on shelves around the room. Labels giving the costs they had caused were clearly placed on them. The sight undoubtedly remained in everyone's mind.

Example 3: The parts from the products of various designers were spread out on the same table. Everyone wondered why there were cables with only a couple of centimeters' difference in length or why other parts were not common.

2. A second learning method is to bring together experts in a particular area and have the group visit each member's plant in turn. The objective is to identify the best technologies and methodologies, so that the others can learn from them.

3. A third method is to have the three Scandinavian units audit each other every year. The auditing plan covers 20 areas the auditing group scores. The objective is to identify the areas that do not meet the standards expected by the group, as well as to find the best methodologies from which the others could learn. The audit lasts two days, including three hours of verbal feedback to the employees.

4. A fourth method is to give the group's business units the key financial and operational ratios and their trends from the other units in the group. This is done at regular intervals. This information, which would not normally be available, could be obtained quickly from group companies by asking them. Common conventions for calculating the figures were agreed, upon.

The Development Process Started Again
Ten years after starting the renewed plant, the Electrolux management decided to invest in updating the products developed in the process just described, maintaining competitiveness and profitability on the planned level.

BENCHMARKING DEVELOPMENT MODEL

Benchmarking is a method of learning from those who are clearly the best. The idea is not new; people have always done this. What is new is the systematic model that can be followed to make sure that learning from others is fast. The roots of benchmarking are in Japan, and Rank Xerox developed the benchmarking process further. Nowadays it is available to everyone through books and courses.

This section presents a 10-step benchmarking development model that can be adapted to improving a business idea, products, processes, and employees' skills. Each stage is illustrated by Elmo, a decathlete who wants to improve his high jump performance by learning from the best (coaching, training, and jumping style). He wants to win the European title first and then the Olympic gold medal.

The model has also been applied to Rosenlew Tools' improvement program.

Benchmarking Development Model

### 1. Determine what to benchmark.  High jump 30 cm in two years	### 2. Identify benchmark companies. Finland's high jump recordholder and his coach
### 3. Measure preformance gap. –Progress –Current –Prediction	### 4. Identify enablers resulting in excellence. *–Coaching process* *–Training process* *–The jump*
### 5. Learn how *we* do it.  –Coaching –Training –The jump –Questions –Speed exercises and recovery	### 6. Learn how *they* do it.  –Coaching –Training –The jump
### 7. Establish performance goals. –High jump performance –Trust –Condition	### 8. Adapt and implement.  –A high jump trainer –To attract sponsors –A new jumping style –A new training style
### 9. Continue development to gain superiority. 	### 10. Start again with higher targets. –Olymipic gold –Long jump

Summary

1. **Determine what to benchmark.**
   Identify a key performance with critical impact on the company's success expressed in performance figures. This performance affects the search for a benchmark company in stage 2.

2. **Identify benchmark companies.**
   Identify a benchmark company or companies that are significantly better than you in terms of the selected performance measures.

3. **Measure performance gap.**
   Identify the performance gap between you and the benchmark company. Identify how performance areas have improved in both companies and how they are expected to develop.

4. **Identify enablers resulting in excellence.**
   Identify the factors that account for the difference in performance and that need development in order for the improvements to be achieved.

5. **Learn how *we* do it.**
   Develop an understanding of your own process. Measure process performance and identify methods and practices that make it easy or difficult to achieve a satisfactory performance.

6. **Learn how *they* do it.**
   Develop an understanding of their process. Measure process performance, and identify and understand the root causes of process performance resulting in excellence. Compare the performances and observe the root causes and enablers, and determine gaps.

7. **Establish performance goals.**
   Establish performance goals for improvements. Determine the ideas to be implemented immediately after the visit, as well as long-term goals.

8. **Adapt and implement.**
   Prepare the plans and schedules and implement them. Adapt and implement the best methods, practices, and enablers into your own process.

9. **Continue development to gain superiority.**
   The aim is to use continuous measurement to ensure that the objectives are achieved and the benchmark level exceeded.

10. **Start again with higher targets.**
    Determine the long-term target, and start again from the beginning.

1. Determine What to Benchmark

Choose an issue that is critical to the company's success. Try to find a development topic that increases both customer satisfaction and internal efficiency. The choice will involve judgment and decision making by senior management. Define the performance measures: how you have improved, how good you are now, how good you want to become, and over what time frame.

Elmo is a decathlete whose dream is to win the Olympics. He has won over 8,000 points, and his performance is relatively even across all disciplines. However, the high jump is one discipline in which he has special strengths. With relatively little practice in the discipline, he has achieved good results. Elmo believes that the high jump could give him a clear advantage over other competitors. He thinks that, in the high jump, he could get most quickly to a stage at which he could win more points than other competitors. Together with his coach, Elmo decides to improve his high jump performance by at least 30 cm in two years. Elmo has also thought about specializing in the high jump later in his career.

2. Identify Benchmark Companies

Identify the best, or at least clearly better, companies in the area you have selected that could be a benchmark. The best may be found in your company, it may be a competitor, or it may be from the same or a different sector. Try to find a permanent benchmarking partnership in which both parties benefit.

Elmo gets in touch with a high jump coach in order to get specific coaching for this discipline. The coach, however, knows the chief coach who recently coached Kalevi, Finland's high jump recordholder. With the assistance of the high jump coach, Elmo contacts the chief coach and Kalevi. They agree to work with Elmo to improve his high jump performance. Kalevi is interested in Elmo's speed and ability to recover from arduous exertion.

3. Measure Performance Gap

Select the best performer, using the appropriate performance measures. Take an interest in current performance: how quickly has it improved and how is it predicted to develop? Compare it with your own.

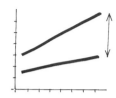

Elmo and Kalevi compare how their performances have improved. Kalevi has improved considerably more quickly. His coach claims that the relatively steep improvement curve will be maintained by using new training methods.

4. Identify Enablers Resulting in Excellence

Identify the benchmark company's processes, skills, and enablers that have been developed to achieve the improvement. There may be one or many enablers that have contributed to success.

> 1. Coaching
> 2. Training
> 3. The jump

Under the direction of Kalevi's coach, Elmo and Kalevi evaluate where the differences in speed of development and the current prognosis stem from. Kalevi's rate of improvement is obviously grounded in his discipline-specific coaching and training. He also learned his present jumping style at a very early stage. Other factors influencing development are also found.

The three factors coaching, training, and jumping style were selected for closer examination.

5. Learn How *We* Do It

Define, describe, measure, and understand your own processes. Only by understanding and mastering your own processes will you be able to make comparisons and learn the best practice. The task should be given to those who own the processes and to the development group selected to improve them.

Elmo and his coach document in detail the coaching method used and Elmo's training and jumping style. The coach writes down what training and experience as a coach he has received. Elmo and his coach write down the principles of how they work together. They describe the training in terms of the training programs followed and the results achieved. Elmo's coach records his jumping style on video. Elmo and his coach describe in great detail the speed exercises and recovery methods that Kalevi is especially interested in. Kalevi and his coach draw up 30 important questions relating to coaching, training, and jumping style.

6. Learn How *They* Do It

Get to know the process you have selected as best, following the same principles as for your own process, so that a meaningful comparison can be made. Since it is a question of learning, involve the owners of the process and the development group in this task. They will be responsible for applying what has been learned.

Elmo sends the most important descriptions and questions to Kalevi and his coach before their meeting. Elmo and his coach meet Kalevi and his coach and present their documented results. Kalevi and his coach are immediately interested in the speed training and recovery methods Elmo uses. The pictures and questions Elmo and his coach sent ahead help Kalevi and his coach prepare for the visit. They are ready to talk about Kalevi's coaching, training, and jumping style and to answer the questions they received. They make comparisons between the methods used and the performances and their improvement over time (figures for thrust, lifting power, speed, and condition).

7. Establish Performance Goals

Set goals that can be achieved immediately and goals that can be aimed for over the short and long term. Setting goals is a central part of the benchmarking process. Even more important is to understand the factors that affect performance.

Enthused by the new opportunities, Elmo and his coach set new goals. The major goal is to win the European decathlon championship. They evaluate the strongest competitors and their development and set annual improvement targets for the high jump and for other performance measures, such as thrust and condition. They also decide to improve in other areas, such as the renewal of the training and competition program, the selection of a high jump coach, and the acquisition of sponsors to safeguard the overall program.

8. Adapt and Implement

Draw up an implementation plan and time-table. Ensure that the process owners and the development group are committed to their tasks and that they have everything they need to implement the plans. Involve as many people as possible in learning and applying best practice. Start a continuous program of measurement to provide feedback on what has been learned.

Elmo and his coach agree on a division of labor to implement the things they have learned. Elmo's coach is able to secure Kalevi's coach as the high jump coach for the next two years. They draw up new training plans and agree on the measurement methods that would be used to track Elmo's progress. Elmo's coach draws up plans to attract sponsors using Keke Rosberg's expertise in this area (a Finnish Formula I world champion and agent for many Finnish sport personalities). For his part, Elmo concentrates on the new competition and training plans and learns a new jumping style under the guidance of his new coach. He often trains with Kalevi and learns valuable lessons. At the same time, Kalevi and his coach are able to follow Elmo's speed training and the recovery methods he uses.

9. Continue Development to Gain Superiority

Ensure that the improvement program is carried through to the end as planned and that the goals set are achieved. Keep up the continuous measurements and make sure that the gains follow the path of continuous improvement.

Elmo closely follows the plan he has made and takes care of the continuous measurement and comparison with the goals he has set. He notices a lot of opportunities for improvement in his training program. New methods are adopted to improve his thrust, and he uses a weight-lifting coach. Elmo improves according to his plan and wins the decathlon European championship in 1998.

10. Start Again with Higher Targets

Benchmarking is a continuous process. Set new goals, look for new benchmark companies, and continue with the other stages of benchmarking. Aim to improve your own benchmarking process continuously by benchmarking the best benchmarkers.

Elmo's dream had always been to win Olympic gold. He chose the long jump and the 100 meters as the main disciplines to be improved. His good experiences with the high jump taught him to apply the same principles.

He turned to his coach to find the people who were clearly better than both of them in each discipline. Elmo decided to win the gold in the year 2000 by always using those who know the most and learning from those who are the best. Elmo and his coach also considered using "medical" videos and methods that would allow them to learn from the best in the world, even if they would not agree to direct cooperation.

Rosenlew Tools, Competitive Benchmarking

In 1987, Rosenlew Tools marketed, designed, and manufactured sophisticated injection molds for the Scandinavian television and automobile industries. It was one of W. Rosenlew's profit centers. The company employed 120 people and had a turnover of about FIM 25 million. Its major competitors were in Finland, Italy, and Germany.

The main thrust of the strategy adopted by corporate management was to transform Rosenlew Tools into a unit that could operate profitably first and foremost as the main supplier for the Nordic TV and automobile industry of large (30–40-ton) injection molds.

All the major European automobile-producing countries (Germany, Italy, etc.) had a strong injection molds industry supplying the automobile manufacturers, except for Scandinavia. Most of the large molds were imported from Germany and Italy. The main objective was to fill this gap.

The Nordic TV industry was growing rapidly as a result of exports and acquisitions. (It was the third largest in Europe.) It was looking for injection molds manufacturers who would be competitive, particularly on delivery times.

In order to meet the overall goals set for the profit center, strategic objectives had been established for profitability, growth, internationalization, product policy, investments, productivity, cost structure, organization, corporate culture, and competitive advantage. We made comparisons with our competitors for all those strategic objectives (performance benchmarking). Full-blown benchmarking processes were used to improve throughput times, productivity, and corporate culture.

The competitive advantages that we were to improve significantly were defined as follows:

1. *Close customer relations:* In order to become the major supplier, close relations would be needed with the Scandinavian automobile and TV industries and with their major suppliers of injection molded parts.
2. *Speed of delivery:* We would have to deliver molds in competitive time-scale and respond quickly to both changes and breakdowns at our customers' plant.

3. *Reliability:* We needed a reputation as a reliable supplier (on-time delivery, quality, customer service).
4. *CAD/CAM:* The geometry of the customer's product had to be able to be transferred to us without technical drawings. This meant using CAD/CAM for simulating the mold, mold design, design of the machining path, and production control.

In order to achieve the overall goal, we had to win a strong position in the market and improve profitability considerably. The company had been making heavy losses for many years, in spite of significant growth. The goal was to achieve a return on equity of 14 percent within three to four years.

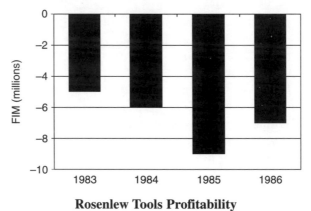

Rosenlew Tools Profitability

The following describes the part of Rosenlew Tools' improvement program that illustrates how the benchmarking processes were conducted.

1. Determine What to Benchmark

We looked for the reasons for our poor profitability in our price level and the information we had on customer satisfaction that affected price level. We obtained customer satisfaction figures from our most important customers. In the following table, a figure of 10 indicates the best, against which the others were measured. We saw how customer satisfaction and price level are correlated.

Customer Expectations	Relative Scores			
	Sweden	Tools	Italy	Germany
Delivery time	9	6	10	7
Product quality	8	8	7	10
Flexibility	9	7	10	7
Customer relations	9	3	5	10
Total	**35**	**24**	**32**	**34**
Price level	8	6	7	10

Since our customers put particular emphasis on the need to halve delivery times, we chose that as our most important factor to benchmark. The other area we chose was productivity, with the target of doubling it.

2. Identify Benchmark Companies

We decided to find benchmark companies from among our competitors. Our customers were our most important source of information. They were keen to support our improvement program so they would have a competitive Scandinavian supplier of injection molds. We were able to benchmark two Italian and one Finnish competitor. From Germany and Japan, we received only country-specific information.

3. Measure Performance Gap

We made the comparisons separately for molds for the automobile and TV industries. Throughput times were based mainly on information received from our customers.

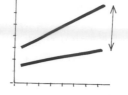

We obtained comparative information on productivity and labor costs from reports of the International Special Tooling Association (ISTA). Tooling companies from around the world send key economic performance indicators to this organization, and these are published annually, arranged by country.

We were not able to make trend comparisons with our competitors, since we had been in this business for such a short period of time.

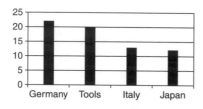

TV Molds 1986—
Throughput Time, weeks

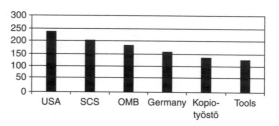

Hourly Productivity, molds,
sales/working hour

4. Identify Enablers Resulting in Excellence

We believed that a fast delivery time was a function of a fast throughput time. We chose the order-delivery process as the one to be benchmarked. The process is started by receipt of an order and ends with the delivery and customer acceptance of the finished mold.

1. *Coaching*
2. *Training*
3. *The jump*

5. *Learn How* We *Do It*

We described the order-delivery process as four subprocesses. We described the operating principles of each subprocess and measured the throughput times measured accurately for each stage. Numerous opportunities for improvement had already been found during the description phase, but they would not have come near to halving the  throughput time, which was the objective set by our customers and which, according to them, our strongest competitors had already achieved.

Mold design	Programming	Manufacturing	Assembly	
6 weeks	1 week	9 weeks	6 weeks	Total: 22 weeks

6. *Learn How* They *Do It*

We were able to visit two of our German competitors with the Finnish Machine Tools Association. The visit enabled us to evaluate their technological level and the principles they applied to customer relations. (They did not regard us as a significant competitor, because they did not know the overall objective of our strategy.)

From our customers, we received copies of their reports on a visit they had made to Japanese mold makers. We learned how the Japanese achieved their speed and high productivity. The guiding factor in our operating philosophy was to achieve as high productivity as possible. This lengthened throughput times. The Japanese, however, had chosen short throughput times as their main target. At the same time, it gave them high productivity and, above all, better added value for the customer.

The Italians were our strongest competitors, and we were not able to visit their plants. In order to discover the secret of their short throughput times, we decided to make benchmarking visits to similar American mold makers. We had gotten wind of their fast throughput times, too. Four of our people visited four mold makers in the United States during the course of a week.

Their throughput times, too, were half of ours. They did not see us as competitors and openly showed us their technology and talked about their operating principles and methodologies, in which are some significant differences that have a decisive effect on throughput times.

Us	Them
The halves of the mold went through the process consecutively. Working time was 2 x 8-hr. shifts. Cost of flexible working was high.	The halves of the mold went through the process simultaneously. Working time was 3 x 8-hr. or 2 x 12-hr. shifts. Cost of flexible working was low.

Then we understood that the Italians must also work like this. We had carried out "indirect competitor-benchmarking."

7. Establish Performance Goals

We returned from the trip eager to set targets for the improvement of our own throughput times. We set corresponding targets for improvement in productivity.

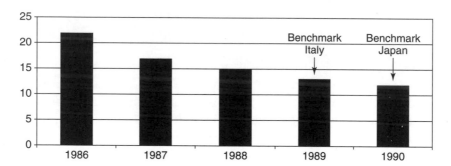

Throughput Time Target (weeks)

As well as taking measures to reduce throughput times, we also instigated a number of other improvements we believed would increase customer satisfaction and lead to improved price levels. The following table summarizes our targets.

Customer Expectations	Relationship Between Customer Satisfaction and Price Level			
	1986	1987	1988	1989
Delivery time	6	7	8	10
Product quality	8	9	9	9
Flexibility	7	8	9	10
Customer relations	3	5	6	8
Total	24	29	32	37
Price level	6	7	7	8

Having seen the price level and productivity improve, we also set new targets for profitability.

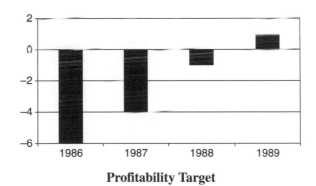

Profitability Target

8. Adapt and Implement

The employees were told verbally about the results of the visit, and everyone was given a detailed report on the trip. In order to achieve the objectives, investment proposals, improvement plans, and a timetable were drawn up and, most important, the people responsible for specific areas were appointed. The most important factors selected as the performance measures were throughput time, reliability of delivery, trial injection quality, productivity, and project-specific profitability.

The measures we implemented included the following, which were adapted from the benchmark companies:

- We concentrated on manufacturing molds and gave up subcontracting and tool making.
- The halves of the molds went through all the stages of the process simultaneously.
- Two designers, rather than one, were assigned to each mold.
- Each designed his or her own half, with one of them having overall responsibility.
- A flexible shift system could be altered in response to changes in capacity requirements.
- Subcontractors were used to help with peak demand.
- A separate week-end shift was introduced.
- Production planning was significantly simplified.

9. Continue Development to Gain Superiority

In spite of having a good business idea, strategic plan, and benchmarking model, we were not improving as quickly as similar projects had. In fact, there was significant progress only in reliability of deliveries. We made a detailed comparison between ourselves and a typical mold-making company (strategic benchmarking). It showed the following differences.

General Features of the Mold-Making Business	Rosenlew Tools
Specialist mold-making companies	Part of a large group
Run by owner-managers	Professional managers from outside the industry
Entrepreneurial culture	Departmental culture
Relatively small companies, 40–150 people	Same size
Light organization	Heavy organization
Director experienced in production control	Mass production control system
Efficient and flexible use of capacity, including three shifts working, week-end working and overtime	Fixed working hours and high overtime costs
Exploit a variety of professional skills	Mass production culture
Multimachine operation common	No multimachine operation
High work morale, high labor productivity	Strong professional departments, low productivity
Systematic training program in mold technology over many years with graded salary system	No training program and small salary differentials

We understood that the task was impossible for us. We lacked the most important requirements for a successful mold-making company. Rosenlew Tools had been created by splitting off the tool-making section of a mass production operation and making it a profit center. That was reflected in its management style and culture.

The jump in improvement was obviously too much for 120 people. Our customers did not believe that it would succeed as long as we were part of a larger group. It also became clear that our customers did not believe Rauma-Repola would keep this kind of operation in the group for long. The strategy chosen was perhaps right at the time, but it was no longer credible.

10. Start Again with Higher Targets

On the basis of the analysis presented and its lack of fit with Rauma-Repola's strategy, the company was sold. The new owner selected new strategies and objectives for the company.

This example of benchmarking did not have the same happy ending as did the earlier example of the Household Appliance business. It shows that operational efficiency (process benchmarking) is of no use if the strategies (strategic benchmarking) are not in place. The example does, however, illustrate the principle that, as with the Household Appliance business, lessons learned from other companies can be applied in a different environment.

SELF-EVALUATION QUESTIONS

Evaluation Critieria Business Development	Priority	Current and Target Performance			
		1	2	3	4
Is there a program of continuous improvement following a systematic methodology and how well has improvement been implemented in the following areas?					
1. Business idea					
2. Product management					
3. Product development					
4. Production and service processes					
5. Other operational processes					
6. Development of employees' practical skills					
7. Development of employees' development skills					
8. Global changes in the company					
9. Cost reduction					
10. Continuous incremental improvement					
11. Are your development resources exploited sufficiently?					
Do you know:					
1. What you should improve?					
2. How good you are now?					
3. How good you should become?					
4. How good you could become?					
5. How you will make change happen?					
Overall grade					

Evaluation Critieria Skills and Learning	Priority	Current and Target Performance			
		1	2	3	4
1. Do you know customer satisfaction?					
2. Do you know your customers' expectations?					
3. Do you know what skills are needed to meet those expectations?					
4. What is the skill level of your employees?					
5. Do your employees learn new things quickly enough?					
6. Is the correlation between continuous and systematic learning and continuous improvement recognized in your organization?					
7. Are sufficient opportunities created for personal learning?					
8. Is continuous personal learning demanded?					
9. Are there sufficient opportunities for the organization to learn?					
10. Is there a transfer of skills from one unit to another within the company?					
11. Is there a transfer of skills from other companies?					
12. Are you able to acquire information and experience from consultants and other experts?					
Overall grade					

x Your evaluation of the current performance level o Your target	Priority 1 Not significant 2 Significant 3 Important 4 Very important 5 Competitive advantage	Current and Target Performance 1 Poor 2 Adequate 3 Good 4 Very Good 5 Exceptional

Part 3

MANAGEMENT OF CHANGE

Determination, Leadership, and Execution

As a leader, I create the conditions for change.

QUICK NOTES

Pages 229–245: Read the complete text.

Chapter 6

MANAGING CHANGE PROCESSES

Using cases, this chapter describes various change situations and the required management skills. It emphasizes the importance of recognizing various change situations and the ability to manage each. The cases do not constitute an exact classification but stress how broad the variety of cases is. The cases describe significantly different change programs.

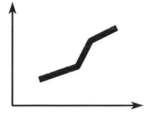

Why is Managing Change So Difficult?

Many managers have been successful in situations in which major changes have not been necessary. Others have succeeded in situations in which continuous development has not been of crucial importance. They have simply efficiently exploited their existing skills, and they have found suitable clients for whom these skills have been sufficient.

These managers don't necessarily succeed when existing skills are insufficient, when customer needs have changed, when the competition has become decisively keener, or when companies have been acquired but their integration has not been implemented.

Sooner or later, every manager must manage change. In those situations, they don't necessarily realize that change is not managed the same way as is day-to-day business. Managers are used to managing through a hierarchical organization. Management tools have consisted of goals, responsibilities, authority, and delegation. In significant change, it is specifically the management tools that are undergoing continuous change.

Operative Focus	Change Focus
Established operating principles	Changing operating principles
Established values	Changing values
Clear parameters	Changing parameters
Established performance level	Rising performance level
Established results	Changing results
Results that are rewarded	Even a good try is rewarded
Established limits of responsibility	Changing limits of responsibility
Delegation	Involvement and coordination
Ability to produce results	Visionary ability
Management by subject matter	Management by will

Managers cannot delegate all change processes. Change does not happen overnight or by itself. Change may affect everything from structures, chains of command, responsibility limits, and incentive systems to company culture and values. Development results come from long change processes that have to be managed by someone.

Different change situations require their own management methods. Big leaps in development are managed differently than is continuous development. Cuts are managed differently than quality program management. Local changes are managed differently than are global changes. The manager must recognize what kind of change is in question and manage the change accordingly. Some examples appear in the following sections.

CHANGES IN COMPANY

In 1986, Rauma-Repola was an enterprise involved in the paper, sawmill, and metal industries. During a little over three years (1987–1991), the company was given a completely new structure.

- Fifty percent new businesses
- Fifty percent new employees
- Fifty percent new assets

The company changed from a very Finnish and eastern-trade-oriented operation to a global enterprise, with over 50 percent of its operations abroad and only 17 percent of its production sold in the Finnish market. At the same time, a marked transition took place from project type production to serial production.

The main objective was to concentrate on four business areas, each with a global market of FIM 5 to 10 billion. In these areas, the target was to obtain the number one or number two position in the world. This goal was met.

The structural change was executed by abandoning the units that were noncompatible with the group structure and by acquiring new units that were compatible with the new strategy. The size of the investments with all costs was about $500 million U.S.

The current Rauma Group emerged with its four business areas: forestry machines, stone crushers, industrial valves, and machines for the pulp industry through these choices and acquisitions.

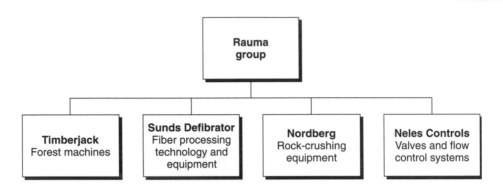

Big changes at the group level require their own methods of change management. Initiatives for change generally come from the operational management, who also generally execute the change. However, the scope of the change is such that the main responsibility lies with the owner, who has to convince lenders to commit to the change. Without the participation of the owners and the lenders, changes of this magnitude will not succeed. In these changes, decision makers must have the following skills:

- Visionary ability
- Global thinking patterns
- Risk-taking ability
- Financial resources
- Ability to divest, select, and acquire
- Long-term horizon

We had to concede that in the 2 to 3 years' time we certainly had not learned how truly international companies operate and exploit their global presence. In global competition totally different rules apply. We had not even identified them, let alone learned them.

This is how one of the group managers described the situation:

> After the acquisitions we thought we were an international company, although essentially we only owned companies in several countries. Mere ownership does not bring the competitiveness required in the global marketplace.

In 1990, Tauno Matomäki, the group chairman, compared the Rauma-Repola situation to an unfinished building. The business areas had been chosen and the leading positions, measured by sales, had been acquired. But the internal structures of the divisions were still unfinished, and common operational strategies for products, production, and other areas were still lacking.

Inside walls and fittings are still lacking.

A rapidly altered company is like an
incomplete house at roof height:
outside it looks finished, over one-quarter of the building work
completed, but most of the furnishings, which are
essential to the residents' comfort, have not even been started.

To illustrate the building of the interior walls, the following section describes the structural changes and cost cuts in one of the Rauma Oy business areas.

COST CUTTING

Rauma's forestry machine division (currently Timberjack) developed and produced forestry machines in Finland. It became the largest in its field by acquiring three Swedish producers of forestry machines around the change of the 1970s and 1980s. Two of the units were shut down some years later.

The remaining units continued however with overlapping products and overlapping production. They even competed with each other to some extent.

The company was the largest in Europe, but it did not make use of its size. Its business units operated independently, as before. Cooperation took place in the spirit of a match between Finland and Sweden.

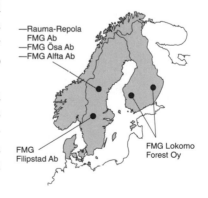

The industry is very sensitive to fluctuations in forest industry conditions. As a result of the heavy cost structure, financial calculations showed that, in the worst case, a loss of FIM 100 million would be incurred in the next recession. Even if delayed, the recession was forecastable.

Rauma group management started an investigation in order to carry out structural changes and to cost cuts. The plan that was devised contained new product and production strategies and the necessary organizational changes. Overlapping products and production would be eliminated to avoid costs and to lighten the structures. Hundreds of people had to be laid off. The change was calculated to reduce costs by FIM 100 million annually and the invested capital by the same amount.

The change program was started and interrupted. Times were still too good and pressures for change too light. A recession and change of leadership were needed before the change was carried out. During the years 1990–1993, the forestry machine group went through the necessary changes and clearly exceeded the targeted savings.

A company can be facing cost cuts for many reasons: after acquisitions, having grown fat, having overdiversified, or having changed its strategy significantly:

- Significant change is always undertaken too late. Changes are carried out only when the pressures have become intense enough.
- Managers have learned to recognize the signs of crisis only by the result, not in advance by other indicators. The actual profitability is far too slow to be an effective crisis indicator.
- It seems that even a bad strategy can succeed in good times and even a good one has problems when the market is experiencing bad times. The forestry machine group produced good results up to the end of 1980s. The supposition was that it was due to a good strategy and skill.
- On the other hand, it had been known for a long time that changes should be made, but it was not known what changes and how they could be accomplished. Once these were known, no decisions could be made.
- The objective is generally to improve profitability by increasing sales or improving efficiency. Creation of structural flexibility has not been an essential concern. The good times lasted too long in the marketplace.
- First, a common strategy has to be created and redundancies eliminated. For those simple methods, quick decisions and a strong executor are required.
- Cutting costs has to be based on a changed strategy. After the cuts, programs to develop cost-effectiveness and quality must be executed.

The manager has to have the courage to carry out structural changes, even globally, when they are necessary, regardless of how hard they are. The change manager has to be able to gain the commitment of the management, whose responsibilities are most affected by the change. These are difficult operations with many differences in culture. The change manager needs skills that are different from those needed in the structural change process of the group, previously described. The change manager must have the following management skills:

- Knowledge of the field
- Global thinking patterns
- Mastery over the cultures of various countries and companies
- Stress resistance
- Ability to execute

Changes of this magnitude are done only under intense pressure. The pressures come from the owners, the market, and the competition. Only exceptional managers are able to create sufficient pressure for change on their own before outside pressures come to bear.

A typical cost-cutting program creates the groundwork for a profitable operation and the development of competitiveness. Cost-cutting programs certainly do not generate additional competitiveness in the market. Neither do they increase cost-effectiveness (profitability). They only cut costs, and mere cost cuts rarely produce the desired long-term results. Costs have been cut and the key figures improved, but profitability and efficiency have actually decreased. Cost cuts have been executed hastily in the wrong areas, and cuts always have significantly negative side effects.

After the cost cuts, a development program must be started to give people hope in the future and to increase confidence in the management. Such a program can produce real improvements in cost-effectiveness and quality. Following is an example of such a change program geared toward development.

DEVELOPMENT OF THE OPERATION

Rosenlew Household Appliance business was sold in 1981 to Electrolux (I moved to Sweden with my family to take over as president of the company.); in exchange, Rosenlew obtained a harvester factory in Sweden. It was one of the first industry rationalization projects between Sweden and Finland. It was also Rosenlew's first company acquisition abroad. Electrolux wanted to concentrate on household appliances, and Rosenlew's objective was to become the world's largest manufacturer of small and medium-size harvesters. Electrolux abandoned the harvester segment, closing one of the factories (Volvo) and selling the other (Aktiv-Fisher) to Rosenlew. The program was executed using the JIT production philosophy and learning from superior units via benchmarking principles. The key indicators were halved or doubled, and enormous losses were converted into a small profit.

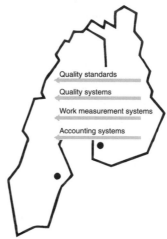

Production of the Swedish harvester models was discontinued. The Rosenlew models were divided between the Finnish and Swedish harvester factories. Rosenlew experienced problems in the transfer of production from Finland to Sweden. Some functions were concentrated, some were decentralized, and some of the production components were manufactured for each other.

Because we discontinued product development and the Swedish harvesters, it was very difficult for the personnel of the Swedish company to accept the decisions. Their newest model was even superior to the Swedish factory's and the product development staff was extremely professional. The Swedish factory had to shut down what was best in the company and thereafter develop what was weakest—namely, production. Its development had been neglected, because the factory had changed ownership three times during the past 10 years. In addition, development resources were absent.

There were dozens of unnecessary positions. The staff knew this, and it caused great uncertainty. The staff also feared the closing of the factory and the concentration of all activity in Finland. The staff's mistrust of the new owner was complete by the beginning of the development project, and problems began to appear accordingly. When significant investments in production were announced, the first precondition for trust was created.

It became apparent that salary costs in Sweden were 25 percent higher than in Finland. We at the Finnish factory set our target to limit the unit costs to the same level as in harvesters produced in Finland. We had to create a factory that could produce the same number of harvesters in four days as the Finnish factory produced in five days. It was obvious that we could not copy the factory and work methods of the Finnish factory.

One of the managers from the group management visited Japan, saw JIT factories, got excited, and got some of us excited, too. We started the project without knowing exactly what we were doing. In 1981, JIT was still a totally unknown concept in Scandinavia. We had only the knowledge that one of us had gained based on what he had seen and heard in Japan.

Our task was not made easier by the fact that we had to interrupt the introduction of the Finnish harvester. We had to dig up the tools for discontinued harvesters and produce an additional two series of two models.

In the old factory, the batch-type production was more storage and transportation than serial manufacture. We tore down unused buildings and linked the two remaining ones. In the new streamlined JIT factory, the throughput time fell from months to 10 days.

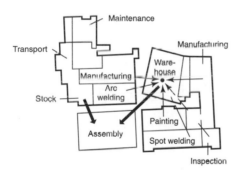

The Bach Production was more storage and transportation than manufacturing

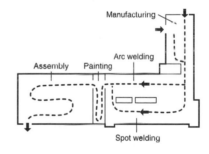

Streamlining of operation

When we finally finished the factory, we could not get it to operate. The factory looked as it should, but it did not work. We had copied what we had seen in Japan. We had not understood what made factories work. JIT was no longer an unknown concept. We read articles and books that showed what we were doing wrong. We realized that a JIT factory is not managed by the same control methods as our old factory.

Many of the required control systems had been started, but not as speedily as they should have been. We were in a hurry to develop them and put them into use. Luckily, we had the sense to learn from those superior to us. We studied Japanese JIT knowledge from books, we got to know ASEA Kanban control experiments in Sweden, and we learned the standard time and quality systems from Finland. We learned the salary system from Volvo and four other companies, management principles from SAS, and financial training systems from Saab Flygmotors.

Development of the JIT philosophy was primarily a process of unlearning the old idea of serial production. Since our models were in Japan and books and courses on the subject were not available, we learned too many things through trial and error. When we finally finished the factory, it contained almost all the principles we found from the book written by the JIT guru, Richard J. Schonberger, toward the end of the project.

Throughput time had fallen from months to 10 days, productivity had been multiplied by two and a half, the inventory turnover of the component and shop floor inventory had risen from 2 to 10, and enormous losses had been converted into a small profit.

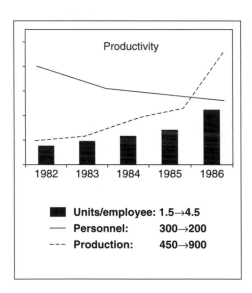

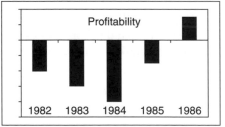

Above all else, the project taught us that a functional JIT model would have been of excellent use. We would have known what we were doing and we would have been able to explain it to others as well. In addition, involving everybody was difficult, as we were unable to explain where we were heading and why. (At a later stage, we documented a JIT model that we had used in later projects.)

On the other hand, because of other issues, we were often in a state of near chaos. Conditions changed rapidly and plans were revised. Changing conditions is an inevitable fact in all major projects that just have to be accepted. In certain situations, it even has advantages. If there is a development model available that can be applied, it is much easier to get back on track and regain control.

Required Management Skills

In a change aimed at development, the change manager requires skills that may be different from those in the preceding examples. He or she is required to have a knowledge of the products, technology, and processes. He or she is required to have a knowledge of development models and of organization of development activity and the ability to work toward long-term goals. In particular, the change manager must be able to motivate people and to get everybody involved and committed.

During the project, the company ownership changed, the product range changed, and the manufacturing technology and production philosophy were renewed. These changes were not merely physical but required a complete change in thinking. All this took years.

A company can get to the point at which rapid improvements are necessary. However, the company has a very limited time to execute them, and there is no time for significant changes. Then the question arises: "Can we together produce the extra effort that would suffice for the necessary improvement and overcome the crisis?" The following case answers this question.

An Extra Team Effort

The Riihimäki glass works had been discontinued and merged with the Ahlstrom Karhula Packaging Glass Works. After the merger, the company produced nearly all of the packaging glass needed in Finland.

The operating principles of the merged glass works had differed considerably from each other. Their company cultures were almost opposite of one another, and the merger resulted in enormous problems in quality and profitability. The integrated quality and profitability of the two operations was well below the level they had been capable of independently.

The situation went on for a year and a half. Customers were dissatisfied, looking for alternative suppliers abroad, and profitability was miserable. The situation was not made easier by the fact that deep conflicts existed between sections of the operation and between management and staff. The production manager had been changed twice. Something had to be done and quickly.

When I took over as production manager for the company, our task was to bring quality and capacity to their earlier level. There was no time for big changes. There was know-how in the organization. It just did not appear in customer satisfaction and profitability. The only way left was to bring out the know-how. Based on this assumption, we started to make a plan.

In the course of three weeks, we succeeded in preparing a plan for reaching our objectives during the following three months, in collaboration with the personnel. The plan was given the name Operation Straighten Out. The following figure lists the four cornerstones of the program, the contents of which had been agreed upon jointly with the personnel.

The central elements of the program were mutually agreed-upon targets, open target settings, monitoring, and rewarding for results. The program was simply based on the idea that, when we simultaneously straighten things out, leave the quarrels behind, and get all staff members to do their share as well as they can, the results will be unprecedented. I used a program I had executed at Rosenlew Packaging for rapidly and radically increasing the plastic bag production as a benchmark for myself and others.

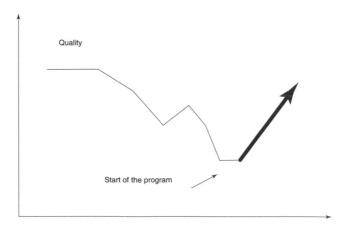

Quality

Start of the program

Our objective is satisfied customers.

With perfect and consistent quality and short, flexible, and reliable delivery times.

At a competitive price, too.

We will raise the acceptance percentage to 84 percent.

We are dissatisfied with our quality, but we will be proud of it someday.

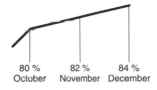

| 80 % | 82 % | 84 % |
| October | November | December |

We will certainly experience setbacks, but we won't let them discourage us.

I will take care of my share.

Without prejudice, creating good conditions, foreseeing problems, and with a strong performance.

I will have a responsible attitude toward my work, I will be willing to cooperate, use all my professional skills and will constantly develop my skills.

There will be rewards for everyone for success.

We will gain customer confidence and come a step closer to a more secure job.

We will get our work to run smoothly, we will feel better, and we will be proud of our work and our results.

Operation Straighten Out

Management, department heads, and each department prepared a list of measures to which they were ready to commit themselves. We monitored the progress in joint sessions, in which it was emphasized that we were responsible, primarily to each other, for reaching the objectives. It was our own jobs that were at stake. We reported to each  other about matters, not to the management, as we had been used to doing. The marketing manager often opened the session instead of the general manager or production manager. He explained customer reactions.

In this way, we tried to break the "employer-employee" setup and change it to "company-customer" setup. We applied many other procedures in order to emphasize the importance of the common responsibility and joint effort.

Required Management Skills

In change processes of this type, managers must be able to gain everyone's trust and belief in the important effects of an extra team effort. Managers must put themselves on the line and show that they will carry their share of the program.

The targets were almost reached during the planned three months. This type of program produced quick and significant results, but not necessarily lasting ones. To accomplish a lasting change and continuous improvement, the program described in the following section was initiated. Its primary goal was to catalyze the continuous improvement of the whole personnel.

CONTINUOUS IMPROVEMENT

We admire major jumps in improvement. Their achievers are heroes. However, major leaps such as these are not recommended. They require great professionalism and contain considerable risks. Despite the need, a big leap can prove to be too much to accomplish within a reasonable time period.

The continuous improvement was initiated at Glass Works with the following rules:

- Each department must be able to identify 10 of its worst problems.
- The department must know to choose one area to be improved and to define an improvement team of three to five people for it
- The problem must be possible to solve within one to three months.
- When the problem is solved, it will go off the list.
- The next problem area will be selected for improvement.

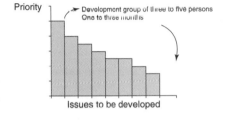

Everybody participated in problem identification, and the search took place using double team techniques. Three people were trained to chair the double team meetings. One of them (the best of the floor managers) was freed for six months to support the start-up of the continuous improvement program full-time. Everyone was expected to participate.

In the first stage, the targets for improvement (for example, "improving the quality of the molds") were chosen by each department independently. In addition, management started projects that concerned the entire production process and in which everyone participated (for example, a "chip killing program" for guaranteeing the absolute purity of the products and "how to become the best shift" by benchmarking the best shift in the plant).

Improvement by continuous small steps has to be created within the company. Every major change has to follow a path of continuous improvement. Nothing stands still; a company either develops or declines. Through continuous improvement, many of the seeds of more significant and dramatic changes can be eliminated.

Continuous improvement is managed differently than is the management of a major change. The following lists some of these points.

Required Management Skills

- Participation by everyone
- Improvement of what already exists
- Management attention to people and processes, rather than to results and innovations
- Continuous improvement comparison with continuous production
- Definition of standards and exceeding them to create new standards
- Improvement training
- Processes that are comprehensible and visible
- Improvement in the direction of the production flow
- The customer as the next stage
- Continuous follow-up
- Appreciation of even small improvements

The culture of continuous improvement is not born in a moment or by itself. It arises as a strategic decision by the company management with the need for corresponding investments. But what improvements are we talking about?

Continuous Learning

Development is learning. Continuous learning guarantees continuous development, and thus companies survive. Learning twice as quickly the competitor leads to success. If we want to accelerate the improvement, we have to accelerate the learning.

Corporate learning starts from personal learning. A company improves only when each person improves. A company may have significant amounts of individual know-how without its being reflected in customer satisfaction and profitability. It becomes apparent only when people learn the same things. That is organizational learning.

As managers, we have had it easy by sending our subordinates to courses to improve their personal knowledge and skills. This will still be necessary. However, imagine the following situation.

A manager is given the task of cutting the throughput time of a tender by half, from four to two weeks. She finds out that the tender goes through three other internal departments, two subcontractors, and one government office. A total of 15 people participate in the tender. Cutting in half happens by *learning* new ways to operate; learning can also be supported with technical solutions. The problem of learning is not solved by sending one's own subordinates to courses. It has to be solved following the principles of process improvement, in which all 15 people participate.

Required Management Skills

Organizing learning opportunities is a new challenge for managers and supervisors. They have to understand the correlation between success and learning. They must learn to organize conditions in which learning speed increases and to continuously inspire themselves and everybody else in the continuous learning—they must also make it happen. A learning organization must be created.

SKILLS REQUIRED IN CHANGE MANAGEMENT

A manager must recognize the nature of a required change and manage the change according to its nature. The company must be able to achieve both the budget goals and the long-term development goals. Only a few companies are capable of that. It is a skill that sets the winners apart from those that are mediocre. It also separates the real leaders from the bureaucrats.

The skill of continuous development is primarily a question of attitude. Do we develop to earn or earn to develop? Which one are we talking about? The following comment is heard: "We can't afford to develop. Just now we have to concentrate on making profit." Development is something that is done if we have the time and money. However, our customers constantly demand better and cheaper products, our owners ever higher earnings, our staff better wages, society more tax revenues, and so on. Consequently, we should say, "Our main task is development. To do that, we must also have other activities and income in order to generate the capital for improvement."

Chapter 7

SYSTEMATIC FRAMEWORK AND SPECIFIC TARGETS

If you want to achieve something of importance, you have to undertake it decisively and with a plan. You have to be systematic in your improvement. Nevertheless, development often takes place even in chaos. Chaos is inevitable, sometimes even necessary, at some stage of the development program. Chaos may give rise to the best and the most creative solutions. However, you will not remain in chaos permanently, if you carefully follow the guidelines in this chapter.

QUICK NOTES
Pages 247–258: Read headings, text boxes and the text in *italics*.

IDENTIFY THE TRUE NEED FOR CHANGE

Without an accepted need, there will be no action. Recognize the need coming from outside, and motivate others to believe in the need for change.

Help everyone to see the need at a three-year distance. Maintain this need throughout the change process. A visible and accepted need is the precondition for the initiation and continuous progress of the development program.

> If there is no identified need for change, a development program will not be launched.

There is always three times more opportunity for development than what there is time for. We undertake only what we consider to be necessary. How does a lasting and visible need for change come about? Is it created by changes in market conditions? Yes, if they are typical for the industry and they are prepared for by internal changes. Most of the time, that is not the case. An already started program is interrupted when the next boom starts and forces are concentrated on sales and generating capacity.

A lasting need is not created by the manager's fascination with new ideas not by the obligations of a union agreement, by the owner's new profit requirements, by a management bonus system, or by the dissatisfaction of the personnel. A lasting need comes from changes outside the company. It comes from changing customer expectations, competitive conditions, environmental demands, or other external changes.

The need must be understandable and accepted by people. A need that motivates the manager to start the change is not necessarily enough to become a lasting driver for others. The manager must be able to recognize this need and to communicate it to the whole organization. The need must also be consciously canvassed in order to keep change happening.

CREATE A CHALLENGING, INSPIRING VISION

Vision is our common image of the state of the future as we desire it. It is our common conception of what we want to become. Our vision is the source of our inspiration; all personnel see themselves in it and understand their own shares in its realization.

> Development without vision feels forced and meaningless—it leads to boredom and stagnation.

If a significant change is to be achieved, economic measures and rational reasoning are not enough for a vision. They will have changed before the change has been accomplished. Targets based on calculations are adjusted downward, when the first difficulties appear. A vision must also include emotional stimuli. A vision coming from the heart is not (immediately) compromised.

An effective vision is like the desire to obtain a pretty cottage on a lake surrounded by clear waters and forest, something most people want to acquire. The manager has to create this picture and convey it to everyone.

A vision is a final target at which efforts are directed. It avoids the definition of the means. On that opinions may differ. Take enough time to create the vision and its expression. Do not create it only to correspond to your own desires. It must not be the source of inspiration only for you; It must correspond to everyone's wishes.

Avoid discussion on the means. You can agree on that at the next stage. On the other hand, it is difficult to share the vision, if one has no idea how it can be reached.

SHOW YOUR COMMITMENT THROUGH YOUR INVOLVEMENT AND INTEREST IN LEARNING

Commitment means continuous, active involvement. It is doing your share, anticipating problems, and supporting other people. Commitment is also knowing how to develop and continuously learn. At their best, managers set an example and act as the development coach of their organization, showing the way.

> A development program without management commitment cannot gain staff commitment.

Management must be committed to its vision, targets, and plans. Commitment is not only endorsing a cause and speaking on its behalf. It is not only allocating resources and rewarding performances. It is not only leading the development team.

Commitment is learning methods that enable target achievement. It is a constant evaluation of the adequacy of resources, of the development know-how within the organization and the active influencing of these factors. It is a continuous allocation of resources between the operational and the development activities. It is ongoing support of development resources to overcome the worst obstacles. It supports constant communication and sensing of problems in advance. Commitment means changing your own thinking and sometimes even your values and showing the changes visibly.

> One of my key roles is to identify areas of ABB where management has become complacent or where activity seems to be drifting. When I spot such an area, I shake things up to create an environment of learning even in operations two or three levels below.
>
> *Göran Lindahl, a member of ABB's top-level management team*

Commitment must be seen, felt, and heard. It must be visible in your time allocation and in your calendar. Managers are not judged by what they say but by what they do.

BE READY TO COMPROMISE

You cannot do everything at once. Something has to give. Abandoning ship can be permanent or temporary. Sometimes it is sensible to abandon budgetary targets, growth, product ranges, customers, flexibility, an entire development program, or some internal routines.

If you are not ready to give up some things, the development chokes.

Change programs are often started only when the organization is already under heavy pressure. The problems have grown and accumulated. All the organization's time is taken by the struggle to stay afloat. If we are already doing the maximum amount of overtime, how can we squeeze in another development program? Two of them are already running—something has to give. Abandonment means weeding out products and customers and outsourcing or even shutting down a production unit. Abandonment can also mean barring engineering changes for half a year, leaping over one planning cycle, or making an accurate profit report only every two months during a whole year.

Often some of the operational targets must be abandoned during the development program. If the time and energy are consumed by internal changes, do not aim for strong growth. If you have targeted a new quality and/or productivity level, do not require a high degree of flexibility until those operational targets have been met. Wait until the quality and profitability targets have been met. If the development requires investments and recruitment, the costs have to be approved in the budget.

Allocating resources and energy to an extensive change means abandoning something else. A showy abandonment of something that had a higher priority earlier, even temporarily, is also the best sign of management commitment. The change manager has to stop the game and set new rules, so that making the change can begin.

Raise Your Targets

Discover the magnitude of your development needs and what others have already achieved. Set unrealistically high but achievable targets. Only tough targets are interesting. Only their achievement means realizing significant visions.

Development without targets does not lead to anything worthwhile.

Many have demonstrated that reaching unrealistic targets is possible. They have been reached, for instance, by MTM and JIT methods, modularization, process development, and benchmarking. Doubling returns demands a totally different solution than 10 percent to 20 percent targets. Radical improvements are created only by radical changes. Required solutions are unearthed only with tough targets.

Start benchmarking processes. Investigate how others have achieved their challenging targets. Lower your target only when a clear basis for surrender exists. It is better to improve the chances of success than to lower your targets.

In setting targets, be bold but not stupid. Recognize what is impossible. In certain situations, high targets are not even necessary. You can achieve a marked competitive advantage even with a smaller improvement. If the company is being prepared for sale, positive cashflow may be sufficient. Even demanding targets are achieved one step at a time.

If you have been entrusted with the execution of a challenging change program, find out what the expectations really are. What is intended with them? What are the conditions? Who sets them? In what time frame do they have to be executed? Is there a consensus? Have the targets been explained to everyone? Are others ready to do their share? Can the targets change? You will be surprised by the variety of perceptions people have about targets.

PREPARE CHALLENGING PLANS

Targets are mere dreams without plans. The planning of development has to be as natural and unconditional as that of budgets and production programs. We compete with the quality of the plans and the speed of execution. Make the timetable unrealistic but still possible. Develop a sense of urgency.

Without plans, development does not really start.

You should organize your development project for ventures that have all the signs of a good project. Define the project organization, targets, responsibilities, and powers, as well as timetables, resources, and monitoring and reward systems. You are not competing only with plans but also with the speed of their execution. Make the timetable extremely tight but still possible. The task will take the time it is planned for. Start benchmarking processes, for that is how others have achieved their high targets in less time. Lower the time target only when it has become obvious that it cannot be met.

Differences in development speeds are multiple. Reaching the same target in a year instead of two certainly requires a different solution. What is crucial is not the amount of resources but their quality. Have the resources been chosen correctly? Do the persons selected for the development have sufficient motivation and development skills, and have they been given the tools to succeed? The solutions that bring speed are found only with demanding time limits, often only under intense pressure. The daily business and development activity always competes for the same resources and usually for the best ones. In the project plan, these resources have to be allocated and their use constantly monitored.

We often have no development plans. Why? Because it is not necessarily easy. The organization may not have the experience. If you are not capable of making an exact plan for three years, plan in shorter periods, the nearest periods with great accuracy. Improve the accuracy of the next period during the preceding period. Give a clear approval for the preceding period and a clear order to start the next one. You can learn many practical "planning tricks." Planning can be learned only by doing it. Plans and their follow-up tell us whether we are on the development path. At the same time, they function as a feedback system for learning.

TIMING IS EVERYTHING

The winners are those who spot the needs and possibilities for change before others do. You have to group change processes chronologically, organize them in steps, perform each step in the right order, and avoid running too many processes at the same time. Time management has become one of the most critical competitive factors.

> Without the right timing, gains from development can remain marginal.

The right timing is critical to change processes. Many issues are interconnected. Mastering the process does not happen without mastering the product, and mastering the product hangs in the air without a clear business idea. Product development and production must happen simultaneously to ascertain production-friendliness and to reduce the throughput time of the product development process. In a global company, the product range and product structure significantly impact the development of the company structure and organization.

Simultaneous cost-cutting (such as downsizing) and development work rarely succeed. When you start a rationalization program that is considered necessary, you should simultaneously present the development plans. In this way, you show what has to be done and that there is life after rationalization. As Jan Carlzon, the CEO of SAS, stated to his personnel, "Our profitability is in crisis, but we are not, since we know what we should do."

Do not try too much at the same time. Do not start a large internal development program concurrently with a new product launch or with a large-capacity increase. Do not start too many development programs at the same time. If you do, make sure that the burden of development is evenly allocated or that the development programs support one another.

When you bring a new concept to the firm, try to tie it to something already familiar, accepted, and already running. Emphasize to your people that it does not mean new targets but tools with which the targets already set will be easier to reach.

IDENTIFY AND EXPLOIT DEVELOPMENT RESOURCES

The amount of development resources around you is almost unlimited. The question is if you have the ability to identify and exploit them. Development resources include you yourself, everyone in the firm, external experts, business organizations, national and international development programs, financial institutions, your customers, your suppliers, and your benchmarking partners.

Tough targets without resources lead only to frustration and nonproductive work.

If you apply for the local quality award, you might be able to get quality award analysts to work almost for free for you for several weeks each in order to make a reliable evaluation of your strengths and weaknesses. ISO 9000 auditors also work as development resources.

Successful managers recognize potential development resources and are able to make use of them. Successful firms have strong know-how of their own. It is strengthened continuously and developed by learning from those who have the best skills and by using those who know most.

If the aforementioned resources are not enough, you can always acquire more. In every firm, there is an unlimited amount of development resources. It is a question of recognizing them, choosing people that are skillful enough to exploit, and of knowing how to manage change. How often do we hear, "We don't have the money for development"? It would be better to say, "We can't afford not to develop, but we don't know how."

One principle of Japanese firms is to maintain a constant overcapacity. This creates both functional flexibility and continuous development. Nothing comes for free. You have to invest. The best resources must be invested in development.

Your most important development resource is yourself. Regardless of your firm's organization and job distribution, you are the development manager of your firm.

INVEST IN DEVELOPMENT PROFESSIONALS

Development belongs to every job description. In addition, full-time development professionals are necessary. They can be outside or inside experts who continuously develop themselves to stay at the top of their own area of expertise.

Without development professionals, development remains a hobby.

We would be fooling ourselves if we were to believe that first-class results are achieved with second-class development know-how. Product developers are development professionals. Development of information systems requires its own professionals. Development professionals are needed also for the development of the business idea, product management, business processes, and personal skills or learning.

In Japanese industrial firms, the relation of the number of product development engineers to process development engineers is 1:1. The corresponding figure in the Western countries is 10:1. This is one of the main explanations for the supremacy of the Japanese process over those of Western firms.

Significant new ideas do not take root in a firm without sufficient study of theory, or finding out who masters the substance best, and how it can be applied to the firm's own operational environment. The kind of persons we need are those who will become the leading experts in their fields. We need people who are willing to learn new things continuously and are not afraid of the adversities involved in showing direction to others.

Managers must be one of the development professionals in their firms. They are the chief architects of the business idea and the development of strategies. They are the primus motors of the necessary development programs and the guarantors of their continuity. Managers must have the skills and the willingness to delegate operational activity. Otherwise, they will not be able to perform their most important function—the development of the firm. In addition to their time allocation, they must know and sufficiently master development models by which substantial changes and continuous development can be achieved.

PROVIDE DEVELOPMENT TRAINING

Train and learn from the best. Use the best experts. Select proven development systems. Make use of existing know-how and transferred experience. You must take the role as the principal coach of development. Give responsibility. Trust your people and motivate, train, appreciate, and reward them.

> Tough development demands without development know-how creates only stress and anxiety.

"I don't have the time." In essence, we do not know what should be done. Generally, we do what we know how to do. We explain our lack of know-how by lack of time. We do not admit that we do not know how and we do not have the time or will to learn.

Even a pressing need, exciting visions, and challenging targets do not take us far, if we lack the development know-how. You must organize benchmarking processes in order to learn how successful organizations develop their operations. Send your staff members to high-level courses for inspiration and learning. Acquire the best books and magazines. Motivate everyone to read and study. Send your subordinates to teach others. Recruit the best experts, and make sure that their know-how stays in the firm.

Act as a coach who is also a player. Set an example as someone who has the desire and practical knowledge to learn continuously. It is the duty of a development professional to become the best in the field and to share knowledge with others. Select developers from those who are the most driven. Give development the same appreciation as performance. Give challenging development tasks, trust people, and reward even a good try. Support the sharing of development experiences within the organization.

Development is not necessarily difficult. The way we learn to develop may be difficult. Development must be organized in such a way that development becomes a learnable routine. Learning will be faster and the possibility of replication will improve if you apply proven development models. Aim for continuous development in small steps. This creates repetition, which is the basic precondition for learning. If development projects are always organized according to these targets, learning will take place. Investing in development training demonstrates management's commitment to the development process and gives the process credibility for the staff.

ORGANIZE FOR CHANGE

The organization has to support the change process. It has to change according to the requirements of the change process. Responsibilities and authority have to be in balance for the execution of the change to succeed.

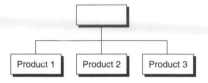

> Without authority and responsibility, the change will not happen.

An organization is not a means in and of itself. It is there for a task and an objective. The organization must be able to change when the tasks and objectives change. An organization is normally unable to change by itself, however, and even less able to discard useless elements. The task of the change manager is to change the organization's limits and power structures.

An organizational change may be necessary at the planning stage of the change process. It can support the planning and accelerate the start of the process. At the latest, the organization should be checked before starting execution. A change of organization does not, however, produce change. A physical reallocation of resources is more decisive than an organizational change; know-how is more important than authority.

An organization that supports change is not necessarily the best one for managing operational business activities. For instance, the change could require a centralized organization and managing the business a decentralized organization. The change might require an organization by product lines, whereas the effective use of capital might require a functional organization. Changing the organization must be possible as the change program progresses. Organizational changes should not come as surprises, but they are a part of change program planning.

Reorganizing is also a good way to free up development resources. Be prepared for personnel changes as well. Some managers simply cannot handle change management. One of the most common reasons that the change does not start is a change resistance in the structure of the organization. The essential requirement is to get a "development organization" and a "line organization" to interact effectively.

Chapter 8

LEADERSHIP BRINGS CHANGE

Development plans are not realized by plans alone. Change is not created merely with tough targets. Change must be managed. On the other hand, without careful planning, change management alone will not succeed. No manager's skills, energy, and time would be enough.

Change demands leadership. Good leadership is simple, naive, and from the heart. But who would like to be simple, naive, and emotional? That is why we make it complicated, stiff, formal, cold, and matter-of-fact. This chapter will show that a good change manager is a "driven leader" who leads the change.

The manager must have the desire to lead the change but also must have the skills to get out of the way of change, once the change has begun.

QUICK NOTES

Pages 259–272: Read headings, text boxes, and the text in *italics*.

The Driven Leader Has Vision and Can Pass It On

Driven leaders have the ability to see, hear, and feel what they want. They can also transmit this picture, sound, and feeling to others.

> Unless driven leaders can communicate their visions, the visions will inspire only the leaders themselves.

We experience and learn in various ways. Some people see things, some hear, and some can experience things best through their feelings. A driven leader is able to define desires through a vision and can visualize it through images, sounds, and feelings in a way that everyone can understand.

The driven leader is able to distinguish different sides of the vision, making it seem, sound, or feel exciting to everyone. One person dreams about the beauty of a cottage, another about the serenity of the surrounding nature, and still another about the comfort of the cottage furniture.

Make visions simple and understandable. Managers often do not do that. Some people believe that, if they speak of simple things in a simple way, others will think they are simple.

THE DRIVEN LEADER HAS DESIRE

The driven leader has a powerful will to make change happen and dares to be more ambitious than others. This desire is authentic. It is convincing. You can see, hear, and feel it. It sticks to everyone. Desire is contagious.

Without the desire of the driven leader, common desires are not created.

Enterprises have generally started from the owner's product idea, which he or she had the burning desire to realize and bring to market. The desire has often overcome warnings, financial difficulties, and other limitations. A sufficient desire has driven these founders over the worst hurdles.

In many firms, this will of the owner, this burning desire, is still enough to maintain ongoing development. A driven leader dares to desire more than others; the desire is genuine and can be demonstrated. In big companies, managers should inherit this original strong desire and convey it to others.

The Driven Leader Listens to Others

The driven manager does not push only his or her own desires but also finds out what others want. The driven manager builds the organization on people's strengths and positive desires.

If you do not want to listen to others, others do not want to listen to you.

The easiest way to start a change is to recognize what others want and to make it possible for their wishes to come true. Ask them such things as, "What are your ideas and proposals you wanted to get through but the management hasn't approved?" Start the change from there. Start especially with changes on which everyone agrees. With them, you build a solid base for the next series of changes. Only very seldom do people want the wrong things, yet not everyone can recognize which matters are the most important for the company's success.

The driven leader gets everyone involved by realizing their desires. The driven leader has everyone on his or her side: "I see important things are developing here. My desires are being taken into account. I want to hear what the manager has to say."

The development picks up speed and can continue in matters that are important for success and in the driven leader's desires. Granted, those desires have been changed. Part of others' desires seem new, interesting, and really important. It is easy to agree with them.

If you go in as a new leader to describe your fine new plans to the organization, find out what others want, what they are already doing, and what they have already accomplished. Pushing ideas as new and your own only irritates others and can even prevent the acceptance of your whole plan.

THE DRIVEN LEADER SEEKS CHANGE IN HIM- OR HERSELF

Driven leaders constantly seek to develop and improve themselves. Thus, they set a good example for others. This, in turn, plants in others the desire to change. The firm can develop only if each person develops him- or herself.

> If you do not want to change yourself, why should others do so?

Driven leaders start with themselves. Driven leaders do not assume that others will change if they have not intended to change themselves. They evaluate their own routines and think openly. They make changes in a way that everyone will notice.

Driven leaders know that development is learning. Learning is something that can be seen. Driven leaders want to show themselves being the first to learn and set an example to others. We always imagine that others have to change, not ourselves. The programs we start do not concern ourselves. They concern our subordinates. Others have to learn; they have to become like us.

If you want to start the change from the center of the universe, start from yourself.

THE DRIVEN LEADER RISES TO A CHALLENGE

The driven leader transforms a vision into an absorbing challenge. Challenges are tangible. They give people an opportunity to use all of their skills and to develop themselves continuously.

Visions without personal challenges do not take flight.

A driven leader knows that the mere desire is not enough. No matter how much you want, you cannot achieve the change. The driven leader deals out responsibilities and authority, while giving others the opportunity to learn and develop themselves. The driven leader gives opportunities to those who want to show their skills, opportunities to manage an important change process and opportunities for advancement. The driven leader also gives them opportunities to succeed, but also to make mistakes and to learn from them. The challenges provided by the driven leader are so interesting that people volunteer for them.

THE DRIVEN LEADER FINDS CHALLENGE LOVERS

The driven leader can pinpoint the kind of people who are ready to take on challenges. He or she makes sure that the challenge lovers get whatever tools they need to get the job done correctly.

Without challenge lovers, driven leaders have no allies.

One of the key qualities of the driven leader is to find challenge lovers unafraid of anything. They are generally persons who have both line responsibility and responsibility for the planned change program. These persons can be either profit center or department heads already appointed or process owners. They can be young "lions" who are appointed to a more responsible position that includes important development challenges. These challenge lovers can be found at different levels of the organization and from different units of the Group.

Management has to know its staff well enough to be constantly aware of hungry challenge lovers who long for challenges. You have to search for them systematically and develop them for responsible line and development duties. It is not enough that challenge lovers are good business leaders or good superiors. They also have to master development methods and the change management skills. These combinations are rare.

When a competent challenge lover is found, he or she is generally one of the so-called indispensable persons of his or her current superior. Management has to have enough courage to reassign such a person where needed at any given time, in the interest of the whole firm.

The driven leader does not trust only the power of challenge and inspiration. He or she personally ensures that the challenge lover has the necessary ingredients of success: professional skill, time, resources, and training opportunities.

CHALLENGE LOVERS GET THINGS DONE

They can plan, but they are, above all else, doers.
They make things happen. They are unafraid. They
work quickly. They make mistakes, but they recog-
nize their mistakes and correct them.

Without challenge lovers, nobody takes responsibility for execution.

Challenge lovers meet challenges head on. They love a challenge. They take it personally, and they ignite this spirit in others. Challenge lovers have powers and the courage to use them. Because people want to work with them they produce results quickly. When things get stuck somewhere, the challenge lover is there to help.

Challenge lovers know that, if you move fast, you make mistakes. If you move slowly, you make mistakes, anyway, but there is no time left to correct them. Making mistakes can generate reactions that help you better understand the issues at stake. Find out where the limits are and what people really think. Challenge lovers are responsible not only for results but also for people.

Challenge lovers are not afraid of mistakes, but neither do they take unnecessary risks. That is why they have several plans in reserve. Make it clear to everyone what is meant by acceptable mistakes and by learning from mistakes. Many make mistakes but do not notice them and never learn from them.

Everyone Must Get Involved

Everyone must be a part of change. Everyone must belong to it. Only participation creates understanding and commitment. Make use of expertise and bring it to fruition. Train to develop. Turn producers into developers. The will to participate is much greater than you think.

> If everybody is not involved, the project will stall because of the resistance to change.

The execution of a major change program requires extensive participation to make use of all know-how, to make sure everyone is committed, and to execute the plan. These are conditions *sine qua non,* if you have challenging targets.

When perfection is your target, everyone is a "key person." A real JIT approach cannot work without the participation, understanding, and acceptance of everyone concerned. The processes will work when every internal supplier-customer relationship works. A strategy will be realized only when everyone knows how it can be used at his or her own workplace. The operation is customer-oriented when everyone knows what it means for him or her. "Everyone involved" does not mean only company personnel. It can also include the owners, lenders, associates, society, and even the company's customers.

Many have superb professional expertise and are proud of it. Harness this energy and channel it into development work. People are not problems; they are opportunities.

When you try to get everyone involved, you will encounter many difficulties.

Reluctance may result from the management history of the firm. Participative management may raise doubts in the beginning, if people are not accustomed to it. It is difficult to involve people in something that they do not understand or accept. Passivity is the most common symptom of resistance to change. The transition from a doer to a developer also requires development training. When you start to involve people, do not give up too easily. Results do not come overnight. When you start participative management, it is difficult to deviate from it in an accepted way. If you use line people for development work, reserve their time in cycles of at least a day. Development "on the side" is self-deception.

CHAMPIONS HAVE WHAT IT TAKES

They are individuals who push for change with everything they have. They believe in what they are doing and have the determination to set the last stone in its place. Champions can be found every-where in the organization. Identify them; give them support.

Without fighters, new ideas are neither started nor finished.

Important new matters will not take root in a firm without dedicated people. These "champions" have been used when firms are introducing, for instance, the MTM technique, JIT production philosophy, process management, benchmarking procedures, and quality management.

Champions are persons who are destined to become leading experts in their field. They are unafraid of adversities, what showing the way to others implies. They familiarize themselves with theory and locate the people who know most about the matter and those who have the most knowledge. They want to share their know-how with others. They are excited about their cause, get along with others, and inspire people.

Champions believe in their cause and act even against the will of the management. Despite all the resistance and prejudice, these champions fight for the approval of their cause. The level of their commitment is the highest of all. They are people who know that all the pieces have to fall into place before a particular operational philosophy works. A champion is the kind of person who fights on when others give up. They refuse to accept things "halfway." They are fanatically committed to bringing things to completion.

Management should identify these fanatical change agents and encourage and support them. (Regrettably, often they are considered troublemakers in the organization who confuse already established management principles.)

PREPARE FOR CONFLICTS

When people take things seriously, it creates conflict. Do not be afraid of conflicts—look at them as opportunities. However, avoid personal conflicts. They only take up energy. If needed, intervene.

If no conflicts arise, no results are achieved.

Superior vs. subordinate, superior vs. superior, colleague vs colleague, department vs. department: in all organizations, both people and issues collide. If a change program has been initiated and you have not encountered a single problem, you should be worried. The change has not been started yet. The first significant problem or conflict is a sign of the beginning of change. A change is always a conflict to some extent. It may be a conflict between people's perceptions, even values. It may be a conflict between old and new ideas. Important changes mean conflicts.

Accept and explain to others that conflicts are one of the natural features of change, that they need not be afraid of or run away from them. In certain situations, there is even reason to create conflicts in order to uncover real opinions: present unfinished, sometimes even false plans to people. People react, tell their opinions, and you get feedback to improve your plan. If you knowingly create a conflict situation, reserve enough time for its resolution.

Conflicts between people absorb energy. On the other hand, their successful resolution creates energy. Maintain a balance. In a well-functioning project, conflicts exist, but not quarrels. Especially useless are conflicts in which people argue about people rather than issues. The worst is if conflicts accumulate and are not solved or even noticed.

INFORM AND COMMUNICATE

If you do not inform people, they imagine negative responses to their unanswered questions. Information about where you are headed minimizes opposition and speeds up the change process. Only through ongoing communication can you figure out what people think. Jan Carlzon, SAS CEO stated, "If people have enough information, they can't avoid taking responsibility."

A lack of information creates harmful rumors.

Tauno Matomäki, Rauma Group CEO said, "For some change is like sitting in the back seat of a car. There is a solid wall between the passenger and the driver. Seen through the back window familiar scenes are left behind and the view through the side windows is flickering and blurred."

Include information and communication as one of the tasks of the project plan. Define its various forms and the responsible persons. Specify to whom, where, when, and what should be informed. Communication happens through all possible formal and informal means. The change manager must constantly wander around, inform, listen, and communicate. People want answers to these questions: How will the change affect me? Will my job be maintained? Do I have to learn new things? Will I learn? Will I survive? Many questions require personal discussions.

Do not rely only on the initial provision of information. Keep everyone aware of the progress and the results of the project. Do not make the mistake of making pep talks to big crowds, no matter how charismatic you might be. On those occasions, no communication happens. Do not cultivate too many slogans popular with management. You excite only yourself. People want to hear concrete messages. Generally, people want to get the information concerning themselves from their closest superior. Organize the information flow accordingly. Improve the information and communication skills of everybody in a leading position. The wildest rumors start from those not directly concerned, so inform even them. Information does not concern only your own personnel. The information must also reach the customers, the suppliers, the owners, society, and the most varied stakeholder and interest groups. No matter how much you communicate, it never seems to be enough.

MAINTAIN THE NEED FOR CHANGE

Without pressure, there is no action. You must motivate both yourself and others to believe that a change is necessary. Help everyone to see the need three years ahead. Maintain this need for change throughout the change process.

> Without pressures, needs, or inspiration, the change does not progress.

Poor profitability may create sufficient pressure to initiate a change program. This pressure will suffice only for a year, no longer. People get used to poor profitability. Some do not even believe it. The operation seems to go on, anyway. Quick and visible changes have not been made. If any, they are dismissals, and actual development has not been started. Management's energy level is low, and because of the dismissals the atmosphere is bad and people are reluctant to participate in development.

Tense conditions create fears and anxieties. For that reason, you need to convert this tension as rapidly as possible into the excitement of development. The sooner the necessary dismissals have been done, the sooner people will feel secure and willing to participate in change and development. As development know-how grows, the enthusiasm for development grows, culminating when the first results are recognized and rewards are given for them.

The need for change can be maintained by constantly monitoring competitors and customer needs. We must do benchmarking both within and outside our own field and we need to find completely new methods and procedures. The basic idea is to look out from the firm, so that we can see the real needs for change, as well as the opportunities. Everybody gets a clear picture of the fact that we are in a constant race with the target to satisfy customer needs better than the competition and to do it efficiently. The clear and open presentation of the owners' expectations must not be underestimated, either, even if they seem to influence primarily the management, rather than the other parts of the organization.

The Right Values Lead to the Best Solutions

Targets and plans are not enough. A person's primary motivator is his or her basic value structure. Develop a value structure that supports daily operations and development work. As a manager and leader, you are in the key position to affect these values.

> Without the right value structure, management chokes on guidance and control.

Significant change often starts with limitation of liberties. At its worst, this means constraints and dismissals. However, we are striving toward a learning organization and continuous development where everyone is involved. To this end, everyone's freedom to make decisions has to be increased. In a situation of free choice, people act in accordance with their own value structure.

The most significant results have been achieved with the development models presented in this book. These models are not only development methods but also management philosophies. They require not only learning new development methods but also changing your way of thinking. Many things that we have believed in and have acted upon are no longer competitive. The need for change is enormous. Under those circumstances, the traditional guidance and control systems are not sufficient.

Most of our actions happen on a subconscious level. Our decisions are ruled by our values and beliefs. It is not enough to learn new things on the conscious level. They have to be absorbed on the subconscious level, to become automatic. Confirming the right values takes time. The right values are not created by themselves; they emerge and develop only through real action. You can say what you like, but if your values are different and you even act against them, it would have been better if you had kept your mouth shut. If you have to make tough decisions at the beginning of a change, do not say anything about values. Who is going to believe in them after that? When you speak about them, make sure they can also be observed in your actions. Otherwise, you will be seen as a hypocrite.

Chapter 9

RESULTS, NOT PLANS, PROVIDE SOLUTIONS

The world is full of plans, some better than others. Of these, very few are ever implemented. Still fewer are implemented early enough and at a sufficient pace to lead to a substantial competitive advantage. By applying the principles in this chapter, you can increase the chances that your development plan will materialize.

QUICK NOTES
Pages 273–286: Read headings, text boxes, and the text in *italics*.

THE PERFECT PLAN DOES NOT EXIST

It is better to have imperfect planning and perfect implementation than the other way around. Release the plans, even unfinished, for experimentation and testing. Start when you know 60 percent about what is required.

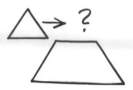

> The perfect plan never starts.

As leaders and managers we are supposed to know and be able to do all things. Even though this thought is an illusion, we believe it because we have projected this image about ourselves for so long. Because we are afraid of losing face, we no longer have the courage to show our ignorance and lack of skills. This illusion of perfection prevents those with innovative ideas from presenting them for fear of being less than perfect.

Important change programs are lengthy processes. You cannot know exactly what the results will be. Both the external and internal conditions will change. Your own conception of the development plan, targets, means, and methods can change, or there can be a lack of good models to follow. You may think that your plan is perfect, yet this is only a belief, blind faith.

Tell people about these principles of uncertainty. Tell them that the race is about the speed of the development and the ability to recognize that 40 percent of the plan may have to be adjusted. Everyone's duty is to implement the plan, but it is also to recognize when the plan must diverge from its original form.

Have the courage to plan with others. With unfinished plans, you concede that you need help from the others, and they experience a genuine feeling of participation. Create visions, but not illusions. When you have to deviate from the official plan, explain the reasons to the organization and present an adjusted plan.

Make Sure Everyone Is Committed

Take a last look to make sure that a consensus exists on the visions, targets, and measures. Do not count on something that does not exist.

> Make sure you have not been abandoned.

It is too easy to believe that everybody understands what the plan is about, is enthusiastic, and thinks as we do. We have attended courses, have been informed, have learned, have participated, and are impressed. We get excited and, for some strange reason, we believe that everybody else is excited, too. Everyone may still agree on the plan we presented. Only when something should be done or changed in some way does apathy appear. In reality, others are not even aware of the training management has received. The seeds fall in uncultivated soil, and we end up wondering why people are not committed, even if the cause is important and the benefits substantial. This is resistance to change.

When you are the change manager, the commitment concerns your subordinates, but with significant changes your superiors will also be affected. Find out who really has set and approved the targets for the development program. Have they been set by yourself, your superior, the general manager, the board of directors, or the owner? Demanding targets are set for the project manager. When the situation changes, the expectations of the top management may change. Keep yourself informed. If your authority is not sufficient, make sure you know where information can be obtained. Make sure top management is ready to make tough decisions if the targets you have set so require. Radical improvements do not happen without radical changes, and they often require unpleasant decisions.

Demonstrate your own commitment, but do not overdo it. It will limit your flexibility; you will become pigheaded and difficult. You may overdo trying, start to feel indisposed or even sick, and, in the worst case, no longer be needed.

MOVE FROM SEVERAL DIRECTIONS SIMULTANEOUSLY

*Many things are interdependent. To pro-
ceed and progress simultaneously in several areas, you must understand the interdependencies, gain time, and involve the
whole organization from the outset.*

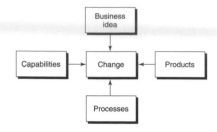

Without simultaneous activity, the project takes too long.

In a change process, several things have to be known and done simultaneously. Renewal of the business idea requires getting to know new markets and
pondering the possibilities brought about by new technology. Developing the
product management requires knowledge of customer needs. We like to proceed with things in a systematic and logical way: first the big things, then the
small; first the top management, then the middle management and floor managers, then the others. If you have grasped where you are headed and with
which means, you can start from several directions at the same time. When as
many people as possible participate in the development from the beginning,
you will also avoid the "This doesn't concern me" attitude.

Multiple start-up also has its downside. The organization may choke.
Some people are capable of handling several things at once, others only one
thing at a time. As a change manager, you must have the skill to handle several things simultaneously. On the other hand, many managers limit the
amount of simultaneous programs. They cannot handle their amount, trust
other people, or delegate. They want to be in charge of everything. People's
ability to solve problems is enormous if they are given the opportunity,
responsibilities, authority, and development training.

Simultaneous development may seem to lead to chaos. It is, however, not
a true chaos—it only seems like it. Things just are not in the customary control of the managers and supervisors. One of the key skills of a change manager is to realize when the situation only seems to be chaotic and when you
have to pull in the reins. Now and then, you have to redetermine what is going
on; everybody has to be given the whole picture of the situation; the direction
has to be changed a little. Then you have to inspire people and loosen up
again.

START OPEN MEASUREMENT IMMEDIATELY

Open and visible measurement tells everyone what things are important in this firm, how good we are, and what the targets are. Measurement directs attention at the right issues and creates common objects of interest. It tells where we want the change.

> Without yardsticks, the target is not concrete.

Measured results should not only be written down or fed to the computer system and examined at management team meetings as "secrets." They should also be registered immediately on big and visible boards. For example, when a dispatcher sends a finished harvester from the assembly hall to a client, he marks the event himself on the board. When a salesperson has closed a sale, she registers it on the board herself.

At the initial stage, you should select one or at the most three yardsticks to be monitored visibly. The yardsticks describe things that can be influenced by the majority and that everyone can influence significantly. The yardsticks measure things that are targeted for change.

Make sure each yardstick leads to the right kind of behavior. In a foundry, "tons per hour" does not lead to the reliability of deliveries, measuring profit does not lead to customer satisfaction, and measuring productivity does not lead to quality. Unfortunately, we tend to measure what is easy to measure or what is important for the results of our own department. If we are part of a chain of companies or part of the firm's internal process, traditional yardsticks are generally only detrimental. They optimize only partially. The wrong yardstick leads to the wrong behavior. The visible start-up of measurement illustrates the importance of the issue, but the reverse is also true. When measurements no longer appear on the board, it also tells that it is no longer important. If you start an important measurement, make sure that it continues.

START AT ONCE

Describe what has already been done. Start the implementation immediately after the announcement of the first solution. Sweep obvious problems out of the way first.

> Without a striking launch, the plans are just manager talk.

It is downright damaging to tell about measures that are never started. Start at once. When you tell people about future measures, tell what management already has done for its part. It will add to everybody's feeling of participation. The program is not just for the employees. It concerns everybody, and management has already started its part. You create a feeling of a quick start by describing what has already been done. Put new ideas immediately to the test to bring results. You will get feedback, and you can correct possible faults. The idea is to minimize the time taken by the cycle of experimenting and adjusting. Radiate feelings of success toward everyone; that increases people's self-confidence and encourages them to continue.

When you try to motivate people, they respond with a variety of doubts. "If only we could finish what we have already started." In creative organizations, more development projects are started than what the time allows to finish. Unfinished work absorbs energy, but finishing a task successfully creates energy. The question is not always about time, but energy. The best way to free up energy is to concentrate on finishing the projects that have been started already, either successfully or by killing them off as unnecessary.

"So many things have been agreed upon and promised, but not executed." Review as your first measure all the things in the organization that have been started, agreed upon, and committed to. Agree upon which ones are to be executed today, which within a week. Describe the timetable of the others or discard them from the list. Many problems are simply the result of negligence or inefficiency. This is how you make a clean sweep for new things. This is also a test for yourself before a major effort. If you cannot fix these small things, how can you handle bigger ones? Without this phase, you are doomed to failure. For instance, start with an orientation project—that is, have the place cleaned and fixed and monitor the progress with a visible indicator. Spread the news about successes.

INITIATE A PILOT PROGRAM

Select a development target from which you can get results quickly and test ideas and development methods in practice. The team learns the skill of development, and the experiences can be transferred to others.

Without a pilot, you end up biting off more than you can chew.

Even bold ideas can be tested and risks controlled through pilots. When you choose one, be sure that the targets can be attained. It must be critical, challenging, and interesting but not too difficult. When you pick a development team, its voluntary nature creates a good chance of success. As leader, choose a challenge manager who will concentrate not only on profits but also on other aspects of the pilot targets. This person must have enough skills to improve the development method and enough respectability to sell it to others.

Give the pilot the opportunity to succeed by arranging optimal conditions. Leave no room for explanations. Do not give the pilot the slightest chance to fail. Do not resort to too much supervision. Give sufficient responsibilities, authority, and freedom. The pilot group must know its targets, and it must be sufficiently trained in the application and further improvement of the development model. It will consciously evaluate the progression of its development know-how and its results during the development process. It will document its development methods and its results in order to facilitate the transfer of its experiences.

The pilot group has to be conscious of its responsibility in all four objectives from the outset. The transfer of experience makes the otherwise unpleasant documentation necessary. The transfer of experience to others has to be planned in advance. A date fixed in advance does wonders. During and after the execution of the pilot, the results in relation to the targets must be analyzed. Training and outside help should be used without hesitation, if necessary. The swiftness of the results is more important than their scale. Quick results help people believe in their abilities to solve problems. Informing others about the results can spread the enthusiasm for their own change processes.

Go for Quick Implementation

Limit the target of the development program to allow implementation within a reasonable time. Use all means to accelerate the implementation of the development process.

> Without speed, the plans become outdated and the benefits decline.

Even many Western firms have halved the throughput times of their product development. Many have done it by benchmarking Japanese product development methods. The starting point for the product development process was a study done by MacKinsey & Co.:

A 6 months' delay in the introduction of a product will reduce by one-third the life-long profit of the product.

If a firm is able to be the first to introduce a successful product to the market, it will achieve the following benefits:

Additional Profits
- Increased product life span
- One hundred percent market share in the beginning
- Liberty in pricing
- Creation of customer loyalty

Cost Benefits
- Cost benefit by process innovation
- Reduced development costs
- Reduced resource requirements

Quality Benefits
- Shorter time span for forecasting
- State-of-the-art technology
- Higher degree of innovation

HAVE A LONG-TERM HORIZON

You will not be able to achieve significant and lasting changes in less than three years. In development programs lasting more than three years, the organization runs out of patience, the customers need change, or competitors get ahead.

> Without a long-term plan, only acute problems are solved.

A significant change takes "exactly" three years. In a shorter time, no real and lasting changes can be achieved. *Changes* means not only cuts or repairs but also change programs aimed at achieving a sustainable competitive edge and requiring a change of thinking throughout the organization. In successful firms, success is not purchased. It is achieved through constant learning. Everything learned in less than three years can easily be learned by others and does not constitute a lasting competitive advantage.

On the other hand, if the change takes more than three years and does not produce significant results, the owners, customers, and company personnel start to become nervous or bored. The competitors get ahead. Customer expectations or other environmental factors have changed, and the results do not bring the benefits that were planned.

The change manager has to see three years ahead and be capable of conveying this window to others. He or she has to have the skill to cruise continuously between now and three years from now, to know which factors affect the end result, and to see from today's signs whether the project will succeed. The change manager is in a hurry to start things, because he or she knows that their learning and taking root will take years.

The change manager is impatient to produce quick results but also has a long-term horizon. He or she is ready to wait for concrete results.

REWARD EVEN A BRAVE ATTEMPT

Use rewards as a means of encouragement. Reward even a good attempt that ends in failure. Rewarding is a sign to the whole organization of the right direction and of the expected mode of action.

Without rewards, people lose interest.

We are accustomed to reward results, but not attempts. Rewards are not only a recompense but also an incentive. Incentives are needed during the project, not afterwards. A fair reward for the right things requires that you know people and their performances. Productivity measurements do not always indicate the change in performance or they may not yet have registered it. Mere delegation and waiting for results are not enough. If you want to encourage people, reward them, even for a good try.

If people are rewarded only for results, they are interested only in tasks for which quick results can be generated. Results bringing a substantial competitive advantage are not produced in a moment. They are long-term processes, trial and error, losses and gains.

In rewarding people, use diverse methods, but be logical. Include rewards as a separate issue in the program. Management interest is one of the best ways of rewarding. Create good reward systems collaboratively and share the experiences of their effects.

How can you reward for a failure? One person's failure can give another an idea. It is silly that the one who made the mistake is punished and the one who learned from it gets the credit. In product development projects, often the first person is fired for a crazy idea, the second for poor technical execution, and the third for poor marketing. The fourth person finally succeeds and gets all the credit.

Move toward Ongoing Improvement

You are not really finished until you have brought the program onto the path of ongoing improvement. Nothing stands still. Either development takes place or regression sets in. Change must be guided onto the path of continuous development. Make sure things are not left unfinished.

> Unless you finish what you have started, you will regress.

When the project reaches a certain stage of development, other problems will have grown bigger and resources will have been transferred to more important problems. Moving to the new does not happen if we still get along with the old. The project is not finished. Heroic deeds have already been accomplished, and there is no glamor in the remainder. This is routine work. The issue in question may even be removed from the project management, and it is assumed that the rest takes care of itself. Some people wait for the project to end and they return to their old ways. There are always those who have not accepted the new ideas. They are just waiting to be able to show that their doubts were justified. In a year, we can be back where we started.

Rooting the change is a disciplined process of effort and completion. The objectives of the change include both the implementation of the change and the bringing of the development to its "path of continuity." The target is not only an honorable completion of the project but also the beginning of the struggle for perfection: 0 errors, 0 disturbances, 100 percent delivery reliability, 100 percent personnel and customer satisfaction. Moving onto the path of continuous development means that everybody participates, the development methods have been learned, development is rewarded, development has as high a status as operational activity, and development results are produced at a constant and steady rate.

The world is full of plans, some better than others, few of which are implemented and even fewer brought to a real completion. The fighters mentioned previously still have strength when others have exhausted theirs. With their obstinate determination, projects are taken to completion. They never give up, and neither should you.

Chapter 10

SELF-EVALUATION QUESTIONS

Evaluation Criteria A Systematic Framework and Specific Targets	Priority	Current and Target Performance				
		1	2	3	4	5
1. Has the constant need for change been recognized and accepted extensively enough in the organization?						
2. Does management have a vision that everyone is inspired by and can identify with?						
3. Have the targets been set high and are they challenging and interesting enough?						
4. Are the timetables of the project plans challenging and interesting enough?						
5. Is there the courage to give up something when important new projects are started?						
6. Can you time the changes right?						
7. Is there skill to make use of all available development resources?						
8. Is there courage to invest in development professionals?						
9. Is there a constant investment in improving the development skills of all personnel?						
10. Can the organization change flexibly and in accordance with the pressure for change?						
11. Does management show its commitment by participating in the development and learning?						
Overall Grade						

Evaluation Criteria Leadership Brings Change	Priority	Current and Target Performance				
		1	2	3	4	5
1. Can management convey its vision in an inspiring way widely enough?						
2. Can management show its desires in an inspiring way and does it get others to share its excitement?						
3. Does management listen to others' desires and take them into account?						
4. Does management show its own desire to change and can it do it?						
5. Can management translate its visions into interesting challenges?						
6. Does management find skilled, inspired, and performing doers from the organization?						
7. Are the professional skills of the development project leaders sufficient and do they reach the targets?						
8. Is the organization involved extensively enough in development programs?						
9. Does the organization have "fighters" who take on new challenges and complete them?						
10. Are the conflicts created in the organization properly handled and exploited?						
11. Is there enough discussion about development and change?						
12. Can the need for continuous change be maintained?						
13. Do the prevailing values support continuous change?						
Overall Grade						

		Current and Target Performance
x Your evaluation of the current performance level	Priority	1 Poor
	1 Not significant	2 Adequate
o Your target	2 Significant	3 Good
	3 Important	4 Very Good
	4 Very important	5 Exceptional
	5 Competitive advantage	

Evaluation Criteria Results, Not Plans, Provide Solutions	Priority	Current and Target Performance				
		1	2	3	4	5
1. Are planning and implementation in the correct proportions?						
2. Has the commitment of management and personnel to start-up been ascertained?						
3. Can development be started simultaneously from several directions?						
4. Can personnel's attention be directed to the right things through visible follow-up?						
5. Can development projects be started quickly without unnecessary delays?						
6. Can pilots be used at the initial stage of the development program?						
7. Are quick and visible results attempted and achieved?						
8. Is the development activity taking place along a long-term horizon?						
9. Is even a good try rewarded, or are only results rewarded?						
10. Can the projects be completed?						
Overall Grade						

x Your evaluation of the current performance level	Priority	Current and Target Performance
o Your target	1 Not significant	1 Poor
	2 Significant	2 Adequate
	3 Important	3 Good
	4 Very important	4 Very Good
	5 Competitive advantage	5 Exceptional

Part 4

MANAGING MY OWN CHANGE

Vision, Belief, Passion, Action

Each of us takes care of his or her own change.

Content Summary

This chapter describes how human behavior and human values are understood in NLP models. They are useful principles in the planning and execution of managing personal change. NLP includes a number of prerequisites selected from system theory, linguistics, information theory, psychology, and the top experts from various areas.

This chapter describes the personal change model. It is an application of the ideas presented by successful American Olympic athlete Marilyn King regarding the factors leading to a top performance. Many of the more detailed models for self-improvement are based on these principles.

This chapter applies the presented model and describes the composition of the book *Managing Change:* the author's vision, what he believed in, what excited him, and what made him implement his project.

The list of questions enables the evaluation of the current situation and the targeted level of the reader's *personal change management* skills, a consideration of the gap between them, and the creation of an action plan.

Chapter 11

INTRODUCTION TO MANAGING MY OWN CHANGE

NLP ideas can be used in every sphere, including human intellectual growth and interaction. NLP has been used in management, coaching, training, personnel administration, business, health care, therapy and guidance work, and self-improvement.

The basic principles, the presuppositions, of NLP are called presuppositions because you presuppose them—that is, you act as if they were true and observe what kind of results they generate. NLP does not claim the results are literally true. They may be true, but not necessarily. The point is not whether they are true but whether they are useful.

Without the understanding of these presuppositions and their integration into one's own behavior, NLP is just a number of mechanistic models that will not lead to the desired change.

QUICK NOTES

Pages 289–315: Read headings, illustrations, text boxes, and text in *italics*.

THE COMPANY DEVELOPS ONLY WHEN I DEVELOP

The operations of an organization must be constantly developed, yet the organization develops only when we change and our professional skills improve. The organization's development targets are reached only when our own development targets are reached, assuming that they match the organization's development targets.

In this context, professional skills mean the following:

1. *Intellectual skills,* consisting of the information we have adopted, our problem-solving skills, and our ability to think logically
2. *Technical skills,* meaning motor performance in various tasks
3. *Ethical skills,* allowing us to define what is right and what is wrong
4. *Interactive skills,* manifested in the ability to communicate intelligibly and to create a good atmosphere that facilitates communication
5. *Emotional skills,* or the ability to identify and handle one's own feelings

The joint effect of these skills builds our total personal professionalism. Often we consider these skills as gifts given to us, yet each one of us can develop every area of our skills. Each separate area requires its own development targets and models. The use of these models cannot be managed by the organization's leader, but their application is the responsibility of each person. Personal change cannot be delegated to our superiors; everyone has to do it him- or herself.

It is customary in the organization to define yardsticks and set related development targets. We believe in the importance and usefulness of targets and yardsticks. But how many of us have defined yardsticks and set development targets for ourselves?

NLP has methods and thinking patterns that you can apply in the management of personal change. The following will introduce you to the key presuppositions.

Modeling Is the Core of NLP

Like the other development models covered by this book, NLP also came about in response to practical needs. NLP was born when mathematician Richard Bandler and linguist John Grinder asked what sets the master apart from the average individual. They did not seek the answer from inborn talent or from training but from the structure of 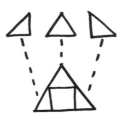 *people's actions and experiences. When investigating superior skills, Bandler and Grinder succeeded in dissecting skills into parts down to their intuitive and subconscious elements. They argued that any kind of human behavior can be conceived as a skill that can be dismantled into parts, learned and repeated.*

First they modeled top therapists, such as Milton H. Erickson, Virginia Satir, and Fritz Perls, and found that the therapists acted differently than what they taught and claimed to do. They also modeled quite ordinary people that were skilled, for instance, in handling negative experiences or in changing their behavior.

Modeling brings us to the world of experiences, where many things happen unconsciously. The use of the subconscious is one of the basic features of NLP. Modeling can happen both by observing and by interviewing. As a matter of fact, we are already unconsciously good modelers. We are best at it in childhood. Most of our learning has happened by modeling, by imitation. NLP does not necessarily bring anything new. It makes us more conscious of the things we already know and are skilled at.

NLP has methods that enable us to make better use of the enormous capacity of the brain and to use both halves of our brains in a more balanced manner. The left half concentrates on the rational side: logical thinking and deduction. The right half handles imagination, creativity, and intuitive action.

NLP Helps Manage the Individual Thinking Process

*According to the principles of NLP, our perfor-
mance comes from ourselves. NLP starts from the
supposition that we choose our own thoughts and
our state of mind. Our environment easily influences our state of mind. However, we can choose
our state of mind. We can choose self-confidence
over stress. We can choose to be relaxed instead of
being frustrated.*

Traditionally, people have tried to influence us and improve our performance by many means: teaching, training, participation, motivation, manipu-
lation, and even force. These have been means to influence us from outside.
We have been indoctrinated by visions and targets of the company (management), which we have not recognized as our own. In the use of these methods,
sufficient attention has not been paid to the inner processes that affect our
motivation, our performance, and our overall behavior.

Our states of mind are created by our mental pictures. Since our state of
mind can easily be spoiled, why couldn't it be improved as well? For instance,
the waiter reports that the cook has a bad cold and that something may have
gotten into the soup he has just served. (Imagine how the soup appeals to the
customer after hearing the waiter's report.) A bit later the waiter returns to the
table to assure the customer that the story was just a joke. (Do you think the
soup will taste any better to the customer?)

Both the real events we experience and those created in our imagination
use the same cerebral neurology and the same nerve channels, and in principle they have the same effect on our behavior. In that sense, there is no difference between the real and the imaginary. At best, this is seen in actors' performances in which the actors can even feel what they are acting. Also, a high
jumper and a ski jumper build a mental picture of a successful performance
before the jump. In NLP, we model our good states of mind and try to transfer them to situations in which we do not feel well. Every state of mind, bad
or good, has a structure that can be broken down into its components. The contents of the components can be changed; consequently, our mental pictures
can be changed.

SUPERIOR PROFICIENCY CAN BE MODELED AND TAUGHT

In NLP, modeling happens by observing, interviewing, and asking specific questions about how a person builds up his or her skill. The questions cover the different levels of experience, such as the methods used, beliefs, values, and mind maps. Modeling helps us understand the factors that make success possible. Pay attention to what works, not to what does not work. In corporate life, we generally dwell on things that do not work, and we try to fix them. Why wouldn't we investigate how some people succeed? "If it ain't broke, don't fix it" is our common management philosophy.

The benchmarking concept *internal benchmarking* can be compared to *internal modeling,* in which I learn from myself. I ask myself, "How do I do things that I do well?" and "How could I transfer these skills to my other tasks?" By modeling, or benchmarking, my own skill, I can transfer it to other situations.

I realize that I learned English easily. How did I do it? Can I transfer it to learning Swedish? I am always calm with Richard. What makes me calm with him? I do not expect too much from him; I appreciate him and listen to him. Can I transfer this way of thinking and behavior to situations in which I communicate with Lisa?

External modeling can be compared to *external benchmarking,* in which the model that could teach us is sought from outside ourselves. "How could I recognize how the person I admire does things and how could I learn from him?" I will model his strategy, beliefs, values, and mental system. I will learn to understand why he acts in a certain way and will try to learn from him and apply what I have learned in my own situation. I will change my own strategy of action, my beliefs, and my mental systems.

In NLP, it is assumed that, if one person can do something, "anyone" can do the same. The question is how the successful mode of operation is modeled and dismantled. When modeling succeeds, the skill or mode of operation can be taught to people that have not managed it before.

WE ALREADY POSSESS THE RESOURCES TO MAKE CHANGES THAT ARE IMPORTANT TO US

A key supposition is that we already have the resources we require to manage our performance and to make the desired change. The point is just how they are recognized and implemented when needed. A considerable part of NLP is simply various means and methods to find and activate the personal and individual resources we all have. The target is to model our successes and transfer them to situations where we have not been successful.

We all have experiences of personal success. The sensations of success may have been long-lasting or only momentary. Some have experienced a feeling of success from getting along with another human being, from bravery, or from self-confidence. Others have experienced having a good sense of humor in a tough situation, and others have noticed in themselves the ability to concentrate and persevere in a challenging task. The list is endless. We have countless evidence of our ability to succeed.

NLP therapy does not mean that somebody else solves our problems for us but that someone helps us find and capitalize on all the resources we already have.

THE UNCONSCIOUS MIND OUTPERFORMS THE CONSCIOUS MIND

The unconscious mind is stronger than the con-
scious mind. It accomplishes much more. The
unconscious mind forms most of our decisions,
thoughts, and deductions. It decides almost every-
thing we do, as if it were in our control. The fact is
that the conscious mind is capable of receiving a
very limited amount of information, and most
information comes through the unconscious. We do many things consciously,
for example, set targets and analyze situations. At the same time, we use many
of our skills unconsciously; these skills have become automatic and fade from
consciousness.

In the management of personal change, we bring our way of thinking, our
beliefs, and our mode of action to the conscious level, where we try to change
them and further train them, so that they again become automatic and return
to the unconscious level.

The unconscious part of our behavior is often more important than the
conscious. This becomes especially apparent when we want to change some-
thing in ourselves and do not succeed. In that case, the unconscious side of the
mind controls the action.

Many beliefs are unconscious. When we have formed a basic belief ("I am good at learning new things"), we later act unknowingly by the same belief, without consciously reminding ourselves of it.

Even in interaction, there are two levels, the conscious and the uncon-scious. They are generally the verbal and the unspoken levels. We may plan our words and control our facial expressions, but inadvertently our tone of voice and body language may convey a totally different message. People often tell two stories: their speech tells one story, while their silent communication tells a different one. If the spoken and the unspoken messages are in conflict, people generally believe in the unspoken.

NLP methods enable interaction with our unconscious mind, when we want to change something in ourselves.

THE MIND AND THE BODY ARE PARTS OF THE SAME SYSTEM

People's analytical thinking has separated the mind and the body. In reality, they are only two sides of the same action, and there is no fundamental difference between them. They are parts of the same system.

The mind works through bodily phenomena, and the body through the mind. By imagining different things, it is possible to control how the body feels or what happens in it.

What we think affects our body, and the health and condition of our body affects our sense of well-being and our thoughts. The body cannot cope without the mind and vice versa. Humans are the result of this cooperation between body and mind. The body expresses what we believe in ourselves and what the mind is experiencing. While we are depressed, the body reacts just as if shrinking, whereas the body acts as if embracing the world when the mind shines.

The mind shapes the body and vice versa. People can change their state of mind through changing their body's experience and actions and vice versa. Try it: walk with your head hanging, with short steps, and hunched over and you realize how easy it is to get yourself depressed. Raise your head, straighten your back, lengthen your steps, increase your speed, and you will notice a big difference.

You can learn to use your body as a "tool" for your mind. In NLP, the phenomena of interaction of the mind, language, and the body are investigated from the viewpoint of a system.

NLP Can Be Used to Improve Communication Skills

NLP came about while modeling the skills of top therapists. A therapist's work success depends wholly on communication skills. These skills were based on the therapists' ability to communicate with their clients. In the same manner, in almost all work assignments, communication skills form an important part of the chances of success.

Communication skills are the most important tools in the work of a leader and a manager. What sets successful leaders and managers apart from less successful ones is their communication skills.

NLP includes many pragmatic principles for the development of communication skills. The key element is establishing a condition of mutual trust. We are all unique in our own beliefs, capabilities, and identities. We all see the world in our own ways. In order to establish rapport, we have to meet other people in their own world. The question is, how does this happen? Rapport can be established in many ways. We can practice using NLP techniques, such as body language, choice of words, and tone of voice.

Skillful salespeople settle into the customer's world. I well remember a realtor who we were waiting for in the hot weather. We were dressed according to the weather, light and casual. The realtor approached us wearing a suit and a tie tight around his neck. His first gesture, after our greetings, was to remove his jacket and tie. He came onto the same level with us with his clothing. While walking, about a hundred meters, he asked questions and listened carefully. He skillfully found out the way we communicated and changed his style accordingly. Instead of trying to make a hard sell, he found out our needs and tried to understand our world. Our meeting did not result in a deal, but he created an impression of a salesperson I would like to buy from.

THE WORLD AND PERCEPTIONS OF IT ARE TWO DIFFERENT THINGS

For someone, the room is too cool; for another, hot; and, for a third, comfortable regardless of the fact that everyone can see the same thermometer reading. Someone finds a proposal exciting, another person finds it objectionable, and a third is indifferent, even if we are talking about the same proposal. We do not react directly to reality; everyone  *has his or her own way of forming the world around his or her own world view. By changing our map of reality, we can change our relation to the world.*

We teach the way we want ourselves to be taught. We motivate our subordinates with arguments that motivate us. A manager is motivated by profitability, since it means more bonuses. For middle management, profitability means more work and sweat. When the employees hear the word *profitability,* they expect layoffs. These are examples of how differently people build their reality, their picture of the world. There is a difference between the world and our perception of it. The terrain and the map are not the same thing. No map pictures reality perfectly. There is no right or wrong map. Many different maps work. Granted, different maps lead us to different goals.

Reality does not limit individuals but, rather, the possibilities they consider realistic, based on their own map. When we build our experience of the world, we make unconscious choices. We include some parts of the world in the picture and remove some other parts. We draw a personal map of the terrain with our personal mapping technique. Communication becomes easier when people use their own maps flexibly and understand that the other person's map is different from their own.

The key question in NLP is, how? How do we build our map and our experiences? How do we create our depression or lack of motivation? What elements around us do we pick up or dispose of so that, for instance, a feeling of motivation or demotivation is created? How do we create a desired feeling?

PEOPLE MAKE THE BEST CHOICE THEY CAN

People make the best choices based on the available information. Every kind of behavior—even if it seems bad—is the best based on the information or map available at the time. If they are offered a better alternative, they automatically choose it, if it fits in their map or if they succeed in extending their map. Thus, everyone acts perfectly—nobody is broken.

We easily criticize the decisions made by others, without knowing the information or circumstances that their decisions were based upon. With the same information and in the same circumstances, we might have made the same decisions.

Instead of evaluating decisions, we judge the decision makers by giving them such names as change resistant, guardian of her turf, lazy, profiteer, selfish, and so on. True, the decision has been selfish in the mind of others, but the decision maker has not experienced it or meant it to be so.

A supervisor was against an idea of reducing the size of manufacturing batches. I supposed it to be natural change resistance and his will of comfort to produce long series. However, through more thorough thoughts, his opinion was based on long setting-up times consuming too much capacity, resistance of operators, increased transportation, and possibly some other arguments. My proposal, in turn, was based on developing setting-up times, changes in the incentive payment system and other improved conditions for shorter manufacturing batches according to JIT principles. His opinion was based on the prevailing circumstances, and my opinion was based on plans in my mind of which he had only a slight idea. I, in turn, was more interested in opportunities in the future than in prevailing conditions. We both formed the best possible opinion based on the facts we had.

WE CREATE OUR WORLD WITH OUR FIVE SENSES

We hear, see, feel, taste, and smell. We convert our sensory experiences through language, enabling us to speak about our experiences. When we wonder what somebody's communication is based on, and when we ask often enough what lies behind or underneath the speech, we will have the answer that the person's speech is the result of his or her sensory experiences.

The function of this system of conceptions is different, individual, and correct for every human being. This difference also explains to a great extent why we experience such different maps. We make our observations mostly via sight, hearing, or feeling. The experience of a person perceiving objects—for instance, in an art show or a concert—can be totally different from somebody else's perceiving the same objects auditively.

> Everybody learns best through his or her own favorite system.

We learn and remember through different systems. Everyone has a favorite system, even if he or she is able to learn by other systems, too. In certain situations, we do not even understand, if we do not receive the information through our favorite system. I called a meeting in writing. Not everybody showed up. I called and asked about the reasons. "I didn't come, because I haven't heard anything about it," was the answer I was given. The message is received, but it is immediately forgotten, if it is not delivered by the favorite system. Some people prefer a telephone call and others a letter. It is possible to be in all three systems simultaneously, but one is always predominant.

The visual person is surprised when others do not see the same picture. Because of the difference in pace, visual people do not like to communicate with kinesthetic people.

If the communication is difficult, it makes sense to ask whether we are operating in the same conceptual system. Visual people learn with their eyes, the auditive with their ears, and the kinesthetic by doing. Kinesthetic persons are often labeled as troublemakers, even very early in life. They are told not to touch, but they touch, anyway.

THE MEANING OF THE COMMUNICATION IS IN THE REACTION IT CREATES

In interaction, the recipient defines the meaning. Since the map and the terrain are different and people have different pictures of the world, I cannot assume that things have the same meaning for me and the person I am dealing with. If I were to make that assumption, I would extend my own picture of the world to other people. Contact between people is created when the other person is met in his or her own world.

Interaction should not be considered as a success or a failure. Instead, observe what kind of feedback the message gets. In communication, there are no failures, only interesting results. Thus, there is no good or bad feedback, either. There are only different kinds of feedback and different results. Whatever happens, it is interesting.

If something you do does not work, use that as feedback and try something else. Change your behavior until you get the result you want. One of the characteristics of a top communicator is flexibility—the ability to change his or her own behavior and way of interacting until the desired reaction is created.

Ongoing resistance is a sign of inflexibility in the communicator. In NLP, it is assumed that resistance is not due to any feature of the other party but, rather, is a sign of the communicator's inflexibility in taking into account the world map of the other person. Generally, the person who is the most flexible has the best success in interactive situations.

ALL BEHAVIOR HAS A POSITIVE INTENTION

A positive intention is there, however inappropriate, negative, or useless the behavior may seem. This NLP presupposition separates the positive, important intention and the negative/useless means by which someone tries to reach a goal.

The idea of positive intention allows us to approach, in a positive way, the sometimes strange behavioral patterns of both ourselves and others. Every reaction is useful in some connection.

When the positive intention behind the action and the means used in its execution are separated, we often end up with useful results. For instance, the young want to become independent. This is a positive intention. The means may vary: someone starts to take drugs, another fights with his parents, and a third takes responsibility for her own life. If we approach these young people on the level of the means they use, we easily define somebody as bad, another as good, and we advise, evaluate, and judge. If we see, instead, the positive intention behind the means, we can approve the important intention and begin to negotiate about means that support that endeavor even better and are acceptable to everyone.

> The roots of self-assurance are in the presupposition that people's intentions are basically positive.

I was starting a seminar with an extended management team from one company. The CEO opened the session. He explained why the session was necessary, told about the targets, and encouraged everyone to participate actively. After a good opening, however, he sat down on a couch at the back of the room, not wanting to participate actively in the small assignments we were doing in pairs. His behavior was in clear contradiction to his own words. Everyone noticed it, and the matter irritated me enormously during the day. In my mind, I gave him the "dodger of responsibility" label. At the end of the day, I tried to find out why he behaved the way he did. His excuse was that he did not want to affect the activity of the others, which he knew would happen if he had participated too actively. He made the best choice based on his own knowledge, rather than mine.

Chapter 12

DEVELOPMENT MODEL FOR MANAGING MY OWN CHANGE

This chapter presents a model for managing personal change. It is an application based on the ideas presented by American Olympic athlete Marilyn King* regarding which factors lead to top performance. Marilyn King is an Olympic athlete, a member of the U.S. team in the 1972 and 1976 games competing in the Pentathlon. While preparing for the ill-fated 1980 Olympics, she suffered a back injury, which resulted in her being bedridden for four months. She spent most of that time watching films of successful pentathletes, visualizing and feeling herself going through the same events. Despite her lack of physical preparation she placed second in the trials thanks, she feels, to her psychological state. Many of the more detailed self-improvement models are based on the same basic principles that King used.

This provides an example of how, through modeling another's success, you can create your own success formula. Another model might suit you, but this model works for me as presented in my example on pages 309–314.

* This information is based on an interview with Marilyn King from an article by Marjatta Jabe in *Fakta,* a Finnish business magazine, in November 1996.

How Do You Generate Maximum Performance?

"Maximum performance requires at the same time a vision of what we want to become and a belief in the value of our cause and in our possibilities. When we add the enthusiasm that also leads to real action, you are ready for peak per-formance," says Marilyn King, successful American pentathlete.

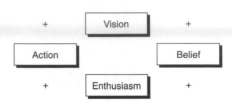

Marilyn King also says, *"Even ordinary people can accomplish great things that seem almost impossible, as long as they have a vision of what they want to achieve, they have the right attitude or a strong desire, passion, and they have the ability to act, i.e. they can transform their vision into reality. The end result can be nothing short of a top performance."*

Even when only one ingredient is missing, the whole thing can be spoiled:

- We may be enthusiastic and hard-working and even believe in what we do. However, if we do not have a vision, a mental picture of what we want to achieve, we are only workaholics.
- We may have a vision, but we do not quite believe in the chances of its becoming real, our enthusiasm fades gradually, and our ability to act weakens.
- We may have a vision we believe in, but we do not get things done. We are dreamers.
- Most of us have visions, dreams we believe in, but we do only the nec-essary minimum, because we lack real enthusiasm. There are great ideas and even creativity, but nothing happens. The task remains unfinished.

In programs for managing my own change, it is exactly these factors that programs try to develop. The following are the top performance factors.

CREATE INSPIRING VISIONS FOR YOURSELF

What is crucial is what we want to become. *Someone wants to become a top company leader and another a consultant. Someone wants to become the best priest and another the best grandmother. Our aspirations are very individual. Those that have become the best have not reached their position by chance, but they have been supported by a recognizable, exceptionally strong desire to excel at what they have set as their targets.*

    Vision is the ability to imagine. *Winners form a vision of what they want. They have visionary talents. The art of creating a vision is the courage to dream of something that is not within easy reach and that cannot even be proven quite simply by calculations. It is something that comes not only from the brain but also from the heart.*

Marilyn King has aptly stated, "Everybody carries dreams. We have the necessary knowledge, heart and energy. But how many have thought every day of being an Olympian or some other kind of winner? We don't even dare to think we are something special."

Marilyn King had set her own target at participation in the Olympics. Her vision came true. She took part in two Olympics and set a world record. Marilyn King stresses—as have many others, having reached an important goal—that a good vision is not only a picture; it is also something that works through many senses. It can include sounds, scents, and feelings. Marilyn King states, "If you cannot imagine what you can accomplish, you won't reach it. In my experience a mental picture always precedes an extraordinary performance."

A company must become spiritually rich in order to become materially rich. Everybody is capable of a hundred times more than what he or she can do or is given the chance to make use of. We only lack the courage for visions and targets and the perseverance to make them come true.

> Everything else can be bought, but not good visions and targets.

Dreams and hopes should, however, be separated from targets, because dreams and hopes do not come true, but targets do.

YOU HAVE TO BELIEVE IN YOUR VISION

You have to believe in the value of your vision. The vision has to be desirable enough. It fulfills your deepest aspirations. The vision is a stepping-stone in your journey toward an even more important target. It has to be valuable enough for you in order to be a source of inspiration.

You have to believe in yourself. You have to believe in your own possibilities—of making the vision come true. The losers lose because they do not believe that they can win. Those who win believe they can win. By changing just one thing in yourself, the belief in your abilities and possibilities, you have already made over half of the necessary changes.

When successful "risk takers" have been asked about their courage, they have not understood the whole question. Never once have they had the experience of taking risks. They have believed in their cause and their vision and have done everything for it. They have encountered setbacks but have not experienced them as failures or risks. The failure is created when there is no more faith and surrender has ensued. Risk is the feeling of possible failure, and that is something they have never felt.

If we do not have faith in our cause and in ourselves, enthusiasm can be short-lived. Enthusiasm dies out at the first major setback.

We all have our own beliefs. We have a certain idea of what we are and what we are like, what abilities and resources we have, what we are capable of, what we can and cannot do, and what we will and will not learn. A belief can support and help a vision or set limits for it. Beliefs guide our thinking and strongly affect our behavior. Beliefs such as "it is impossible to make any difference here," "the boss calls the shots here," "there's no point in trying too hard here" are examples of beliefs that set limits. Instead of such beliefs, recognize beliefs that inspire challenging visions and drive you toward brisk action.

FIRM BELIEF GENERATES ENTHUSIASM

When we believe in the value of our vision and in our ability to make it come true, that belief creates enthusiasm and a strong desire to do something meaningful about it. When we really believe in our cause, enthusiasm becomes passion and can make even extraordinary performances happen. Passion is a burning desire to achieve something, and outwardly this passion manifests itself in enthusiasm and impatience but also in perseverance and tenacity—sometimes at the expense of flexibility.

Enthusiasm can also be picked up from somebody else's vision, visible faith, and enthusiasm. Passion is created only from a totally adopted vision. When I get excited, I get others excited, too. When others see that I have faith, they start to have faith, too. This, in turn, adds to my faith in my cause, reinforcing it.

Not only a lack of faith but also behavioral norms and narrow beliefs may impede excitement. That is what some old perceptions tell us: "I might lose face if I show too much enthusiasm. People will think I'm full of myself. I'd better keep a low profile. If I show too much enthusiasm as a leader, I'll be seen as naive. I'd better just keep my feet on the ground."

When you dare to show your excitement, it starts to attract others that are interested in the same things. You find allies for your cause.

Only Action Leads to Success

Success is not made of vision, faith, and excitement alone. It will not happen only by dreaming. Only action leads to success. Everyone has his or her own visions and means to make them come true. Even the same vision can be reached by quite different methods.

According to studies, winners have the patience to wait for real and final results, but, at the same time, they are impatient to get quick results. The utility of many things is defined by how soon or with what speed they have been executed. In many areas, we do not have to be better than others, if we are just a little quicker than others. The patience to work for the long haul is needed, because important changes do not happen overnight.

Some of us make plan after plan, trying to draw up the perfect one, yet without the courage to execute them. Important change programs are long-term processes. You cannot know precisely what the end result will be. Circumstances will change. Your own idea of the development program, the targets, the means, and the methods will change. You may think that your plan is perfect, but it is still just a belief. You can never know for sure which plans will work. Only by experimenting or acting can you find that out. It is better to have an imperfect plan and a perfect execution than the other way around.

In change management programs, we raise unconscious ideas to the conscious level. We try to develop them further, so that they are again transferred to the unconscious level. Most of the changes we initiate will remain unfinished, because our perseverance is not sufficient to take the changes to the unconscious level and to yield unconscious development.

Chapter 13

CASE STUDY:
COMPOSING *MANAGING CHANGE*

Modeling is at the core of NLP. In that sense it is similar to benchmarking. Both involve observing and asking questions. The following is a hypothetical interview between me and my NLP teacher. It is intended to demonstrate the development model created by Marilyn King, one type of modeling.

Create Inspiring Visions for Yourself

My Vision Developed during the Job

You have written a book called Managing Change. *It has been a hit product for you and your publisher. You have also developed public and company-specific seminars based on the book. Many organizations have used them to start or speed up their own development programs. Organizations have ordered the book in the dozens for their personnel. The book has been published in the United States in English by ASQ Quality Press.*

— *What gave you the idea to write a book?*

— I had simply developed the need to write it. There were obviously reasons that I wasn't even quite conscious of. They have later become clear to me and I would formulate them as follows.

I had accumulated quite a lot of experiences and case studies and lectures based on them. I wanted to mold them into an entity that I felt the managers and consultants I know were missing. I had moved from line duty to consulting. In my mind, something had been left unfinished. A comprehensive entity hadn't been composed, which I then put on paper. I also had the need to collect my experiences and ideas on paper in order to better concentrate on learning new things (such as NLP). I also have always had an enormous need to share my experiences, even in situations where they were not asked.

— *What kind of target did you set for yourself?*

— In the first stage only that I get my ideas and experiences on paper. The idea was, right from the beginning, to create a book from them. In the phase when I almost gave up, I applied the model of managing my own change that I had developed on the basis of my NLP knowledge and by which I set quite detailed targets. The goals were not only hard targets but also mental pictures and feelings of a situation in which I would have known I had succeeded. Some examples of how I know that I have reached my targets follow:

— An abbreviated and an extended version of the book have been published.

— The publishing seminar of the book was highly acclaimed.

— One to two thousand copies of both books have been sold.

— The book is one of the most profitable books of the publisher.

— It has generated other "products" as well: the same book for small companies, service organizations, courses, handbooks, and so on.

— It is used by consultants and training and corporate organizations.

— The book has supported the development programs of many organizations.

— The book has brought me training and consulting assignments.

— I have evolved considerably through the writing of the book.
I feel relaxed, since my own knowledge has been documented, it has benefited others, and I am ready to learn new things.

— Readers are looking forward to the publication of my next books.

You Have to Believe in Your Vision

I Really Believed in It

— *What kind of benefits were you expecting from your book?*

— I believed that mastering a total concept, or combining different development models, and theory and practice, was something that nobody had done before. I believed I was doing something exceptional. I believed that I was doing something that would also be useful to others. I could satisfy my desire to be able to share my experiences.

I believed that the book would become like a business card for me. I dislike marketing myself, and the book would become my marketing tool. By marketing the book, I would do the same for myself. I could also organize my papers and thus they would be easier to utilize in my consulting. I could more easily concentrate on learning new things, when the experiences would be documented.

— *What made you think that you would succeed in writing the book?*

— I had earlier written a book about benchmarking. Granted, it had a model; this one hadn't. It was also a product that served as my business card.

— *In your opinion, what were your most important strengths in your effort to reach your target?*

— I believe they are my varied practical experiences and the relevant track record. I believed that set me apart from others. I also knew that I had generally demonstrated the tenacity and perseverance required with the book, sometimes to the point of being a nuisance. I am used to winning through hard work. By working hard, I have compensated for my weaknesses.

FIRM BELIEF GENERATES ENTHUSIASM

My Enthusiasm Became a Passion

— *What got you excited about the project?*

— A book based on my own experiences and their description according to the Kolb learning model seemed to me really challenging and got me excited. Writing was quite a learning process. I realized continually new things and old things in a new way. For instance, when I had the idea of using the Kolb model of learning from experiences in structuring the book and discussed it further with Professor Jorma Heikkilä, I became even more excited. Writing with a very tight timetable, I got involved with my book and got more and more excited.

— *How did others encourage you?*

— At a very early stage, I submitted the book for test reading, discussed with the test readers, got some encouraging feedback, and got again more excited. I gave one section of the manuscript to five different publishers, held discussions, got tips, encouragement, and again more enthusiasm. I chose a publisher that was able to help in finalizing the content of the book and kept my enthusiasm high.

— *How have you maintained your enthusiasm now that the book is selling?*

— When the book was published, I sent in my excitement 20 books to the people that had most affected the release of the book during my career. In addition, I sent flyers to all of my acquaintances; I have asked for written feedback from the readers and distributed them around in my excitement. I have carried the book with me, almost always presenting it excitedly to everyone and sold the book at my seminars. I have also noticed that my sheer enthusiasm has made people buy my book.

— *Do you think you can maintain this level of enthusiasm?*

— Continuous positive feedback and new surprise customers keep my enthusiasm up. When I noticed that one organization ordered 50 books, I almost fell off my chair. When I recognized the enormous ensuing opportunities, such as translations for the international market, seminars, and the completion of the fourth edition, my excitement showed no sign of fading. Even writing this adds to it.

ONLY ACTION LEADS TO SUCCESS

New Targets Maintain My Momentum

— *How did you get started in writing?*
— There just was some kind of pressure that got it started. I can't explain it. True, it happened to be a rainy summer, which helped quite a bit in starting.

— *How did you keep up the writing?*
— My faith and my excitement grew continuously, and I developed an enormous desire to see what this could really become. Since I kept quite a pace and was writing whenever I could, my train of thought wasn't broken, which made writing easier.

— *You said that you almost gave up writing. How did you get over it?*
— When I had to start writing the third version and my other work was demanding attention, I was close to giving up. At the presentation of my benchmarking book, I held a one-hour presentation of the topic of my book. The leader of a big corporation came over to me, asking me to give a lecture, saying, "We invite our personnel and customers to the Tampere Congress Hall once a year. We have generally used foreign lecturers, but could you come this time to give the lecture?" Both this feedback and memories of the successful Tampere event gave me the strength to go on when I was fed up with writing my book. I had told so many people about the book that even that created some pressure.

— *How did you make sure that the project was finished?*
— I have pushed my publisher to be more active almost to the point of annoying him in order to promote my own ideas and to further the marketing of my book. In fact, there seems to be no end in sight for the project. It has generated the start-up model of a development program based on the questionnaires in the book and one- and two-day public and company-specific seminars, and furthermore the clientele has extended from industry to the service sector, and even to the development of education. The book and the products it generated exist also in English. The fourth edition has been extended with a fourth part ("Managing My Own Change") and some appendices. ASQ Quality Press in the United States has published the book and ILO has distributed it through their own channels. In addition, the idea has been presented to place the events of the book in one company and to tell it in the form of a story. I already went through a story-writing course. We will see if this idea is eventually implemented.

Chapter 14

SELF-EVALUATION CRITERIA

Evaluation Criteria	Priority	Current and Target Performance				
		1	2	3	4	5
1. I have a mental picture (vision) of what I want to develop in my work assignments.						
2. I have formed my desires into distinct and measurable development targets.						
3. I believe that my development target is valuable for myself and for my environment.						
4. My development target is challenging to me and I can grow with it.						
5. I believe in my chances of reaching my development targets.						
6. I have made my development targets public, and others have supported me.						
7. I am excited about my development target, which has been noted by others.						
8. The people important to me are also excited about my development targets.						
9. I start my development work briskly and execute it within the planned timetable.						
10. I monitor my progress and make the necessary changes.						
11. I always finish my development tasks and reach the agreed upon targets.						
12. I get encouraging feedback on my achievements.						
Overall Grade						

x Your evaluation of the current performance level	Priority	Current and Target Performance
o Your target	1 Not significant	1 Poor
	2 Significant	2 Adequate
	3 Important	3 Good
	4 Very important	4 Very Good
	5 Competitive advantage	5 Exceptional

Epilogue

With What Do We Actually Compete?

1. **Total concepts compete with each other.**
   Competition in the market does not happen only in products, but firms compete with their overall concepts: how the firm markets, produces, and services and how quickly it launches new products, to the market.

2. **Tomorrow we need new weapons.** Today companies compete with the existing products and operations. Tomorrow they will compete with new products and processes that should be under development today.

3. **Tomorrow's competition has already arrived.** It happens with development programs underway today. Tomorrow's competition is won by the firm that selects the right development targets and implements the programs with speed and quality.

4. **The ability to change must be developed.** Development always means change. A firm must systematically develop its ability to make rapid and often extensive changes and the ability to develop itself continuously.

We Can Learn from Experience—Our Own and Others'

We can learn from experience—however, only under the condition that we have the patience to observe them and to understand the cause-and-effect relationships. We must keep an open mind in order to avoid repeating models that have worked at some point but that are not suitable for our current situation. It may also become apparent that no experience or model you know of will help you find the right way to proceed. The model must then be discovered from completely new and creative development and management models. Instead of staying with models that have already become familiar, this book should encourage you to venture toward something completely new and unknown.

Development can and must be managed. This book tries to describe issues and phenomena that the development manager can and must influence. Fundamentally, change is the change in every individual. Your own change can be managed only by you. The manager's task is to create opportunities for everyone to develop the skills of managing his or her own change.

I hope that my book has given you even a fraction of what writing it and going through the experiences and development models behind it have given me. Finally, I would like to remind you that:

> You do not become a change manager only by reading books.
> You become a change manager by exerting strong will, managing change, and learning from your own and others' experiences.

MANAGING CHANGE AND MALCOLM BALDRIGE NATIONAL QUALITY AWARD CRITERIA

Taking a practical approach and using some simple models, the book describes the subject areas that are also found in the categories of the Malcolm Baldrige National Quality Award. The book is well suited as a tool for all organizations that are developing their operations using the Malcolm Baldrige National Quality Award criteria.

All the chapters of the book look at the operations of a business in its entirety and divide them using models that have been found to work well and clearly in practice. Following are the main points in common between the book and the quality prize criteria. Although the approaches diverge to some degree, the contents of the book broadly cover the subjects of the quality prize model.

1. *Leadership.* In Part 3 of the book, "Management of Change," practical examples are used to describe various change situations and the management principles that are needed to cope with them. They reflect the importance of management responsibility and skills in planning, managing, and  implementing significant change. Using the principles presented, managers can create the conditions required to implement a quality program and set leadership criteria.

2. *Strategic Planning.* Chapter 2, "Strategic Management," outlines the central concepts of strategic management. Simple models and examples are used to remove the mystique surrounding strategic 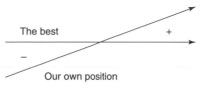 planning and make it understandable to the whole organization. The ABB Customer Focus program is used to demonstrate how strategic plans can be turned into objectives and practical action.

3. *Customer and market focus.* Chapter 3, "Product Management," describes how the demands of global markets and Aquamaster-Rauma Oy's customers are identified and taken into account when product properties and competitive advantages are  defined. The example shows how the competency needed to fulfill customers' needs is identified and incorporated into an organizationwide development program.

Chapter 4, "Process Management," describes process improvement from the customer's standpoint. Using the example of Ahlstrom Pumps, the implementation of a process improvement program based on the customer's purchasing criteria is outlined. The example shows how purchasing criteria can be used to define the process flow chart, the processes requiring improvement, and the competencies required to support fulfillment of the customer's expectations.

4. *Information and analysis.* Chapter 2, "Strategic Management," uses a simple model to describe how a business operation's strategic objectives feed into the organization's competency objectives. The chapter goes on to depict the competency hierarchy of the whole company and the interrelationship among the various parameters. The chapter provides the basics for an understanding of this category.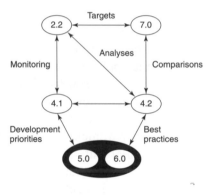

Chapter 3, "Product Management," uses the example of Aquamaster-Rauma to give a broad description of the most important parameters in a business operation and how they interrelate, as well as how they are used in the planning of an improvement program, in justifying it, in motivating people, in monitoring competitors, and in implementing the program.

Chapter 4, "Process Management," describes how Prostec selected competency objectives for its product development that supported the overall objectives of the whole organization.

Chapter 5, "Development Management," presents the concept of benchmarking and a development model. Corporate examples demonstrate the selection of competency measures, their comparison against the best in the field, and how one learns from them using benchmarking. The examples are drawn from Rosenlew Tools, a manufacturer of injection molds; Rosenlew, which manufactures household appliances; and Elmo the decathlete.

5. *Human resource focus.* Chapter 4, "Process Management," describes process management and process improvement. Both stipulate the required conditions for the efficient mobilization of resources toward the organization's objectives.

In Part 2 of the book, "Development Models," all the chapters describe how the competencies in the organization need to be directed toward the commercial objectives and customer requirements. This ensures that the development of competence at the level of the individual is based on the major objectives and plans of the organization.

Part 3, "Management of Change," and Part 4, "Managing My Own Change," present the principles that can be used to increase the development competence of individuals.

6. *Process management.* Chapter 4, "Process Management," describes the principles of process management and development, which are refined using many case studies. The examples in this chapter demonstrate the application of many evaluation issues.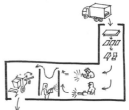

7. *Business results.* The case studies in all the chapters illustrate the interdependence between profitability and the improvement measures that have been implemented. They also present many examples that show organization-specific results in each category.

Chapter 5, "Development Management," illustrates the principles underlying the comparison of the results of different operations.

LITERATURE

This book is based on the writer's own experiences and those of his interviewees. The book has been influenced by the following books, which may allow the reader to go deeper in the matters handled by the book.

Camp, Robert C. 1995. *Business Process Benchmarking.* Milwaukee, WI: ASQC Quality Press.

Hammer, Michel, and James Champy. 1993. *Reengineering the Corporation.* New York: Harper Business.

Hannus, Jouko. 1993. *Prosessijohtaminen.* Jyväskylä, Finland: HM & V Research Oy.

Harrington, H. James. 1991. *Business Process Improvement.* New York: McGraw-Hill.

Heikkilä Laakso, Kristiina, and Jorma Heikkilä. 1997. *Innovatiivisuutta etsimässä.* Turku, Finland: Turun opettajankoulutuslaitos.

Kolb, D., J. Osland, and I. Rubin. 1995. *Organizational Behaviour: An Experimential Approach.* Englewood Cliffs, NJ: Prentice Hall.

Rummler, Geary A., and Alan P. Brache. 1990. *Improving Performance: How to Manage the White Space on the Organization Chart.* San Francisco, CA: Josscy-Bass.

Stalk, George, Jr., and Thomas M. Hout. 1990. *Competing Against Time.* New York: The Free Press.

Tuominen, Kari. 1993. *Benchmarking—prosessiopas.* Helsinki, Finland: Metalliteollisuuden kustannus.

Tuominen, Kari. 1993. *Benchmarking—yhteenveto yritysjohdolle.* Helsinki, Finland: Metalliteollisuuden kustannus.

Watson, Gregory H. 1993. *Strategic Benchmarking.* New York: John Wiley & Sons.

About the Author

Kari Tuominen has been working in managerial and development functions at the Rosenlew, Repola, and Ahlstrom companies both in Finland and abroad for 26 years.

In addition to operational responsibility, his duties have always included the planning and implementation of extensive development and change projects. He has been president of Oy Benchmarking Ltd since 1995 and, as a management consultant, has trained and managed operational development projects and benchmarking processes for industrial, service, and public sector clients.

Kari Tuominen's previously published books are *A Guide to the Benchmarking Process* and *Benchmarking, a Summary for Managers*. He served as chief auditor of the Finnish Quality Award from 1995 to 1997 and has a NLP trainer degree.

Work Experience

W. Rosenlew Ltd.

1968–1974	Director of Management Development and Industrial Engineering
1974–1978	Plant Manager, Combine Harvesters
1979–1981	Plant Manager and Director of R&D, Household Appliances
1982–1985	President, Combine Harvesters, Svenska Rosenlew AB, Sweden
1986	General Manager, Rosenlew Packaging Division
1987	General Manager, Rosenlew Tools Profit Center

Repola Ltd.
1988–1992   Vice President, Business Development, Rauma Group

A. Ahlstrom Corporation
1992–1993   Plant Manager, Glass Containers
1993–1994   Vice President, Operations Development, Ahlstrom
             Machinery

Benchmarking Ltd.
1995–Present President, Oy Benchmarking Ltd.

CONTACT INFORMATION

Kari Tuominen
Oy Benchmarking Ltd.
Läntinen Pitkäkatu 18 B45
20100 Turku, Finland
Tel and fax: +358 2 2330 406
GSM: +358 400 594 738
E-mail: kari.tuominen@benchmarking.fi
Internet: www.benchmarking.fi

Index